A Dangerous Journey

BOOKS BY THOMAS HAUSER

GENERAL NON-FICTION

Missing
The Trial of Patrolman Thomas Shea
For Our Children
(with Frank Macchiarola)
The Family Legal Companion
Final Warning: The Legacy of Chernobyl
(with Dr. Robert Gale)
Arnold Palmer: A Personal Journey
Confronting America's Moral Crisis
(with Frank Macchiarola)
Healing:
A Journal of Tolerance and Understanding
With This Ring (with Frank Macchiarola)
Thomas Hauser on Sports
Reflections

BOXING NON-FICTION

The Black Lights
Muhammad Ali: His Life and Times
Muhammad Ali: Memories
Muhammad Ali: In Perspective
Muhammad Ali & Company
A Beautiful Sickness
A Year At The Fights
Brutal Artistry
The View From Ringside
Chaos, Corruption, Courage, and Glory
I Don't Believe It, But It's True
Knockout (with Vikki LaMotta)
The Greatest Sport of All
The Boxing Scene
An Unforgiving Sport

Boxing Is . . .
Box: The Face of Boxing
The Legend of Muhammad Ali
(with Bart Barry)
Winks and Daggers
And the New . . .
Straight Writes and Jabs
Thomas Hauser on Boxing
A Hurting Sport
A Hard World
Muhammad Ali: A Tribute to the Greatest
There Will Always Be Boxing
Protect Yourself At All Times
A Dangerous Journey

FICTION

Ashworth & Palmer
Agatha's Friends
The Beethoven Conspiracy
Hanneman's War
The Fantasy
Dear Hannah
The Hawthorne Group
Mark Twain Remembers
Finding The Princess
Waiting for Carver Boyd
The Final Recollections of
Charles Dickens
The Baker's Tale

FOR CHILDREN

Martin Bear & Friends

A Dangerous Journey

Another Year Inside Boxing

Thomas Hauser

The University of Arkansas Press
Fayetteville
2019

ISBN: 978-1-68226-107-1
eISBN: 978-1-61075-676-1

23 22 21 20 19 5 4 3 2 1

♾ The paper used in this publication meets the minimum requirements of the American National Standard for Permanence of Paper for Printed Library Materials Z39.48-1984.

The following articles included in this book were originally published by *Sporting News* (www.sportingnews.com): Unbeaten: Rocky Marciano, Regis Prograis and the World Boxing Super Series, Jacobs-Derevyanchenko and the Operating Room, Curtis Harper Goes Viral, Deontay Wilder vs. Tyson Fury in Perspective, The Ring Walk, The Contender: 2018, The Mouthpiece and Boxing, The Sporting News Tradition, A Conversation with Bear Bryant, What Would Arnold Palmer Think of Donald Trump Today?, A Boy Learns to Love Books, A Plea for Spence-Crawford Now, The Heavyweight Triangle: Anthony Joshua is Still The Man, and CompuBox and Muhammad Ali.

Library of Congress Cataloging-in-Publication Data

Names: Hauser, Thomas, author.
Title: A dangerous journey : another year inside boxing / Thomas Hauser.
Description: Fayetteville : The University of Arkansas Press, 2019. |
   Includes bibliographical references. |
Identifiers: LCCN 2019003518 (print) | LCCN 2019014563 (ebook) | ISBN
   9781610756761 (electronic) | ISBN 9781682261071 (pbk. : alk. paper) | ISBN
   9781610756754 (ebook)
Subjects: LCSH: Boxing—United States. | Boxers (Sports)—United States.
Classification: LCC GV1125 (ebook) | LCC GV1125 .H293 2019 (print) | DDC
   796.83—dc23
LC record available at https://lccn.loc.gov/2019003518

Trainers are teachers. Over the years, I've been fortunate to be able to pick up the telephone and call some of boxing's best trainers for their insight and guidance. This list isn't all-inclusive. But special thanks for sharing their knowledge to Eddie Futch, Emanuel Steward, Angelo Dundee, Gil Clancy, Victor Valle, Bouie Fisher, Don Turner, Freddie Roach, Pat Burns, Harry Keitt, Barry Hunter, and Teddy Atlas.

Contents

Other Sports

Issues and Answers

Author's Note

A Dangerous Journey contains the articles about professional boxing that I authored in 2018 and also a section that includes a handful of pieces written about other sports.

The articles I wrote about the sweet science prior to 2018 have been published in *Muhammad Ali & Company*; *A Beautiful Sickness*; *A Year at the Fights*; *The View From Ringside*; *Chaos, Corruption, Courage, and Glory*; *I Don't Believe It, But It's True; The Greatest Sport of All*; *The Boxing Scene*; *An Unforgiving Sport*; *Boxing Is*; *Winks and Daggers*; *And the New*; *Straight Writes and Jabs*; *Thomas Hauser on Boxing*; *A Hurting Sport*; *A Hard World*; *Muhammad Ali: A Tribute to The Greatest*; *There Will Always Be Boxing*; and *Protect Yourself At All Times*.

Fighters and Fights

Over the course of twenty-four hotly-contested rounds against Gennady Golovkin, Canelo Alvarez proved that he's an elite fighter.

The Validation of Canelo Alvarez

On September 15, 2018, Saul "Canelo" Alvarez and Gennady Golovkin did battle at T-Mobile Arena in Las Vegas for the middleweight championship of the world. It was the kind of match-up that boxing needs more of. Two elite fighters ranked high on every pound-for-pound list and the top two fighters in their weight division, one of them boxing's biggest pay-per-view draw.

It was a legacy fight for both men. But for Alvarez, it was something more. One year earlier, he and Golovkin had fought to a controversial draw. That fight had been for history and glory. This one, because of a positive test for a banned drug, was for Canelo's honor.

Alvarez is a fighter at heart. He's a tough SOB with a great chin. And he can fight. He turned pro at age fifteen and, in the thirteen years since then, has fashioned a 50–1–2 (34 KOs) ring record. On many occasions, he has gone in tough. But with each big win he achieved in the past, there was a caveat attached. This opponent was too old. That one was too small. The decision wasn't right. And there was a 2013 loss to Floyd Mayweather when a too-young Canelo was befuddled over the course of twelve long rounds.

Golovkin, now 36, won a silver medal at the 2004 Olympics on behalf of Kazakhstan and had compiled a 38–0–1 (34 KOs) ledger in the professional ranks. More significantly, he'd reigned at various times as the WBC, WBA, and IBF middleweight champion and still held the WBC and WBA crowns. While Gennady had been tested by fewer world-class inquisitors than Canelo, he'd never shied away from a challenge. At his best, he relentlessly grinds opponents down.

Alvarez and Golovkin met in the ring for the first time on September 16, 2017, in the most-anticipated fight of the year. That bout generated a live gate of $27,059,850 at T-Mobile Arena, the third largest live gate in boxing history. The 22,358 fans in attendance comprised the largest indoor crowd ever for a fight in Las Vegas.

It was a spirited bout with most observers believing that Golovkin deserved the decision. Dave Moretti scored the contest 115–113 for Gennady. Don Trella scored it even. Adelaide Byrd turned in what might have been the worst scorecard ever in a major fight: 118–110 for Canelo.

Clearly, a rematch was in order. But on what terms? Despite being the challenger, Alvarez had been the driving economic force behind the first fight. That was reflected in the slightly better than 70-to-30-percent division of income in favor of Canelo and his promoter (Golden Boy). The differential was narrowed to 65–35 as negotiations for the rematch proceeded. A contract for a May 5 encore was signed. But while Canelo-Golovkin I had been conducted in an atmosphere of mutual respect, the atmosphere was different now.

Alvarez is a hero in his native Mexico, while Team Golovkin has gone to great lengths to position Gennady as a "Mexican style" fighter.

"There is no such thing as a Mexican style," Canelo noted. "There have been many fighters from Mexico with different styles. My style is mine. I'm Mexican, and that's what is important."

But at the February 27, 2018, kick-off press conference for Canelo-Golovkin 2, Abel Sanchez (Gennady's trainer) roiled the waters, saying, "I hope Canelo was able to see a transmission specialist for the rematch because in the first fight he was stuck in reverse. He was a runner. It behooves Canelo, with as much talking as he's doing about his legacy and how he's going to be remembered, to at least make it a fight."

"I outboxed him," Canelo said in response. "I went on the ropes. I made him miss. I controlled the center of the ring. I'm not a jackass who just comes forward, throwing punches and gets hit. He believes he is a great coach. He does not know what boxing is. He does not know what it is to have technique, what it is to box, what it is to make a move, knowing how to adapt to the circumstances of the fight, not just going forward throwing punches. I hope he goes home tonight and really thinks about what he says. Because he's saying stupid idiotic things."

Then there was a problem. A big one. On March 5, it was revealed that urine samples taken from Canelo by the Voluntary Anti-Doping Association (VADA) on February 17 and February 20, 2018, had tested positive for clenbuterol.

Clenbuterol helps the body increase its metabolism and process the conversion of carbohydrates, proteins, and fats into useful energy. It also boosts muscle growth and eliminates excess fats caused by the use of certain steroids. Under the World Anti-Doping Agency Code, no amount of clenbuterol is allowed in a competitor's body. The measure is qualitative, not quantitative. Either clenbuterol is there or it's not.

The Alvarez camp maintained that the positive tests were the result of Canelo having inadvertently eaten contaminated meat. To this day, Canelo has maintained his innocence. Regardless, on April 3, he announced that he was withdrawing from the May 5 rematch. Then, on April 18, the Nevada State Athletic Commission unanimously approved a settlement agreed to by Alvarez that called for the fighter to be suspended for six months retroactive to the date of his first positive test for clenbuterol. There was no admission of wrongdoing on Canelo's part. But there was an acknowledgement that clenbuterol had been present in his system.

With Alvarez temporarily out of the picture, Golovkin fought Vanes Martirosyan on May 5. Martirosyan had fought his entire career at 154 pounds, been out of the ring for two years, and won only four of eight fights over the previous six years. HBO didn't even put his image on promotional posters for the fight. Instead, it ran a full-body photo of Golovkin down the left side of the poster and relegated Vanes's name to a font one-twelfth the size of the letters "GGG." Golovkin knocked Martirosyan out in the second round.

Then negotiations for Canelo-Golovkin 2 resumed. But now the Golovkin camp was demanding a 50–50 revenue split and pushing the narrative that, having tested positive for clenbuterol, Canelo needed to fight Gennady again to rehabilitate his image. They also argued that Team Canelo should be penalized an amount equal to the out-of-pocket expenses that had been lost as a consequence of the May 5 postponement. On June 13, the warring camps agreed to what is believed to have been a 55–45 division of revenue.

Canelo-Golovkin I was a feel-good promotion and a celebration of boxing. Two elite fighters had fought one another in an atmosphere of good will. "He respects me, and I respect him," Gennady said of his opponent before they met in the ring for the first time.

Canelo-Golovkin 2 was a different matter. The expressions of mutual respect were gone. Leading up to the rematch, the antipathy between the fighters was such that they declined to participate in traditional marketing ventures such as HBO's "Face Off" and, prior to the fight, appeared together only for the final pre-fight press conference and weigh-in. There was no kick-off promotional media tour. In its place, the two teams partic-ipated in a split-screen media conference on July 3 from their respective training camps in Big Bear and Guadalajara.

A deep wellspring of resentment flowed from Golovkin as a con-sequence of the first fight. He came into the rematch nursing a host of grievances. Some of his anger was motivated by having to take short money. He was also upset by the decision in Canelo-Golovkin I.

"Canelo lost that fight," Gennady said. "That's it. He lost the fight according to all standards. I thought I didn't understand something, but then I reviewed the fight. These people [the judges] are like terrorists. They're killing sport. It's not about me. People like that should be in prison. People being cheated like that; it's too much. This is America."

And more significantly, Golovkin believed that Canelo had used illegal performance enhancing drugs while preparing for their first fight. Let it go? In Gennady's mind, that made Canelo as much of a cheater as Miguel Cotto and many others believe that Antonio Margarito was when Margarito fought Cotto with allegedly loaded gloves. Did Cotto let go of that grievance?

Golovkin called Canelo a liar and added, "I told the truth. If he does not like the truth, it is not my problem. It doesn't matter if he likes me, loves me, doesn't like me. I wouldn't say I hate him. It's just that my opinion of him has changed completely. What he says doesn't inspire any respect. The people who support him and stand by him are swindlers, just like him. How could one respect them?"

Meanwhile, Abel Sanchez called Canelo "a man without character" and questioned his credentials as a representative of the Mexican people.

"Abel Sanchez just likes to talk," Chepo Reynoso (Canelo's manager and co-trainer) responded. "He talks too much. At the end of the day, it's going to be Canelo and Triple-G fighting with their fists, not with their mouths. He likes to be the star of the movie, but this is not about him. It's about Canelo and Triple-G. What we need to do as cornermen, as trainers, is to do our job quietly because it's not about us. Learn to be quiet, please."

Chepo also said that Golovkin fought "like a donkey" in that "he does the same thing over and over again." That led Sanchez to counter, "Chepo Reynoso has never had an Olympian. Chepo Reynoso has never had a silver medalist. Chepo Reynoso has never had eighteen world champions like I have had. When he gets to that level, maybe he can speak in an intelligent manner."

Canelo stated the obvious when he observed, "The cordiality we had is over. The respect that I had, that we had, it has been lost. They disrespected me for everything they have been saying, everything they have been doing, all their actions. Now it's different. This fight is personal because of all that has been said, and it will be difficult to regain the respect we once had."

As a general rule, the week of a big fight has a celebratory feel to it. It might be stressful for the fighters and promoters, but most people on site are enjoying the ride.

Fight week for Canelo-Golovkin 2 felt different. There was a sour residue from the ugly back-and-forth between two respected camps. The devastation that Hurricane Florence was wreaking in North Carolina contributed to the malaise. Oscar De La Hoya added silly to the equation when he told TMZ that he was "seriously" contemplating a run for president in 2020.

Canelo tried to tone things down. Taking questions in English and answering in Spanish at media events during the week, he observed, "I expect the best Golovkin for the fight, I will be the best Canelo. There will be no excuses. Some say that he won the first fight, and some say that I won. That is why it was a draw."

Asked about having tested positive for clenbuterol, Canelo answered, "I learned from it. I turned the page on it. And I am done with it."

As for De La Hoya running for president, Canelo noted, "I don't like politics. If he wants to do it, that's his decision and his problem."

All of this led to the question that mattered most: Who would win the fight? Here the war of words continued.

From Abel Sanchez: "On the fifteenth, when Oscar and Canelo are having breakfast, Oscar needs to remind him he needs to bring his courage to the venue that night . . . To win a fight, you have to try to win the fight. You win a fight by doing damage to your opponent and making it a battle . . . If he fights Gennady, he's going to get knocked out. He would have gotten knocked out the first time, but he decided to make it a track meet that night. If he doesn't defraud the fans again, then he's going to get knocked out . . . Canelo Con Carne is finally going to face the music from the man he has avoided most. It will be a public service to the sport and the Mexican beef industry he has selfishly maligned."

From Golovkin: "This wasn't boxing by Canelo. It was running. He always has a way of running in the ring. However, in our last fight, he was really avoiding fighting close to me . . . I felt a couple of slaps. Slap! Slap! I didn't feel real power, punch power . . . He's fast; he's quick. He is good fighter but he is not at my level."

A lot of the commentary from the Golovkin camp was gamesmanship aimed at influencing the judges. It was also designed to lure Alvarez into an ill-conceived firefight.

Canelo was not shy in responding:

★ "It's easy for Abel Sanchez to talk. He won't be getting in the ring and fighting on Saturday. Comments from Sanchez don't really bother me. I find it strange that someone who believes himself to be a great trainer does not know how to distinguish between having technique and what he is saying."

★ "I have watched the first fight several times. The first fight gave me the guideline for the second fight. I know that I can do many things in the ring against him. I know that I can hurt him. I'm going to do the necessary adjustments and the necessary things to win. Instead of making changes, I've added to the strategy. They're trying to get me to do what they want. But I will do what I have to do to walk away with the victory."

★ "Golovkin knows who I am. He knows what I am about. But he doesn't know how much more I have left to show. I'm looking forward to showing him that on September 15."

But neither side was certain who would win.

"It makes me laugh," Canelo said of Sanchez's predictions. "Saying what will happen when boxing is so unpredictable and so hard."

And Golovkin was in accord, acknowledging, "Is not like a show. Is serious business. Every fight is dangerous fight. Even with the same fighters, every fight is different. Nobody knows for sure how it will end. I want. He want. I am ready for him. He is ready for me. This is boxing."

Canelo Alvarez arrived at Dressing Room #1 at the T-Mobile Arena on Saturday night at 5:10 p.m. A five-by-ten-foot Mexican flag hung on the wall opposite a large flat-screen television monitor.

Two hours earlier, a seven-man film crew that works for Canelo had set up in the room. In recent years, the crew has been gathering material for a documentary about Alvarez's life. They also feed content to Canelo's 3.6 million Instagram followers, his 1.3 million Twitter followers, and the 2.9 million people in his Facebook community. The cameras recorded his arrival in the dressing room with Chepo and co-trainer Eddy Reynoso.

Alvarez was a 13-to-10 betting underdog. One day earlier, he'd weighed in at 159.4 pounds while Golovkin registered 159.6.

Canelo sat on a black imitation-leather armchair to the left of the flag. HBO production coordinator Tami Cotel came in and repositioned him for a pre-fight interview with Max Kellerman. When it was done, he returned to the armchair and, arms crossed across his chest, began watching the first pay-per-bout of the evening—Roman Gonzalez vs. Moises Fuentes—on the TV monitor. Gonzalez knocked Fuentes unconscious in round five. Canelo nodded in acknowledgment.

Chepo Reynoso began folding gauze into pads for his fighter's fists. When each pad was ready, he showed it a Nevada State Athletic Commission inspector for approval before bringing it to Canelo to ensure that it fit comfortably.

David Lemieux vs. Gary "Spike" O'Sullivan—the second televised bout of the evening—began. The winner would be on the short list of prospective opponents for Alvarez. Canelo turned his body slightly to the right in his chair, crossed his right leg over his left thigh, and studied the action with his right hand pressed against his chin. The fight didn't last long. Lemieux KO'd O'Sullivan two minutes 44 seconds into round one.

Two fights. Two reminders of how quickly and brutally a fight can end.

Soft Latin music began playing in the background.

The TV monitor showed Gennady Golovkin arriving at T-Mobile Arena. Again, Canelo nodded.

Several sponsor representatives entered. Alvarez rose to greet them and posed for photos before returning to his chair. Video footage from his first fight against Golovkin began to play on the monitor. Canelo watched impassively, chatting occasionally with Diego Alejandro Gonzales (the son of Golden Boy public relations director Ramiro Gonzalez).

At 6:05 p.m., clad in a tuxedo, Julio Cesar Chavez came in to conduct an interview for Mexican television. That was followed by a visit from Nevada State Athletic Commission executive director Bob Bennett, who arrived with several commission dignitaries and referee Benjy Esteves, who gave Canelo his pre-fight instructions.

Golden Boy publicist Gabriel Rivas and matchmaker Robert Diaz appeared from time to time to attend to various matters.

The video of Canelo-Golovkin I ended.

More well-wishers, family members, and friends came and went. Canelo rose from his chair to greet each one with a welcoming smile and embrace.

At 6:20 p.m., Canelo's girlfriend came into the room with his youngest daughter, an adorable toddler named Maria Fernanda Alvarez. Canelo took his daughter in his arms and sat with her on his lap.

"What a beautiful girl," he murmured.

He lifted her arms up and down while nuzzling her cheek and saying "Papa! Papa!" over and over again in a sing-song voice.

Maria rested comfortably in her father's arms. Then Canelo rose from his chair and walked her around the room on her unsteady legs, holding both of her arms above her head from behind.

He looked like a man playing at home with his daughter, not a warrior readying for war.

Jaime Munguia vs. Brandon Cook—the third fight on the pay-per-view telecast—began. Munguia knocked Cook out in three rounds. Canelo put his daughter down and began stretching with Eddy Reynoso, his first boxing-related exercise of the evening.

Miguel Cotto, who Alvarez defeated in 2015 to win his first middleweight belt, came in, hugged Canelo, shook hands with Eddy, and chatted for several minutes with Chepo.

There was more stretching.

At seven o'clock, Eddy began wrapping Canelo's hands with a representative of Golovkin's camp looking on. Right hand first, then the left.

At 7:15 p.m., inspectors Alex Ybarra, Francisco Soto, and Charvez Foger cleared the room of camera crews, family members, and friends. In forty-five minutes, Canelo would leave his sanctuary for the ring.

Tami Cotel returned with the request that Canelo sit for a brief interview for HBO social media.

"I'm sorry," Robert Diaz told her. "This isn't a television show now. He has to get ready for a fight."

Canelo put on a protective cup and black trunks with gold trim. Eddy applied Vaseline to his face. There was more stretching followed by a brief interlude of shadow-boxing.

Eddy gloved Canelo up.

There was some padwork.

Cotel returned. "You walk in twelve minutes," she instructed.

Chepo draped a black serape emblazoned with a Mexican-flag emblem over Canelo's shoulders

The dressing room had been remarkably quiet from start to finish. Now only the soft Latin music could be heard.

Canelo began signing in tune with the music. A love song.

He looked like a boy in a man's world.

A.J. Liebling once wrote of rematches, "The spectator who goes twice to a play he likes is pretty sure of getting what he pays for on his second visit, especially if the cast is unchanged. This is not true of the sweet science."

With Canelo-Golovkin 2, fight fans got what they paid for.

The crowd was divided with vociferous partisans on each side. Chants of "GGG! GGG!" were met with "Ca-nel-o! Ca-nel-o!"

Golovkin looked flat in the early going. Or was it old? Either way, he didn't fight the way the world is used to seeing him fight.

A lot of that was due to Canelo. Looking back on their first encounter, Alvarez had realized that Golovkin was wary of his power. Very wary. In his dressing room after that bout, Canelo had told his team, "The judges think he punches like a monster. My punches were just as hard as his, harder."

So this time, Canelo decided to test Golovkin early with more aggression and see how he responded. By moving forward and holding his ground, he deprived Gennady of the ability to set up at his leisure and gave him less room to mount an attack. This time, Canelo was the man stalking. This time, Canelo moved forward constantly and gave ground more grudgingly while fighting a measured disciplined fight.

And this time, for all of Abel Sanchez's talk, Golovkin was the more cautious fighter. He jabbed effectively. But Gennady has built his reputation and dominated opponents with the power punching that follows his jab. And that power was absent here because, like all boxers, Gennady throws with less authority when his forward momentum is stalled.

Canelo went to the body consistently and effectively, fighting like the more confident man and forcing the pace of the fight. When Golovkin hit him solidly, he didn't crumble. He fired back.

Gennady's face started to show bruising as early as round two. Canelo was cut on the left eyelid in round four

After five rounds, Golovkin was breathing heavily in his corner. He isn't a robot or computer-game figure. He's a real person who's subject to fatigue, pain, and all the other conditions that affect how a fighter fights. And the older a fighter gets, the harder it is for him to summon up the resolve to walk through punches.

After nine rounds, Golovkin looked to be fading. Canelo's power was influencing him more than his power was influencing Canelo. It was clear that Gennady needed another gear to win. And he dug deep to find it.

Midway through round ten, Golovkin shook Canelo with a straight righthand and followed with a barrage of punches. Most of them missed, and Canelo regrouped to fire back.

In round eleven, Gennady shook Canelo again. Round twelve saw toe-to-toe action as both men sensed that the outcome of the fight was in doubt. At the final bell, they embraced. Two men who understood that, in the ring, they're the equal of each other.

If Abel Sanchez had been hoping to influence the judges, it didn't work. Canelo emerged with a 115–113, 115–113, 114–114 triumph.

"I scored the fight even," Sanchez said afterward. "I thought that the twelfth round was the pivotal round. We've got to give Canelo credit. He was able to do the things that he needed to do tonight."

LeBron James, who was sitting at ringside, later tweeted, "One of the best fights I've ever seen! Ultimate competitors in @Canelo and @GGGBoxing! Salute to both of you. Could watch y'all fight any day."

Saul "Canelo" Alvarez and Gennady Golovkin have vastly different personalities and come from significantly different cultures. But they're both elite fighters, and there's far more that unites than divides them.

Katie Taylor is an interesting phenomenon in the #MeToo era.

Katie Taylor Can Fight

Jimmy Wilde reigned as the world's first flyweight champion and is regarded by some as the greatest British fighter of all time. Wilde once declared, "The idea of women in the boxing ring is repulsive and will receive no support from real lovers of the art. Girl boxers will ruin their matrimonial chances. No man could fancy a professional bruiser for a bride."

That was a long time ago. But women's boxing has yet to enter the consciousness of mainstream sports fans. Christy Martin was a blip on the radar screen by virtue of her appearance on Mike Tyson undercards. Laila Ali garnered attention because she was Muhammad's daughter. Lucia Rijker, the best female boxer of her era, was largely unknown. The talent pool is thin. Many women boxers don't know how to slip a punch or where to hold their hands.

Katie Taylor, who fought Victoria Noella Bustos in a 135-pound title unification bout at Barclays Center on April 28, 2018, is changing the perception of women's boxing.

Both of Taylor's parents were involved with the sweet science. Her father was an Englishman who married an Irish woman and moved to Bray, County Wicklow, where Katie was born on July 2, 1986. He boxed as an amateur and was Katie's first boxing coach when she took up the sport at age ten. Her mother was one of Ireland's first female boxing judges. Katie has three older siblings, one of whom is a professor of mathematics at Trinity College.

Katie grew up physically gifted, competitive, and loving sports. She was an elite athlete at a young age in both boxing and soccer. The downside to being a fighter is that fighters get hit. But in the end, she gravitated to boxing.

Later, she would explain, "There comes a point in the life of all junior boxers, when you hit fourteen or fifteen years old, when the punches start to hurt and you have to decide whether you're going to take it seriously or not at all. There's no middle ground."

At age 15, boxing as an amateur, Taylor participated in the first officially sanctioned woman's match in the history of Ireland. Thereafter, she won six gold medals at the European Championships and five at the Women's World championships. She was the flag bearer for Ireland at the 2012 London Olympics and became a national hero after winning a gold-medal at the 2012 Olympic games.

"Listening to the anthem [at the awards ceremony]," Katie later reminisced, "was the proudest moment of my life."

Then came what Taylor calls "the lowest moment of my career." At the 2016 Rio de Janeiro Olympics, she lost in the first round to Mira Potkonen of Finland.

"I just didn't perform well," Katie says of that outing. "It's a simple as that."

Taylor turned pro in late 2016 and fashioned an 8-and-0 record en route to winning the World Boxing Association woman's lightweight title last year. Her trainer, Ross Enamait, describes his charge as being totally dedicated to her craft.

Katie is confident but not arrogant with regard to her ring skills. She has a well-muscled frame with shoulders that are broader and thighs that are more powerful than might appear at first glance. She's poised, gracious, articulate, laughs easily, and is unfailingly polite.

She's also a study in contradictions. She likes attention but is wary of it. There's a private, somewhat shy, person behind the public facade.

"I lead a simple life," Katie says. "It's built around my family and my faith."

The faith is reflected in her strong Christian convictions and commitment to the Church of the Nazarene. Her family life is a bit more complicated. For the past year, Taylor has lived in Vernon, Connecticut, an ocean away from many of her loved ones.

"I love the fact that I'm anonymous in America," Katie explains. "I can go for walks and be left alone when I want to be alone. I can just be myself over here."

All fighters have demons and dreams that drive them. Fame means exposure. And exposure means leaving oneself exposed.

"When you reached an age when the punches hurt and boxing became serious for you," Katie is asked, "was the motivation you were most aware of when you got in the ring to defend yourself or attack?"

"That's an interesting question," she counters.

Taylor-Bustos was on the undercard of an HBO doubleheader featuring Danny Jacobs vs. Maciej Sulecki and Jarrell Miller vs. Johann Duhaupas.

Bustos had 18 victories and 4 losses on her ring ledger but had never fought outside of Argentina. More significantly, in 22 professional fights, she had never scored a knockout. The odds favoring Taylor ran as high as 20-to-1 despite the fact that Bustos had been the International Boxing Federation lightweight champion for over a year.

There was a blip during the medical examinations at the weigh-in on Friday when a New York State Athletic Commission doctor noticed a cold sore on Bustos's lip. One doesn't normally think of a cold sore as preventing a fight. But Victoria was told that she needed a clearance letter from a dermatologist. The dermatologist then sent a letter to the commission saying that the sore was "likely" to be contained. That wasn't good enough for the NYSAC, which consulted next with an infectious disease specialist. It wasn't until 1:15 p.m. on fight day that Team Taylor was advised the fight was on.

Taylor's status as a star and also her gender dictated that she not share a dressing room with other fighters on Saturday night.

Carrying her own gym bag, Katie arrived at room 1B11.09 in Barclays Center at 6:45 p.m. Her long dark hair was pulled back in a single braid. She was wearing black pants, a black T-shirt, gray sneakers, and a black jacket with "Katie Taylor" emblazoned in gold on the back.

Ross Enamait and manager Brian Peters were with her.

The dressing room was fifteen feet long and ten feet wide with black industrial carpet, pale yellow walls, and recessed lighting above. A gray table built into one of the walls ran the length of the room with a wall-to-wall mirror above it. Seven black cushioned folding metal chairs were set against the table. A black leather sofa stood against the opposite wall.

Tomas Rohan (who works with Peters) and filmmaker Ross Whitaker joined the trio. It was a small group. No expanding circle of family, friends, and hangers-on.

Enamait unpacked his gym bag and put the tools of his trade on the table.

Veteran cutman Danny Milano (who would be working Katie's corner for the first time) brought in a half-dozen white terrycloth towels.

"I've been following the women for a while now," Milano had said earlier in the day. "They tend to lose their composure more quickly than the men when things aren't going their way. But not this one."

Katie sat on the sofa, propped her feet up on a chair, and sipped from a bottle of water.

At 7:10 p.m., Enamait asked a New York State Athletic Commission deputy commissioner if Bustos had arrived at the arena.

She hadn't.

"I'll feel better when I know she's here," the trainer said.

At 7:20 p.m., Brian Peters left the room to see if Bustos was on site yet. Five minutes later, he returned.

"She's here."

It was a quiet dressing room. For much of the time that Katie was there, she sat alone on the sofa, watching undercard fights on a TV monitor. Other times, Enamait or Peters sat beside her, engaging in quiet conversation.

Male or female, the rituals for battle are the same. A pre-fight physical examination and the taking of a urine sample were followed by the referee's dressing room instructions.

Occasionally, Katie stood and stretched.

At 7:40 p.m., she put on a pair of black-and-gold boxing trunks, a matching top, and a fuchsia T-shirt with words from Psalm 18 in white letters on the front ("It is God who arms me with strength") and back ("He trains my hands for battle").

Enamait began taping Katie's hands, right hand first. At 8:15 p.m., the job was done.

Katie stretched on her own and shadow-boxed briefly.

Enamait greased her hair with petroleum jelly to hold it in place.

The assumption was that Katie would win. But boxing is boxing. She was about to venture into the unknown. In less than an hour, a woman trained in the art of hurting would try to hurt her.

"I get nervous before every fight," Taylor has said. "I'd be worried if I wasn't nervous. But I feel like I'm most alive when I'm in the ring. You don't know what will happen. That's what makes it so exciting."

There was more shadow-boxing. Katie's face looked harder now. She was transforming into a warrior.

Enamait gloved her up.

Trainer and fighter worked the pads together.

"Don't give her any free shots," Enamait cautioned.

Brian Peters helped Katie into a black robe with gold trim.

At nine o'clock, a voice instructed, "It's time to walk."

The fight went largely as expected.

Taylor has good footwork and good hand-speed coupled with a nasty jab, a sharp straight right, an effective left hook, and a serviceable upper-cut. She's not a big puncher but mixes her punches well.

Fighting at a distance in the first half of the bout, Katie was in total control. In rounds eight and ten, she chose to trade on the inside (which was the only place Bustos could reach her), stayed in the pocket too long, and took some unnecessary punches. The judges were on the mark with their 99–91, 99–91, 98–92 verdict.

After the fight, Katie returned to her dressing room and sat on the sofa. There were ugly welts on her back and shoulders, a bruise on the left side of her forehead, and a smaller bruise beneath her right eye.

"I'm tired," she said.

Pressed for more, she elaborated on her performance.

"I can always do better, but I did okay tonight. She [Bustos] was durable, and it was a different style from what I'm used to fighting. I'm still learning my trade. There's a big difference between the amateurs and the pros. The pros are more physical. But I'm happy with the win, and I'm happy to be a unified champion."

In recent years, championships have been sadly devalued in boxing. That's particularly true on the women's side of the ledger.

John Sheppard, who oversees BoxRec.com, recently reported that boxing's world sanctioning bodies have created 110 different women's titles. This means that, assuming each title is available in 17 weight divisions, the sanctioning bodies have belts for 1,870 women's champions. Meanwhile, according to BoxRec.com, there are only 1,430 active women boxers in the world today. "Thus," Sheppard notes, "there are approximately 1.3 titles available for each female boxer."

How can that be?

The answer is that the sanctioning bodies have an insatiable lust for sanctioning fees. For example, the World Boxing Council has thirteen different denominations for women "champions": World Female, Diamond Female, International Female, Youth Female, Silver Female, Latino Female, FECARBOX Female, FECOMBOX Female, CIS and Slovac Boxing Bureau Female, Asian Boxing Council Female, Asian Boxing Council Silver Female, Asian Boxing Council Continental Female, and Baltic Female.

In this nonsensical world, Katie Taylor stands out as a "real" champion. She now has two world championship belts and, given her druthers, will be in the ring soon competing for the other two quasi-credible titles. By the time women's boxing advances to the point where there's a serious pound-for-pound conversation, she hopes to be at the top of the list.

"Everyone has different skills and talents," Katie says. "This is mine. When people watch me box, I hope they see a boxer, not a female boxer. I would love to bring the sport to another level and take women's boxing to a place where people really respect it."

Men's boxing has a storied tradition. Today's male fighters can look back in time and say, "I would have loved to have fought Sugar Ray Robinson. Or Muhammad Ali. Or Joe Louis." Maybe someday, young women fighters will look back on this era and say, "I would have loved to have fought Katie Taylor."

As 2018 began, the general public still didn't know Deontay Wilder. He could have stood in the middle of Times Square shouting his slogan—"BOMB SQUAD"—and it's more likely that he would have been arrested than recognized. But that might be changing.

Deontay Wilder Walks Through Fire to Win

There were competing fight cards at Barclays Center and Madison Square Garden on March 3, 2018. One fight out of the 21 bouts that were contested—Deontay Wilder vs. Luis Ortiz—was a magnet for media attention and fan interest.

Wilder won a bronze medal at the 2008 Olympics. He was a work in the early stages of progress when he turned pro that year. A decade later, at age 32, he's progressing.

Wilder has a potent right hand that can detonate with one-punch knockout power. He has learned to protect a suspect chin by fighting at a distance. He has benefited from the reality that the heavyweight division is weak at the present time. And he has been able to ply his trade in a parallel universe created by Premier Boxing Champions impresario Al Haymon. All of the above enabled Deontay to pound out a 39–0 (38 KOs) record and claim the WBC heavyweight crown.

Ortiz maintains that he will celebrate his 39th birthday later this month. He might be older. A product of the Cuban amateur system, Luis turned pro in 2010. His career peaked 27 months ago when he demolished Bryant Jennings in seven rounds. Since then, he has looked ordinary. Ortiz has also tested positive for illegal performance enhancing drugs on multiple occasions while remaining undefeated in 28 pro fights with 24 KOs.

The build up to Wilder-Ortiz was characterized by the usual back-and-forth:

★Wilder: "We all know that when Deontay Wilder get under those lights, those cameras, I perform my best. They never had a guy in there so vicious, so mean as me. And it's so real."

* Ortiz: "He doesn't intimidate me. His trash talk makes me laugh. It's just a lot of noise. But I've had it with this guy. He talks too much. He has a big mouth. He has insulted me and has said too many dumb things. He's going to find himself on the canvas before he knows it."

* Wilder: "He dealing with a monster. He dealing with a guy with a killer instinct. I am the king of the jungle. I am the lion of the jungle."

* Ortiz: "He says he's going to kill 'King Kong.' He's going to knock me out. I'm not like those other guys he fought. I'm a real fighter, tough and with a lot of experience."

* Wilder: "I've always said I'm the best. I say it all the time. I speak it. I believe it. I love to hit people in the face. I love to see their body on the canvas."

* Ortiz: "I will tear the skin off his body."

* Wilder [to Ortiz at the final pre-fight press conference two days before the fight]: "I could fuck tonight and still beat your ass on Saturday."

On paper, Ortiz had the better pedigree—362 fights in the Cuban amateur system. But that meant there was a lot of wear and tear on his body. Amateur fights in Cuba are hard.

Then there was the matter of Luis's age.

"We don't know what Ortiz's real age is," Showtime commentator Al Bernstein acknowledged. "He could be an AARP member for all we know."

And Showtime expert analyst Paulie Malignaggi noted the problems that fighters face when they're caught doping and then have to fight clean.

"One thing I got to say," Malignaggi offered. "And nobody is saying this. It's like the big elephant in the room. Ortiz, would he be as effective minus the PEDs? It seems like a lot of the big wins and a lot of the strength may have come from that. The guy failed twice, maybe three times. You have to start asking the question, how good is this guy if he's clean? You have to wonder about this fight that we're all getting excited about. Is the fight really that good or is Deontay naturally that much better? You don't want to downplay Ortiz too much because he does come from that amateur system and he does have skills. But was the power bulked up? That's my question."

There were 14,609 fans at Barclays Center on fight night, most of them Wilder partisans. Deontay had weighed in one day earlier at 214–¾ pounds, the lightest he'd been since his second pro fight in 2009. Ortiz, in line with recent outings, registered 241–¼ pounds and had a roll of flesh around his waist. Wilder was a 3-to-1 betting favorite.

The early rounds were dull. Both men fought cautiously. Wilder spent the first few stanzas throwing rangefinder jabs while looking for an opening to throw his big right hand. Ortiz plodded forward behind an equally passive jab.

The crowd booed the lack of action. But there was an underlying tension because of two variables that attach to Wilder: his power and a suspect chin. Deontay had twelve rounds to land THE right. If he didn't get whacked out first.

Fifteen seconds before the end of round five, Wilder finally landed the right and followed with another that deposited Ortiz on the canvas. Luis rose and, in the first half of round six, weathered the storm that followed. Deontay was swinging wildly, missing a lot. And Luis took the blows that landed well.

Then the tables turned.

Two minutes 20 seconds into round seven, Ortiz stunned Wilder with a hard straight left and followed with a barrage of punches that pummeled Deontay around the ring.

"He had me in a whirlwind," Wilder acknowledged after the fight. "And I had to get out of there."

Deontay appeared to be out on his feet. But he stayed on them.

At that point, the New York State Athletic Commission fumbled the ball.

In recent years, the NYSAC has come under heavy criticism for substandard medical procedures that led to the state paying tens of millions of dollars to settle claims against the commission. In response, the NYSAC modified its medical protocols. Most of the changes have been good. Some aren't.

The NYSAC now requires ring doctors to stand on the ring apron and observe both fighters during all breaks between rounds. If a doctor wants to examine a fighter from inside the ring, he asks the referee to call a time out. This has led to multiple occasions in fights when a boxer is examined and the action is put on hold to the dismay of the opposing fighter and the crowd.

Does the practice make sense?

Dr. Margaret Goodman (former chief ringside physician and former chairperson of the medical advisory board for the Nevada State Athletic Commission) is a neurologist and one of the foremost advocates for fighter safety in the United States. Asked about doctors standing on the ring apron between rounds, Dr. Goodman says, "That's more for show than anything else. If you need to get in there, get in there."

And what about extending the one-minute break between rounds as opposed to a ring doctor examining the fighter during the traditional one-minute rest period?

"I understand the need to safeguard the fighter," Dr. Goodman answers. "But in my opinion, that one minute should only be extended in extreme circumstances. Otherwise, you're interfering with the flow of the fight and possibly changing the outcome of the fight."

After round seven of Wilder-Ortiz, the New York State Athletic Commission tampered with the flow of the fight. Wilder was given an extra twenty seconds to recover while an NYSAC physician examined him. There's no way of knowing what would have happened without that additional recovery time. When the action finally resumed in round eight, Ortiz continued his assault. But his attack was more measured than might otherwise have been the case.

Both men had now fought through adversity and survived.

By the start of round nine, Wilder had fully recovered. A sharp right hand near the end of the stanza shook Ortiz.

One minute into round ten, a Wilder right put Ortiz on wobbly legs. Deontay rushed him and threw the Cuban to the canvas, which gave Luis a few seconds to recover, but it wasn't enough. Two more knockdowns courtesy a big right hand and then a right uppercut ended the battle at the 2:05 mark.

It was an exciting fight. Wilder showed intangibles that a lot of people didn't think he had. We knew he has power. We knew he has fast hands and a long reach. Now we know he has heart.

If you have to work on a Saturday night, hanging out with Evander Holyfield isn't a bad way to do it.

Evander Holyfield: Fight Night is Different Now

In the long history of boxing, only a handful of fighters have earned the right to be called a great heavyweight champion. Evander Holyfield is one of them.

Holyfield fought nine bouts against Mike Tyson, George Foreman, Lennox Lewis, Larry Holmes, and Riddick Bowe and twelve times against Buster Douglas, Hasim Rahman, Michael Moorer, Michael Dokes, John Ruiz, James Toney, Nikolay Valuev, Pinklon Thomas, and Chris Byrd.

No athlete pushes himself as hard as a fighter who's getting beaten up and is still trying to win. Time and again, Holyfield did just that. And not only did he keep trying to win, he won.

If every fighter was like Evander, boxing would be the world's most popular sport.

Fight nights are different now for Holyfield. He's a promoter.

In May 2017, Evander announced the formation of Real Deal Sports & Entertainment. Real Deal Boxing (a corporate subsidiary) is a promotional entity. Holyfield (who's contributing his name and sweat equity to the venture) and Sal Musumeci are equal partners. Several investors own a small percentage of the company. COO Eric Bentley, aided by Kevin O'Sullivan, does most of the nuts and bolts work.

But Evander is more than a figurehead. Longtime Holyfield attorney Jim Thomas says, "Evander is doing much more here than simply lending his name to the company and showing up at fights. He has a good eye for talent and has significant input into which fighters the company signs to promotional contracts. He and Sal talk every day about a variety of company matters."

March 10, 2018, marked Real Deal Boxing's sixth fight card. The setting was Kings Theatre in Brooklyn.

Kings Theatre opened in 1929 in an era when movies were at the core of American entertainment and television didn't exist. In major cities, feature films were often paired with live music in ornate theaters known as movie palaces. Kings Theatre was one five original "Loew's Wonder Theaters." In the closing decades of the twentieth century, it fell into disrepair and disuse. A $95 million renovation completed in 2015 modernized the 3,250-seat facility and restored much of its original grandeur.

The theater is more evocative of a spectacular European opera house than a setting for club fights. It has elaborate statuary, marble stairs, an ornate 70-foot-high ceiling, chandeliers, and a burgundy-and-gold color scheme. The chairs are comfortable. The sightlines are good. Clad in a tuxedo that would have done Michael Buffer proud, fight-night ring announcer David Diamante fit nicely with the elegant surroundings.

But for the fighters, all that mattered was what happened on a small square of illuminated canvas.

Dressed in a blue suit and white dress shirt open at the collar, Holyfield arrived at Kings Theatre at 6:30 p.m. Soon after, he went to the dressing rooms to visit each fighter. There were handshakes and words of encouragement.

"When I started boxing," Evander counseled, "I was told I could be something I wanted to be . . . The best thing about being a fighter is that it's all on you. You can control your own situation . . . You got to fight every fight like it's the biggest fight of your life . . . Courage is trying as hard as you can. One of the reasons I was good was I wanted to win so bad."

Most fighters live on dreams that will never come true. Some of the fighters who listened as Evander spoke are prospects with a future in boxing. Others have no realistic chance of becoming more than an opponent. The young prospects know they're good. The question is how good. After each loss, the opponents tell themselves, "The next one will be different. I can make adjustments." But the next fight comes and it's just like the one before.

"They wouldn't be doing this if they didn't believe," Evander said as he left the last dressing room. "I can't make any of these guys a champion. But I can give them the opportunity to make themselves a champion."

Real Deal Boxing has a "showcase" series and a "championship" series. This was a showcase card. The promotion was hurt when two good ticket-sellers who had been scheduled to perform on March 10 were scratched. New York super-middleweight Edgar Berlanga underwent an emergency appendectomy. Then, on Tuesday of fight week, Brooklyn super-bantamweight Khalid Twaiti came down with pneumonia. That left eight bouts.

History will note that the first fight ever contested at Kings Theatre was won by a woman when Natalie Gonzalez outpointed Judit Hachbold over six rounds. None of the remaining bouts went the distance.

Cesar Francis stopped Demetrius Wilson in the third stanza.

Joseph Elmore, a former MMA fighter making his boxing debut against local favorite Justin Biggs, got up from a body shot that Arturo Gatti in his prime would have had trouble getting up from. Then, much to Elmore's dismay, his corner stopped the bout.

Two former Olympians from Uzbekistan—Murodjon Akhmadaliev (bronze) and Shakhram Glyasov (silver)—made their professional debuts with first-round knockouts respectively over David Michel Paz and Nicolas Atillo Valazquez. Valazquez was floored by a hook to the body in the first flurry of the fight and counted out at the 15-second mark.

Mathew Gonzalez KO'd Elliot Brown in round two. Josue Vargas did the same to Zack Ramsey in the third stanza. Julian Sosa stopped Wilmer Rodriguez in three.

Holyfield sat in the front row and watched each fight intently. The ring had been erected on the theater stage with VIP seating around it. There was only a one-foot drop from the ring apron to the floor, so Evander was close enough to reach out and touch the combatants. He entered the ring before each bout to greet the fighters and again when the result was announced.

From time to time, he reminisced with those sitting around him.

"My greatest moment in boxing was when I made the United States Olympic team. The last fight at the Olympic trials was over. We were standing in the ring. Then I heard the announcer say, 'Ladies and gentle-men; representing the United States in the light-heavyweight division, from Atlanta, Georgia . . .'"

There were thoughts on his first loss as a pro in an epic battle against Riddick Bowe.

"I sparred with Riddick when I was twenty-two and he was seventeen. He gave me hard work even then. I remember his telling me at the time, 'A good big man is better than a good little man.' Then, when we were getting ready to fight for the first time, Riddick told me, 'You know, I'm not that young kid anymore.' And he wasn't. But there was real respect between us. Through all three fights, we respected each other."

There was humor: "You only get hit if you make a mistake. I guess I made a lot of mistakes because, every fight I fought, I got hit."

And insight: "A fighter has to love fighting to be great."

It's not uncommon for fighters to form their own promotional company. In that regard, Oscar De La Hoya, Roy Jones, Lennox Lewis, and Floyd Mayweather come quickly to mind. But these ventures work best when the fighter in question can leverage his own ring appearances into network television dates. They become problematic when he's no longer an active fighter. Ray Leonard and Mike Tyson were each part of a promotional company after their days as an active fighter ended. Neither venture lasted long. It's hard to turn a profit as a boxing promoter in today's environment.

Jim Thomas puts matters in perspective when he says, "Evander has a deep emotional attachment to this. He's offering more than his name. He's working hard to build this from the ground up. At the end of his career as a fighter and after he retired, Evander was drifting. He was looking for his place. And he feels now as though he has found it. He believes in his heart that Real Deal Boxing can become the biggest promotional company in the world. If you shoot that high and get halfway there, you're doing well."

There's reason for optimism and reason for skepticism. Sort of like when Holyfield fought Mike Tyson.

For sixteen years, Russell Sullivan's biography of Rocky Marciano stood alone at the top of the list of books about the Brockton heavyweight. But in 2018, Unbeaten *by Mike Stanton earned equal billing.*

Unbeaten: Rocky Marciano

The story of Rocky Marciano has been told so many times for so many years that it's hard to find something new. Mike Stanton, in an excellent biography entitled *Unbeaten* (Henry Holt and Company) has found something new.

Rocco Marchegiano spent the closing months of World War II, not in battle, not ferrying supplies to Allied troops in Normandy as was widely reported in later years, but in a military stockade in England. He was imprisoned after being arrested, court-martialed, and found guilty of robbery and assault. While an investigation of the incident was underway, Marchegiano's commanding officer, Major Richard L. Powell, told investigators that Marchegiano was an "untrustworthy, unreliable and unsatisfactory soldier" and that "his derelictions have been consistent and numerous." Powell concluded that Marchegiano was "of no value to the Army."

Marchegiano was imprisoned for 22 months.

Rocky Marciano grew up poor in Brockton, Massachusetts. He got into more than his share of street fights as an adolescent and became one of the most storied boxers of all time. When he announced his retirement from the ring on April 27, 1956, his record was an unblemished 49 wins in 49 fights with 43 knockouts.

Marciano, Stanton writes, "was an unlikely champion. He didn't start boxing seriously until age 24 and was often overmatched in size and skill. He was five-foot-ten and weighed 185 pounds with short stubby arms, clumsy feet, and a bulldozer style that opened him up to fierce punishment."

Charley Goldman, the trainer who oversaw Marciano's transformation from crude street fighter to boxer, told his charge what lay ahead before they started working together.

"It isn't easy," Goldman cautioned. "It's rough. It takes a lot of work, a lot of sacrificing, a lot of bats in the nose. But I think you might be able to do okay. You're a strong kid. That's about all I can say for you right now. You're strong and you're willing. And I can tell that you like it. You gotta like it. Otherwise you just don't belong in it."

Thereafter, Goldman said of Marciano, "I got a guy who's short, stoop shouldered, and balding with two left feet. They all look better than he does as far as the moves are concerned, but they don't look so good on the canvas. God, how he can punch!"

Marciano overcame chronic hand problems that plagued him from his amateur days until the end of his ring career. He was the beneficiary of questionable decisions in fights against Ted Lowry and Roland LaStarza before legitimately prevailing in rematches against each man. He frequently fouled opponents, hitting below the belt, throwing punches after a round had ended, landing blows to the back of the head, and committing other infractions which he said were the unintentional result of his crude brawling style.

The key to his success was what Stanton calls his "indomitable will to win."

Marciano trained relentlessly, and always entered the ring in peak physical condition. "If you were there looking at Rocky's training and the way he lived," Goldman observed, "it was hard to believe that a man could sacrifice so much."

After Marciano reached the bigtime, the weeks leading up to his fights were spent training in the Catskill Mountains. Recounting Marciano's preparation at Grossinger's for his first championship bout against Jersey Joe Walcott, Stanton writes, "Rocky stayed far from the hotel and its glittering nightlife, living in a Spartan secluded cabin high up on the mountain. He shut himself off from the outside world and embraced the wilderness solitude of the Catskills. His opponent's name was never mentioned in his presence unless by an inquisitive sportswriter. In the weeks before the fight, he read no mail and took no phone calls, not even from his wife. The final week, he wouldn't even shake hands, ride in a car, or eat any new foods. He wasn't allowed to read anything about the fight. He didn't allow himself to think ahead to the morning after the fight when he would be freed from this hermetic existence."

"You've got to make boxing a kind of religion," Marciano explained. "You believe in yourself and you believe in the things you got to do. You never forget them for a minute."

As for the fights, Stanton writes of "a relentless style impervious to pain," and says of Marciano, "He had an indomitable heart that enabled him to withstand savage beatings. And he had a punch that was like a near-death experience. He trudged into the ring like a factory worker punching a timeclock and started pounding on the wall in front of him until it crumbled."

Archie Moore, who Marciano knocked out in the final fight of his storied 49–0 ring career, later said of his conqueror, "Rocky didn't know enough boxing to know what a feint was. He never tried to outguess you. He just kept trying to knock your brains out. If he missed you with one punch, he just threw another."

Marciano fit nicely into the culture of the 1950s. A symbol of American optimism, he was perceived, in Stanton's words, as "an All-American postcard from a simpler, more innocent age . . . Immigrant son, strong but soft-spoken . . . Humble and polite and devoted to his family . . . A patriot who had learned to box in the Army while serving his country during the war." *Time Magazine* hailed him with the accolade, "He stands for the comforting notion not that might makes right but that might and right are somehow synonymous."

Marciano, in turn, felt an obligation to boxing to present himself as a worthy heavyweight champion outside the ring as well as in it. And a compliant media played along. A profile of Marciano written for *Sport* magazine by Ed Fitzgerald in 1952 after Marciano dethroned Walcott was typical of its time.

"Rocky," Fitzgerald wrote, "is a neighborhood kid who married a neighborhood girl and thinks the old hometown is the greatest place in the world. His social activities are confined largely to entertaining friends and relatives at home or making the rounds of their houses and the Ward Two Club and the Seville Council, Knights of Columbus. The priests and nuns of St. Colman's parish where he worships call on him again and again to serve as a model for their lectures to the neighborhood kids."

But the truth was more complicated than that. By all accounts, Marciano loved his parents and siblings. But he was an absentee husband

and often ignored his daughter (who was born ten weeks after Marciano dethroned Walcott). He had a penchant for prostitutes and other available woman. In 1968, he and his wife adopted a baby boy who, Marciano later told his brother, Peter, was his own biological child.

Also, Marciano was inextricably tied to the mob. Manager Al Weill took fifty percent of Marciano's purses pursuant to their contract and stole more from him on the side. Weill then shared his take with Frankie Carbo, a high-ranking member of the Lucchese crime family and the most powerful man in boxing at that time.

Marciano socialized with mobsters during his ring career and, after his retirement from boxing, did business with them. Carbo was a guest for Sunday dinner in his parents' home. When Vito Genovese (known as "the boss of all bosses") was dying in prison, he let it be known that he wanted Marciano to visit him. Not only did Marciano visit, he brought fight films to show Genovese.

But these relationships were largely out of public view. When Marciano was killed in the crash of a small plane on August 31, 1969— thirteen years after his retirement from boxing and one day shy of his forty-sixth birthday—the world mourned.

Marciano's improbable rise to the heavyweight championship of the world is a remarkable story, and Stanton tells it well. He conducted an enormous amount of research and has woven his findings into an engaging narrative rather than simply throw information at readers. He recreates places and events in impressive detail and brings them to life. This is particularly true of his description of the environment that Marciano grew up in.

Unbeaten paints an honest portrait of Marciano, who comes across in some ways as a decent man and in other respects as a thug. The trajectory of his ring career is well-told as Stanton takes often-told stories and tells them in a way that makes them feel fresh and new.

People who are just names in history books come alive as vividly-drawn characters. This is particularly true of Weill—Marciano's obnoxious, crude, abrasive, overbearing, very smart, very dishonest, bullying, mob-connected manager.

There's also an informative and moving chapter on the life-altering brain damage suffered by Carmine Vingo in his sixth-round knockout loss to Marciano in 1949 and a dramatic recounting of the fight itself that elevates Vingo to more than just a name on Marciano's ring ledger.

Also, as previously noted, Stanton does what a good biographer is supposed to do. He breaks new ground. That's hard to accomplish with a biographical subject who has been dead for five decades and written about as often as Marciano. But Stanton does it with his recounting of Marciano's military service during World War II.

While stationed in England, Marciano and a fellow soldier named James Murphy robbed two Englishman, beating them up in the process. They were court-martialed and convicted, after which Marciano was dishonorably discharged from the Army and sentenced to three years in prison. He was released after 22 months and then allowed to rejoin the military for the duration of 1946 in order to receive an honorable discharge.

Unbeaten is such a good book that I'm reluctant to cast a shadow on any part of it. But there's one flaw that has to be mentioned. From time to time, there are factual errors in the narrative.

Stanton writes that Sugar Ray Robinson's "St. Valentine's Day Massacre" of Jake LaMotta in 1951 brought him the world welterweight championship. But it was the middleweight crown. Stanton incorrectly states that, one day after dethroning Sonny Liston, Cassius Clay announced that he was changing his name to Muhammad Ali. But it wasn't until March 6, 1964, ten days after the Liston bout, that Nation of Islam leader Elijah Muhammad bestowed that name upon him. More egregiously, Stanton writes that Ali "screamed 'what's my name?' over and over as he pummeled [Floyd] Patterson before knocking him out in 1965." But it wasn't Floyd Patterson in 1965. It was Ernie Terrell in 1967.

Mistakes like this take some of the glow away from a superb book because they lead a reader to wonder what other errors might lurk beneath the surface. That said; *Unbeaten* is a superb book.

And Another Biography of Marciano

John Jarrett has been writing about boxing since 1951 when his first article, a piece about Rocky Marciano, was published in *Boxing News*. Since then, he has been involved with the sweet science in myriad ways including ongoing service as Northern Area Secretary for the British Boxing Board of Control for forty years. During that time, he has written nine books, the most recent of which (*Rocky Marciano* published by Pitch Publishing) brings Jarrett back to his creative roots.

Rocco Francis Marchegiano was born into a struggling working-class family in Brockton, Massachusetts. The first time that he auditioned in the gym for trainer Charlie Goldman (who would ultimately sculpt the rough-hewn block of marble into greatness) Goldman told him, "If you done anything right, I didn't see it."

Shirley Povich of the *Washington Post* later quoted an unnamed observer of the boxing scene as saying, "Rocky Marciano can't box a lick. His footwork is what you'd expect from two left feet. He throws his right hand in a clumsy circle and knows nothing of orderly retreat. All he can do is blast the breath from your lungs or knock your head off."

No fighter trained harder than Marciano. That was one of the keys to his success. Asked to elaborate on his training regimen, Rocky noted, "After a while, you get to hate all the guys around you. You get to hate the sight of their faces and the sound of their voices."

Marciano lost four of the twelve amateur fights that he engaged in. Three decades later, Bob Girard (one of the men who beat him) reminisced, "I beat him because it was three rounds. There were a hundred guys who might have stayed three rounds with Rocco. But no man in the world was gonna beat Rocco in fifteen rounds."

Jarrett offers a particularly good retelling of the September 23, 1952, fight between Marciano and Jersey Joe Walcott when Marciano, trailing on all three scorecards at the start of round thirteen, seized the heavyweight throne with a highlight-reel knockout.

But as is often the case in this book, the most compelling writing with regard to Marciano-Walcott I comes from Jarrett's choice of quotes from others rather than his own prose. Here, the choice verbiage originated with Peter Wilson of the *Daily Express*, who wrote, "Then, like the car you never see on the dark road, the shell which you never hear, shocking, irrevocable, came that tremendous horrifying right. It left Walcott looking down his own spine with eyes that could not see. He crumpled forward, clutching for a rope, knees grayed by the resin dust. A brown paper bag burst by a thoughtless child. A headless, thoughtless, sightless, senseless, paralyzed man. Style, skill, pacing of the fight and good punching, all had availed nothing."

In his dressing room after the fight, Walcott was asked about the knockout punch and acknowledged, "I don't remember anything. He caught me open and that was it. I don't know if it was a right or left. I just don't remember anything."

Jarrett has done considerable research regarding Marciano's fights. But there's no new scholarship in his book, nor does he do much to place Marciano in the political and social context of his times. Also, when it comes to Marciano's personal life, Jarrett tends to view him through rose-colored glasses, painting the portrait of a man who felt ambiguous about boxing because "he hated the time it took away from his family in Brockton."

In truth, the historical record developed by Russell Sullivan, Mike Stanton, William Nack, and others suggests that Marciano was more interested in whoring around than in being a good husband and father.

That said; Jarrett's writing flows nicely and he's passionate about his subject. Fans of Rocky Marciano will enjoy the book.

There are many reasons why boxing has had trouble getting mainstream corporate sponsors. Some of them were on display at Barclays Center on April 21, 2018.

A Night at Barclays Center

Too often, undercard fights fail to give fans their money's worth. But the opening bout on the April 21, 2018, fight card at Barclays Center took things to a new level. Heavyweights George Arias and Tyrell Wright fought a sluggish eight rounds with Arias winning a close decision. However, the fight started before the arena was open to the public. That meant anyone who bought a ticket in the hope of seeing Arias vs. Wright couldn't see the fight. So much for respecting the ticket-buying public.

Eventually, 13,964 fans made their way into the arena. Three fights—Gervonta Davis vs. Jesus Cuellar, Jermall Charlo vs. Hugo Centeno, and Adrien Broner vs. Jesse Vargas—headlined the show.

Davis age 23, has a wealth of talent. He briefly held the IBF 130-pound belt before surrendering it on the scales just prior to his last outing. Cuellar, a 7-to-1 underdog whose previous losses were by decision to Oscar Escandon and Abner Mares, was moving up in weight from 126 pounds.

Gervonta has quick hands and good power. He started fast on Saturday night, dropping Cuellar with a straight left to the body in round two and a brutal body shot in round three. Then he pummeled Jesus some more while referee Benjy Esteves waited for an unnecessary third knockdown before stopping the slaughter at 2:45 of the third stanza.

Jermall Charlo won an IBF 154-pound belt with a 2015 stoppage of 42-year-old Cornelius Bundrage. He relinquished his title last year to campaign at 160 pounds but fought only once in 2017 (a victory over Jorge Sebastian Heiland, who came into the bout with a damaged left knee).

Like the Klitschko brothers in the early years of their career, Jermall and his twin brother, Jermell, have suffered in terms of their marketability because there are two of them. Jermall's response has been to say, "Twin power is better. If you don't like the Charlos, stay out of our lane and keep the hate down."

Centeno is the sort of opponent one expects to find as the non-threatening adversary for a house fighter doing battle for a WBC "interim" middleweight title.

In the build-up to the fight, Charlo expended as much energy on his fellow headliners as on Centeno.

In a March 24 Instagram video, Jermall declared, "Y'all motherfuckers coming to see me fight. Ain't nobody coming to see Adrien Broner fight. I didn't want to be on that fucking card. You think I wanted to be on that fucking card? No. I'm being real. I didn't want to be on Adrien Broner's card again. Every time I'm on his fucking card, he lose. Then its Hispanic vs. Black, and I fight a Hispanic. I still do what I gotta do, but this motherfucker don't do what he gotta do. The main event look like shit. The event don't get no recognition. No, I don't want to be on fucking Adrien Broner's card. I'm sorry, I'm just speaking facts."

Then Charlo turned his attention to Davis, proclaiming, "Tank, that little nigga ain't fought nobody. He with Mayweather and ain't fought nobody. This little fat Tank motherfucker, he think he Mayweather. I read the tweets and the comments [from Gervonta]. He's mad because they moved me to the card. I'm sorry, nigga, that my opponent got a broken rib. I gotta fight him on your card, so that means your TV time is cut short. Stop playing with me, nigga, because every time I see you, you ain't really about that shit, you dumb slow stuttering motherfucker."

Charlo was a 20-to-1 favorite over Centeno. The fight didn't last long. Round one saw Jermall stalking his man while Centeno stayed as far away as possible and held when Charlo got in close. Then, forty seconds into round two, Jermall landed a punishing right hand as the opening salvo in a four-punch combination that ended with a vicious left hook to the jaw that dropped Hugo for the count and then some. It's unclear why referee Steve Willis bothered to count since Centeno had zero chance of getting up.

That set the stage for Broner-Vargas.

Broner has prodigious talent that has been undermined by a notable lack of discipline in and out of the ring. He has stepped up in class to fight a world-class opponent on three occasions. Each time (against Marcos Maidana, Shawn Porter, and Mikey Garcia), he lost.

It has been said that trouble follows Broner wherever he goes. An equally valid hypothesis might be that Broner follows trouble.

TMZ reports that Broner has fathered seven children with six different women which, to Adrien's way of thinking, might evince a commitment of sorts to one of the women.

In addition to a string of juvenile arrests, Broner has been charged
with robbery, aggravated robbery, felonious assault, battery, illegal possession of a weapon, domestic violence, and intimidation of a witness.
On February 13 of this year, he added to his rap sheet with a charge of
misdemeanor sexual battery after a woman accused him of groping her
in an Atlanta shopping mall. The woman, Kaila Crews, is now suing him
in a civil lawsuit for sexual battery.

Originally, Broner was slated to fight Omar Figueroa at Barclays
Center to determine a mandatory challenger for the WBC 140-pound
title. But Figueroa fell out after being arrested on a charge of driving
while intoxicated, Vargas was substituted, and the bout was changed to a
catchweight of 144 pounds.

At the final pre-fight press conference on April 19, Broner called
Vargas a "puto" (Spanish for whore) and Leonard Ellerbe (CEO of
Mayweather Promotions, which was co-promoting the fight card) a
"bitch-ass nigger." But by then, it was clear that Adrien's insults might
lead to consequences more serious than discord within the promotion.

More specifically, Broner and Tekashi69 were engaged in a social
media dispute that began when the rapper called Adrien a "clown" on
Instagram. That led Broner to respond, "Ey 6ix9ine, don't be commenting
no fuck shit under my pictures, boy. Talkin' bout clown, nigga. I'm about
to pull up on you, nigga. I ain't one of these rap niggas you be trollin'
with, nigga, quit playin' with me, nigga."

Tekashi69 then countered by calling Broner a "pussy" before suggesting in solid capital letters, "CHECK IN WHEN YOU GET TO
BROOKLYN TOO. KING OF MY CITY."

Thereafter, an April 18 open media workout was canceled as a security precaution and the final pre-fight press conference (previously scheduled for the Highline Ballroom in Manhattan) was moved to Barclays
Center, where there was heightened security. It was also decreed that the
Friday weigh-in would be closed to the public. At the weigh-in, Broner
floated the idea of asking Tekashi69 to walk him to the ring on fight
night. But that was quickly vetoed by the promotion.

When fight night came, there was a heavy police presence at Barclays Center: uniformed cops, plainclothes cops, gang units. Even then, a temporary lockdown was necessary when a gun was fired in the building.

Details are vague at the present time. But it appears as though there has been bad blood between Tekaski69 and a Brooklyn rapper named Casanova. On fight night, the two men and their associates confronted each other in a hallway near a VIP lounge in Barclays Center. A shot was fired and the perpetrator ran from the building. TMZ later reported that a .32 caliber shell casing was recovered by the police. It's unclear how a man with a gun was able to evade what were supposed to be heightened security precautions.

As for the fight; Broner had been listed as an 11-to-10 favorite over Vargas, but the odds flipped during fight week. Adrien was the more physically-gifted fighter. However, as always, there were questions as to where his head was at. Jesse had lost by decision to Timothy Bradley and Manny Pacquiao. But he was a credible opponent with a ninth-round knockout of Sadam Ali to his credit.

After a cautious first round with little aggression from either man, Vargas began throwing with both hands in the second stanza, mixing punches well to the head and body. The action continued in round three with Broner stepping up his own effort and going low often enough that it didn't seem accidental.

At the midway point, Vargas had a substantial lead on the judges' scorecards but appeared to be tiring. Then Broner began landing sharp effective punches. By round nine, Adrien was unloading and it seemed clear that he could hurt Jesse more than Jesse could hurt him.

But Broner, for all his talk, is a safety-first fighter. He's more effective when fighting aggressively but rarely wants to take that risk. Despite being in control of the fight in the late rounds, he never put his foot to the pedal in an effort to knock Vargas out. Then, in an act of foolishness, Adrien took round twelve off.

That cost Broner the fight. Judge Julie Lederman gave the nod to Adrien by a 115–113 margin. But she was overruled by Eric Marlinski and Kevin Morgan, each of whom scored the bout a 114–114 draw.

In the ring after the fight, Broner confronted Vargas while Jesse was being interviewed by Showtime's Jim Gray. Their exchange unfolded as follows:

Broner: Hey man, fuck all that. Let me see the mic. I beat your
  ass. Look at his face. It looks like I beat him with what they
  beat Martin Luther King with [Note: It's likely that Broner
  meant Rodney King].
Vargas: I'm gonna be honest. I'm an honest man. We went at it
  for twelve rounds.
Broner: We didn't go at it. That's gay.
Vargas: We can do it again.
Broner: I beat your ass like you stole something. I beat your ass
  like you were suspended from school. I beat your ass like you
  stole my bicycle, nigga.
Vargas: You can get some more if you want.
Broner: You're bruised up.
Vargas: I'm ready to fight right now, fool.
Broner: C'mon man. You need peroxide and alcohol.
Vargas: You need to settle down.

Broner then turned his attention to Gray and asked, "Was you watching? You got cataracts? Are your eyes all fucked up? Did you see?"

Broner is more bark than bite. The expectation is that he will continue to fall short of what he might have been as a fighter.

Meanwhile, Gervonta Davis and Jermall Charlo attack like pitbulls.
The open issue on each man's resume is that neither has fought a world-
class opponent.

And a final note: Barclays Center was teeming with law enforcement
personnel on Saturday night. But that didn't keep a robbery from taking
place. A young woman named Iranda Paola Torres was robbed. Thousands
of New Yorkers witnessed the heist.

Torres, like many Mexicans, journeyed to the United States in search
of a better way of life. She was here to fight Heather Hardy, the Brooklyn
native whose 21–0 ring record doesn't reflect the times that opponents
have been robbed in the past.

Torres entered the ring with a 12–2–1 ledger, but those numbers
were deceiving. Her last six wins were against women who have a composite ring record of 3 wins and 29 losses.

Thus, Iranda was considered a "safe" opponent for Hardy. But the way
Heather has been fighting lately, no opponent is safe. Hardy looked out of

shape. She tired early, got hit a lot, and ran for most of the night. When the judges' scores were announced (79–73, 78–74, and 78–74), they seemed to be on the mark. Then Heather was proclaimed as the winner.

The pro-Hardy crowd vociferously booed the decision, which brought to mind an email that I received from a reader years ago after an egregious decision went in favor of a Top Rank fighter.

"Did Bob Arum supply girls for the judges," the reader inquired, "or did he perform the favors himself?"

Hardy bears responsibility for her poor performance. But the atrocious scoring isn't her fault. The blame for that falls squarely on the New York State Athletic Commission.

The NYSAC needs to train a new generation of judges and other commission personnel. But it's so mired in petty politics that incompetence and worse have become the accepted standard.

"Vasyl Lomachenko," Jimmy Tobin has written, "is math, not literature."

Vasyl Lomachenko and the Lure of History

Boxing fans want to believe that they're watching greatness. And today's omnipresent hype machine feeds that desire.

"History isn't what it used to be," Patrick Kehoe writes. "Being historically significant is as overrated as you can get these days. Can't they get it in their agreements with the television networks? All they have to say is, 'This fight is one for the ages.' How hard can that be?"

Within that milieu, Vasyl Lomachenko is making a sincere effort to pursue greatness. On May 12, 2018, as part of his quest, he defeated Jorge Linares at Madison Square Garden to claim the World Boxing Association 135-pound title.

"I want to put my name in the history of boxing," Lomachenko said three days before the bout. "This is one of the steps I have to take. Money and titles, you lose, you die. History is forever. I want to get out of my short boxing career the most I can."

The 30-year-old Lomachenko is one of the best—if not the best— fighters in the world today. After winning two Olympic gold medals and compiling an other-worldly 396–1 amateur record, he turned pro in 2013 and lost a questionable split-decision to Orlando Salido in his second professional bout. Three months later, he outpointed Gary Russell Jr to claim the WBO featherweight crown.

Lomachenko's pro record now stands at 11-and-1 with 9 knockouts.

"I've done this a long time," promoter Bob Arum proclaims. "And he hasn't had those tomato cans you usually feed to guys as you're building them. He didn't get those four-and six-rounders who really don't have a shot to win the fight. He was fighting real guys from the beginning."

Lomachenko hasn't just beaten good fighters. He has broken them physically and mentally. In his four outings immediately preceding the Linares bout, Vasyl watched as Nicholas Walters, Jason Sosa, Miguel

Marriaga, and Guillermo Rigondeaux ended matters on their stool rather than come out for more punishment.

Lomachenko is confident but not arrogant. He dresses casually and doesn't talk trash. He answers questions patiently and without artifice. He has turned his body into a well-honed precision instrument and implements his skill set in a way that's all his own.

Boxing doesn't come easily to anyone. Watching Lomachenko in the ring, viewers have to remind themselves how hard it is to do what he does.

"Lomachenko has toyed with world-class opponents as if he were the alley cat and they were the church mouse," Frank Lotierzo writes. "He's an intuitive fighter with an uncanny sense of anticipation. He's an instinctive fighter who grasps how vulnerable an opponent can be rendered if forced to reach and lunge and miss the target. He has a fighting style along with great athleticism and a high boxing IQ that allows him to match up with most styles. He also has the best footwork in boxing and can pivot on a dime while standing in front of his opponents and make them miss, forcing them to punch from their blind side, leaving them open to counters and flurries. And unlike most flashy boxers with great speed, instead of making you have to look for him, he comes to you and presents a target that appears to be right there. Allowing him to fight at his leisure and pick his spots is ring suicide."

To that, Hamilton Nolan has added, "Lomachenko is what happens when you build an entirely new style on top of the frame of technical mastery. His jab hand is like a snake held by the tail, continually poking and striking up and down while the rest of his body seems to be relaxing on its own. His footwork is matchless. He can be anywhere in a 270-degree radius of your face before you can move to meet him. He's in front, now he's on your left side. And he's hitting you body-head-body-head-head before you can tell what's happening. Even when he is directly in front of you, he is unhittable, constantly rolling his shoulders from side to side and darting behind his own gloves like a man peeking out from between two moving pistons. He slips punches with the ease of a grown man pretend-boxing with a toddler. You can't find him, and if you do, you can't hit him. And the whole time he's hitting you."

Linares (44–3, 27 KOs) was a credible opponent, albeit not a great one. Jorge had won WBA belts in two weight classes but has struggled against solid opposition and been stopped short of the distance by Juan Carlos Salgado, Antonio DeMarco, and Sergio Thompson.

Lomachenko opened as a 6-to-1 betting favorite. The odds in some circles ran as high as 10-to-1. Each man weighed in one day before the bout at 134.6 pounds. However, on fight night, Lomachenko weighed 138, while Linares had rehydrated to 152 pounds.

An announced crowd of 10,429 was on hand for the festivities.

It was a fast-paced fight, and the pace grew faster as the bout progressed. There was a lot of movement from each fighter, but the movement was to get into position to punch, not to avoid confrontation.

Lomachenko fights for three minutes of every round. He gives an opponent no time to rest. And he's willing to trade. When an opponent lands, Vasyl immediately fires back. By round four, it appeared as though he had figured Linares out and knew exactly what he needed to do to win. The area around Jorge's right eye was swelling and he was starting to take a beating.

Then . . . Two minutes thirty seconds into round six, Lomachenko threw a right jab and his protective left hand drifted a shade too far to the left.

Linares fired a textbook counter right.

Vasyl saw it coming, but he saw it too late.

"It was a great punch," Lomachenko said afterward. "It happens."

The blow landed smack in the center of Lomachenko's face and dropped him to the canvas. It was the first time he'd been knocked down since an amateur bout eleven years ago. Fifteen seconds later, the bell ending the round sounded. But now the fight had a new dimension. Vasyl looked smaller than he had before. And a war was raging.

It was a superb fight. Both men dug deep.

The battle ended in round ten.

Lomachenko buried a brutal straight left in Linares's liver.

Jorge went down and was able to beat the count. Barely. If the bell had rung, he might have been able to regroup during the one-minute break between rounds and fight on. But there were 52 seconds left in the stanza and, in the moment, he was in no condition to continue. Referee Ricky Gonzalez appropriately stopped the fight.

All of boxing's greatest fighters have hit the canvas. It's what happens after a fighter goes down that matters. Lomachenko closed the show the way a great fighter should.

Lomachenko seems sincere in his stated desire to fight the best and earn a place in boxing lore through his ring accomplishments rather than hype.

"I haven't shown yet what I'm capable of doing," Vasyl says.

He's not afraid of losing. If it happens, it happens.

So the question now is, "What happens next?"

Becoming the fourth man to beat Jorge Linares is hardly an accomplishment of historic proportions. The fight that boxing fans most want to see is Lomachenko versus Mikey Garcia. A victory over Garcia at 135 pounds would raise Vasyl to a new level (as it would for Garcia were he to beat Lomachenko). Outside of Garcia—and possibly Gervonta Davis—it's hard to think of a fighter at 135 pounds or less who is likely to give Lomachenko a tough fight. And it would be a mistake for Vasyl to move up too far in weight. Lomachenko himself acknowledged that reality two days before facing Linares when he was asked about fighting Manny Pacquiao and answered, "My real weight to fight is 130 pounds. I don't know now how I'll feel at 135. To talk now about a Pacquiao fight at 144 pounds doesn't make sense."

One can play mind games and match Lomachenko against great fighters from the past. But it's impossible to judge a fighter's place in history based on twelve pro fights. So for now, let's say that Vasyl Lomachenko is an exceptionally good professional fighter and hope that he has the opportunity to match his skills against today's best.

Manny Pacquiao was once at the center of the boxing universe.

Manny Pacquiao vs. Lucas Matthysse

The more time goes by, the less Manny Pacquiao feels like a feel-good story. On July 14, 2018, in Kuala Lumpur, Malaysia, "Pacman" knocked out Lucas Matthysse to claim one more in a long line of sanctioning body belts. But the narrative has changed.

Ten years ago, Pacquiao was on the verge of launching a three-fight knockout streak against Oscar De La Hoya, Ricky Hatton, and Miguel Cotto that would establish him as a great fighter. He had risen from the streets and was about to become a global icon. He planned on running for public office and someday becoming president of the Philippines. He was a standard bearer for oppressed people around the world and had a kind word for everyone who came into his orbit.

Times change.

Pacquiao will turn forty years old on December 17. He has won some elections, first for a seat in the Filipino House of Representatives and then in the Senate. But he has been largely ineffective as a congressman, made virulently homophobic statements, and cast his lot with the repressive regime of Filipino president Rodrigo Duterte.

He has also fought too long. As Pacquiao entered his confrontation with Matthysse, his once vaunted power seemed a distant memory. He had lost four of his most recent nine fights and hadn't knocked out an opponent since fighting Miguel Cotto nine years, thirteen fights, and 150 rounds ago. Conversations regarding his boxing skills lingered on the past.

The end of Manny's relationship with trainer Freddie Roach also chipped away at Pacquiao's good-guy image. That relationship was part of the feel-good story. They were together for 34 fights over 16 years.

Earlier this year, Roach learned via a press release issued by Team Pacquiao that he had been dismissed as Manny's trainer. This came five months after Freddie told an interviewer, "I think it's a good time for him to retire. He's doing a good job as a senator right now, but not as a boxer."

"Manny and I had a great run," Roach said when advised of his termination. "Longer than most marriages and certainly a rarity for boxing. I would be lying if I didn't say I was hurt that he didn't contact me personally about his decision. If Manny would have called me and told me what he wanted to do, it would have been a perfect ending. But I learned a long time ago, life is not perfect. I'm disappointed that I had to read it in the newspaper and I didn't hear it from Manny first. That stings a little, but there are no hard feelings. I have no complaints because my life is so much better in so many ways because of Manny Pacquiao. I wouldn't trade any of it. Inside the boxing ring and the political ring, I wish Manny nothing but the best."

Pacquiao-Matthysse was viewed as an intriguing fight with Pacquiao installed as a 2-to-1 betting favorite.

Five years ago, Matthysse (now 39-and-5 with 36 KOs) was a significant player on the boxing scene. His only losses were split-decision verdicts at the hands of Zab Judah and Devon Alexander. Then he devastated Lamont Peterson in three rounds, which set the stage for Matthysse vs. Danny Garcia on the undercard of Floyd Mayweather vs. Canelo Alvarez. Matthysse came up short that night, losing a unanimous decision. Two years after that, he was stopped in ten rounds by Viktor Postol.

The knock on Matthysse is that he has trouble with quick opponents and tends to fall apart when faced with adversity. Also, at age 35, he's past his prime.

In the weeks leading up to Pacquiao-Matthysse, there were questions regarding how solid the financial backing for the fight really was and whether the bout would proceed as planned. By the time the necessary financial components (i.e., money in the bank) were in place, it was too late to undertake a pay-per-view promotional campaign in the United States, so the card was televised on ESPN+. Joe Tessitore, Tim Bradley, and Mark Kriegel called the action off a TV monitor in New Orleans where they were on site for an ESPN fight between Regis Prograis and Juan Jose Velasco.

Pacquiao weighed in at 146 pounds; Matthysse at 146.7. Kenny Bayless was brought in to Kuala Lumpur from Las Vegas to referee the fight.

Pacquiao was the aggressor throughout. As his foot-speed has decreased in recent years, his ability to reset quickly at sharp angles and punch effectively has diminished. But Matthysse's own footwork was so plodding on Saturday night that Lucas was unable to set his own feet and punch with power. And when in range, Matthysse was unable or unwilling to pull the trigger. To say that he looked one-dimensional would be giving him credit for one more dimension than he showed.

Pacquiao dominated the action. In round three, he scored a knockdown with a sharp left uppercut. Toward the end of round five, Matthysse took a knee after being on the receiving end of what appeared to be a glancing right hand up top. In round seven, a left uppercut dropped him again, at which point Lucas spat out his mouthpiece and Kenny Bayless stopped the fight.

Speaking from an ESPN studio, Teddy Atlas put the bout in perspective.

"You hit a heavy bag, you look good," Atlas noted. "All you Pacquiao maniac fans out there, no disrespect. Give him a lot of credit. Thirty-nine years old, he got the job done. He looked good, yes. Against a 35-year-old who, in the end, quit, a diminished Matthysse. Matthysse did not fight. He did not try, For the most part, he was a passive guy who looked like he was just getting paid. He took a knee; he looked like he was going to quit in the fifth round when he got hit with that punch that barely touched him. It didn't look like a consequential punch. I'm not in his brain; I know that. But I've been in this business forty-five years. He was thinking, 'Do I continue? All right, I'll continue.' Then he got convinced not to continue with that really good left uppercut in the seventh round. Marvelous performance for a 39-year-old with 69 fights; no doubt about it. But no effort on the other side. No resistance on the other side."

Pacquiao's record now stands at 60–7–2 with 39 knockouts. He'll never be a great fighter again. The question is, "Can he be very good?"

Regis Prograis' nickname is "Rougarou"—a legendary werewolf-like creature said to prowl the swamps of southern Louisiana.

Regis Prograis and World Boxing Super Series

On October 27, 2018, the World Boxing Super Series will break new ground when 29-year-old junior-welterweight Regis Prograis steps into the ring to face Terry Flanagan.

Why new ground? Because Prograis is widely regarded as the best 140-pound boxer in the world today. Some knowledgeable observers think that he'll be the first elite American fighter to emerge from the WBSS.

Prograis was born in New Orleans and has multiple athletic gifts. If he'd been six inches taller and sixty pounds heavier, he might have played in the NFL.

"I was good at football," Regis reminisces. "I played running back and cornerback until I was fourteen. One time, I scored six touchdowns in a game in a New Orleans Park Ball League. We lost because the other team had two brothers—Delvin and Lionel Breaux—who scored seven touchdowns between them. I scored six by myself and the two of them scored seven."

One might note here that Delvin Breaux later played cornerback in college for LSU and in the NFL for the New Orleans Saints. Lionel Breaux played wide receiver at the University of Mississippi.

"I loved playing football," Prograis adds. "But I was small. And the other thing was, I didn't want to practice. Boxing was the only sport I loved to practice at."

New Orleans boxing has a storied tradition. James J. Corbett defeated John L. Sullivan at the Olympic Club in New Orleans on September 7, 1892, to claim the heavyweight crown. Ray Leonard's "no mas" triumph over Roberto Duran and Muhammad Ali's victory in a rematch against Leon Spinks were also contested in New Orleans. Harry Wills and Tony Canzoneri are the best-known fighters to have been born in Louisiana.

Prograis moved to Houston in 2005 after Hurricane Katrina devastated New Orleans. But he plans on becoming a significant part of The Big Easy's boxing tradition.

"Most people are scared of fights," he says. "But as a kid, I loved to fight. It started at school. I was popular in school but you know how it is. Everybody picked on everybody, so you have to fight. Before I started in the amateurs, I was fighting grown men in the streets, sometimes with gloves on, just for fun."

Prograis began fighting in sanctioned amateur bouts at age sixteen. He fought Errol Spence in the amateurs twice and lost by decision each time. "I always had a professional style," he recounts. "My goal was never the Olympics. It was always to turn pro."

Regis is likable, engaging, and confident. He's married with a young son and daughter.

"Because of boxing," he says, "I can go home to New Orleans and do things for my family that I couldn't do if I had a regular job. But it's not just family that I'm interested in. I'm interested in all people. I want to know why people think the way they think. I like meeting people with different kinds of minds who make me think."

Prograis turned pro at age 23 and has compiled a 22–0 (19 KOs) ring record as a pro. He's a southpaw with speed, power, boxing smarts, and a ferocious body attack.

"The most I was ever hurt was five, six years ago," he recalls. "I was sparring with Jermall Charlo and he hit me with a body shot. It was bad. I didn't go down but I was glad when the round ended. And I learned from it. I said to myself, 'If that's how it feels, I got to do more of that myself.'"

Regis beat three undefeated prospects—Amos Cowart, Abel Ramos, and Joel Diaz Jr—on ShowBox. On March 9, 2018, he demolished Julius Indongo in two rounds. He's currently trained by Bobby Benton, one of the better young trainers in boxing. And he can fight.

Several months ago, trainer Freddie Roach was asked, "How good is Prograis?"

"Regis wouldn't be my first choice for one of my guys to fight," Roach answered.

"Who would be?"

"Somebody other than Regis."

Originally, Prograis was managed by Jay Johns. When their boxer-manager contract expired, he signed with a management team that includes Sam Katkovski and Churchill Management.

Churchill was founded in 2016 by director-producer-writer Peter Berg and actor-producer Mark Wahlberg. The group also has six lesser known partners. Other managers offered Prograis more money. But he felt that Churchill would look after his interests, and he has some Hollywood in him.

Asked why he chose to not sign with Al Haymon, Regis explains that (1) he thought he might be regarded as "just one of the fighters" on the PBC roster; and (2) he wants to fight more often than Haymon's fighters fight. Also, he reasoned that Berg and Wahlberg are not without influence.

Lou DiBella has been Prograis' promoter since 2015.

On March 17, 2018, Jose Carlos Ramirez (a Top Rank fighter) fought Amir Imam (promoted by Don King) at Madison Square Garden for the World Boxing Council 140-pound title that had been vacated by Terence Crawford. Prograis was ranked ahead of Ramirez by the WBC and should have been in the ring fighting Imam. But there was an opportunity for additional sanctioning fees, and the WBC embraced a scenario whereby Prograis fought Julius Indongo for an "interim" world title eight days before Ramirez and Iman fought for the "regular" WBC belt. The understanding was that the two winners would then fight each other with a 50–50 purse split between them.

But Top Rank wanted no part of Prograis as an opponent for Ramirez. Instead, Bob Arum began talking about Regis fighting in the main supporting bout beneath a Ramirez title defense in June. Team Prograis said "no" to that. But there were concerns as to whether the WBC would really enforce a purse bid for Prograis-Ramirez. And DiBella was afraid that, if it did, Ramirez would claim an injury and pull out of the fight.

Also, by then, the World Boxing Super Series was beckoning.

Prograis had long said that he wants to bring bigtime boxing back to New Orleans. He'd fought in Louisiana on three occasions but never at home. Thus, he agreed to a July 14, 2018, bout against Juan Jose Velasco as the main event at the Lakefront Arena in New Orleans. The fight card was co-promoted by Top Rank and DiBella. Prograis showed flashes of brilliance in beating Velasco down with a brutal body attack that included three knockdowns occasioned by pulverizing body shots en route to an eighth-round stoppage. In the convoluted world of today's sanctioning bodies, he's now listed as the WBC 140-pound "diamond" champion.

That brings us to the World Boxing Super Series. Season One was a success in that it brought clarity to the cruiserweight division and established Oleksandr Usyk as the best cruiserweight in the world. Also, Callum Smith emerged as a force at 168 pounds. But both WBSS tournaments played out beneath the radar of boxing fans in the United States because of the absence of a meaningful television contract.

That problem now appears to have been solved. Season Two of the WBSS will feature eight-man elimination tournaments at 118, 140, and 200 pounds. All twenty-one bouts are slated to be televised by DAZN. Prograis (who as earlier mentioned, is scheduled to fight Terry Flanagan on October 27) is the #1 seed at 140 pounds. But Regis's ambitions go way beyond the World Boxing Super Series.

"I love the spotlight," he says. "I always have. And I like going in tough. I'm a competitor. I feel like I can do anything in the ring when I fight off my instincts and rhythm. I train hard. I've developed skills. But it comes naturally to me. I'm a natural fighter. My best weapon is my boxing IQ. I set up my shots. I know where to put them. I'm always planning where the next punch will go. I can be aggressive. I can counterpunch. I can be slick. I can be a volume puncher. I have a style that's a mixture of things, a style that's no style. I can be mean too. You got to be mean to be a great fighter. If I hit someone on the elbow, I want to hurt his elbow. If I hit him on the shoulder, I want to hurt his shoulder."

"The best thing about being a fighter," Regis continues, "is the respect you get. And the self-respect. You walk down the street and you feel indestructible. That's not true; I know that. They got bullets. But being a fighter gives you that feeling. Because of boxing, I feel I can do anything. I feel fear before all my fights. The most is usually a week or so before the fight. You never know what will happen in the ring. One punch can change everything. On fight night, I'm still a little nervous. But once I put my hands up, I'm good. I'm not scared of anything."

"Most people don't understand how complicated boxing is," Prograis says in closing. "You're always learning. It's always different when you get in there. You can watch boxing all day long. But until you get in front of that person and they hit you and you're hitting them, you never know what's gonna happen. I watch all the old fighters. Sugar Ray Robinson, Muhammad Ali. Every fighter can be beat. I look at seeing how to beat them as something like a math problem. I would have loved to have fought guys like Roberto Duran, Henry Armstrong, Aaron Pryor, to test my skills and courage against them. Courage is how you react to a situation. Every fighter has courage or he wouldn't be a fighter. The question is, 'What are your skills and how much courage do you have?' For me, the greatest show of courage is when a fighter is getting beaten up and comes back to win. I haven't been tested like that yet, but I will be someday."

New stars come along from time to time in boxing. Regis Prograis is well-positioned to fit into that narrative. "I can't tell you how good I am," he says. "I don't know my limits yet. But I can tell you, I'm a fighter, man. I'm a fighter."

One difference between a prizefight and surgery is that, in the operating room, they knock you out before the action begins.

Jacobs–Derevyanchenko and the Operating Room

Danny Jacobs entered dressing room #6 at the Hulu Theater at Madison Square Garden on October 27 at 9:00 p.m. In a little more than two hours, he would be fighting Sergey Derevyanchenko for the IBF 160-pound title.

The room was roughly eleven feet squared, a size better suited for a small entertainment act readying to go onstage than a world-class fighter's retinue. Six folding metal-framed chairs and two narrow equipment tables were the only furniture. The gray-and-white speckled tile floor, cream-colored walls, and high intensity lights gave the enclosure the feel of a hospital surgical preparation room. That was appropriate since Jacobs will always be defined in part by his battle against cancer.

In 2011, Jacobs felt numbness in his legs and began having difficulty walking. The diagnosis was osteosarcoma: a life-threatening form of bone cancer that had wrapped a tumor around his spine. He underwent surgery and returned to the ring after a 19-month layoff with titanium rods implanted in his back. It's difficult to overstate the magnitude of his accomplishments and courage.

There are more than a few parallels between a boxer's dressing room and a surgical preparation room.

There's an anxious wait.

A select group of family and friends come by to wish their loved one well.

Surgeons, anesthesiologists, nurses, and other medical support staff have specific jobs to do. The same holds true for a fighter's trainer, cutman, and other seconds. Everyone understands the nature of the mission as they review their plan one last time.

The hospital patient puts on a gown. An antibacterial solution is applied to his body. For a fighter, it's boxing trunks and Vaseline. Latex-free rubber gloves are the order of the day for many in attendance.

In each instance, physical danger and life-altering consequences loom. A fighter in his dressing room knows that he will be hurt physically. The question is how badly he will be damaged. For a hospital patient, the threatening physical condition is the opponent.

Jacobs-Derevyanchenko was a significant middleweight bout and a crossroads fight for both men.

Jacobs, a 31-year-old lifelong Brooklyn resident, had amassed a 34–2 (29 KOs) ring record and won what's politely referred to as a "minor" title when he knocked out Jarrod Fletcher in 2014. Thirty-one months later, he acquitted himself well in challenging Gennady Golovkin for the legitimate middleweight crown but lost a close decision. His resume was thin on victories over quality opponents.

Derevyanchenko, a 32-year-old Ukrainian national born in Crimea and now living in Brooklyn, had a reported amateur record of 390 wins against 20 losses. Despite a meager (12–0, 10 KOs) professional ledger, he'd been designated by the IBF as the mandatory challenger for its portion of what was then Golovkin's 160-pound empire. But Gennady declined to fight Derevyanchenko, opting instead for an easier outing against Vanes Martirosyan and a lucrative rematch against Canelo Alvarez, He was then stripped of his belt which left Derevyanchenko in line to fight one of several possible opponents for the IBF crown.

The most obvious opponent for Derevyanchenko was Jacobs. But Danny was locked into a contract with promoter Eddie Hearn and HBO, which limited the home for that fight. Lou DiBella (Derevyanchenko's promoter) wanted to explore other options for Sergiy including a possible IBF title fight against Englishman Martin Murray. That bout would have been less lucrative for Dervyanchenko, but more likely to lead to his winning a belt. However, Keith Connolly (who manages Jacobs and advises Dervyanchenko) preferred Jacobs-Derevyanchenko and instructed Sergiy to cease all communication with DiBella. That led to a great deal of shouting back and forth with DiBella doing most of the shouting.

Ultimately, Jacobs-Derevyanchenko was made. With a twist.

Andre Rozier trains both fighters with Gary Stark Sr as his assistant. It was agreed that Rozier would work with Jacobs while Stark would train Derevyanchenko. Asked at the kick-off press conference if he was offended that Rozier had chosen to work with Jacobs instead of with him,

Derevyanchenko answered. "No. I said to him, 'Andre, I understand. You worked with Daniel since he was a kid.' If I'm Andre, I do the same thing."

More intriguing was the fact that, over the years, Jacobs and Derevyanchenko had sparred more than three hundred rounds together. What were the implications of that for the fight? Former WBO 140-pound champion Chris Algieri, who worked extensively with Jacobs as a nutritionist in the months leading up to the bout, speculated that the many sparring sessions would help Derevyanchenko.

"Danny has had more professional fights and more big fights than Sergiy," Algieri posited. "He has learned how to deal with the pressure of those situations. But the unknown is diminished here for Sergiy because he has sparred so many rounds with Danny. That takes some of the pressure off him."

If Jacobs won, he'd have a marketable belt and be well-positioned for future big-money fights. If he lost, it would be back to the drawing board. For Derevyanchenko, a win would mean that he had a belt and a salable name. A loss would send him back to relative anonymity.

"I want belt," Sergiy told the media at the kick-off press conference. "Danny want belt. If I have belt, guys will say, 'okay, let's fight.' If I don't have belt, they don't want to fight me. Maybe it is the one chance in my life."

The normal pre-fight rituals of boxing proceeded apace in Jacob's dressing room on fight night. There was stretching, the taping of hands, gloving up, padwork. In another room off the same corridor, Derevyanchenko was preparing for his own reckoning.

Soon, the fighters would enter the ring where overhead lights would shine as brightly as those in a hospital operating room. Each man would be both patient and surgeon. Unlike a patient under anesthesia, they would retain a significant measure of control. But in both theaters—the ring and the operating room—things can go horribly wrong.

Even with careful planning, the unexpected sometimes happens. A disease can surprise both doctor and patient with its resilience and reach. Cancer thought to have been contained can be found to have metastasized from the colon to the liver. No matter how well a fighter has prepared for a fight, a chance cut or debilitating blow that seems to come out of nowhere can change everything. There are no guarantees.

The unknown looms for every one of us for every moment of our lives. As former heavyweight champion Larry Holmes once said, "None of us is promised tomorrow." But the stakes are undeniably higher and the uncertainty of life is more obvious at certain moments in time.

In Danny Jacobs's case, seven years ago, some people were going to cut him open, reach into his body, untangle a living organism that was wrapped around his spine, and remove the organism from his body before it destroyed him.

How does Jacobs compare the roles of patient and fighter?

"It's the difference between nerves and fear," he explained three days before fighting Derevyanchenko. "There's no fear in the dressing room. Nerves? Yes. Fear? No. There was a lot of fear when I was getting ready for the operating room. They're as different as night and day."

Jacobs was a 2-to-1 betting favorite over Derevyanchenko. Both fighters started cautiously. Then at the 2:38 mark of round one, Danny landed a sharp right to the top of Sergiy's head. Derevyanchenko kept his feet but his gloves touched the canvas, leading referee Charlie Fitch to correctly call a knockdown.

For much of the bout, it seemed as though Jacobs would have been satisfied with a sparring session. Despite being the bigger faster better athlete and seemingly harder puncher, he often back-peddled and circled away. But when Derevyanchenko forced the issue, Jacobs obliged him.

Also, while Derevyanchenko is a pressure fighter, he's not a big puncher. And Jacobs, who seemed a bit fragile early in his career, now has "man strength." There was always the feeling that he could hurt Sergiy more than Sergiy could hurt him.

As the rounds wore on, the action heated up with both men landing solid blows. From time to time, Jacobs switched to a southpaw stance. He also went to the body effectively although his blows strayed low often enough that Fitch could have warned him for the infractions.

It was a good fight. Derevyanchenko showed a solid chin and took everything that Jacobs landed. They didn't fight like friends. The decision could have gone either way. Jacobs emerged on the winning end of a 115–112, 115–112, 113–114 split verdict.

For Jacobs, the operation was a success.

Boxing fans want to believe that what we saw was special. Some fights we saw in 2018 were; others weren't.

Fight Notes

The January 14, 2018, IBF welterweight title fight between Errol Spence (22–0, 19 KOs) and Lamont Peterson (35–3–1, 17 KOs, 1 KO by) marked another step in the maturation process of a man who appears to be a special fighter.

Young fighters on the rise have a look about them. Their confidence, optimism, and strength are evident in the way they walk, their posture, their eyes.

Spence, who turned 28 on January 13, has that look. This appraisal is bolstered by the way he has outclassed a lot of ordinary fighters plus his May 27, 2017, demolition of Kell Brook (KO 11) and now his performance against Peterson. Boxing might take a toll on him someday. But for the moment, he's riding high.

By contrast, the 33-year-old Peterson has seen better days as a fighter. The high point of his career was a controversial 2011 split-decision verdict over Amir Khan in Lamont's hometown of Washington D.C. The low point came seventeen months later when Peterson was wiped out in three rounds by Lucas Matthysse.

Peterson had been in the ring only once in the 27 months preceding his outing against Spence. The prevailing view was that Lamont had little chance of winning and would be just another name on Errol's resume. The promotion was about Spence, not Peterson and Spence. Errol was a 15-to-1 betting favorite.

Both fighters conducted themselves as exemplary sportsmen throughout the promotion. There was no trash-talking. They're excellent representatives for boxing.

"Errol Spence is clearly a great fighter," Peterson said at a January 17 media workout. "I can see why people revere him in that way. But on Saturday, we're going to give him a fight and he's going to have to prove it."

Spence responded in kind, saying. "I've seen too many fighters look down the road, and the guy standing right in front of them that they don't see beats them." But Errol also put people on notice with the declaration, "I want a dominant performance. I want to look great. I want everybody to talk about this fight after the fight."

Spence weighed in at the 147-pound welterweight limit, Peterson at 146–¾.

A crowd of 12,107 witnessed the proceedings at Barclays Center. They saw a good fighter who's past his prime versus a better fighter who might be moving toward greatness.

My notes, taken during the fight, read as follows:

Round 1: Spence controlling the action with his jab . . . Peterson maintaining a protective posture, throwing next to nothing . . . Spence is too good offensively to just play defense against. As dangerous as it might be, Peterson will have to fight fire with fire.

Round 2: Spence opening Peterson up by going to the body, then upstairs. He's very sound fundamentally, economical with his punches and movement, very little wasted effort . . . Putting on a clinic.

Round 3: Peterson fighting more aggressively now rather than be a sitting duck. Trying without success to get inside and smother Spence's punches . . . Spence landing more often and harder . . . Great punch selection, pinpoint accuracy. And the body shots keep coming . . . Peterson looks hurt and tired as he walks to his corner. No way he goes twelve rounds.

Round 4: Non-stop pressure from Spence. Good defense. Brutal offense. Not giving Peterson any time to rest . . . Peterson's face is bruised and swelling up . . . Spence is painting a masterpiece.

Round 5: Spence teeing off . . . Straight left drops Peterson. A lot of time left in the round . . . Lamont fighting back courageously but he doesn't have the tools to survive. Spence firing bombs. Peterson throwing firecrackers.

Round 6: Spence's methodical assault continues. He has fast hands and pulls the trigger quickly . . . Peterson has nothing to keep him off . . . Peterson won't win. He can't win. They should stop the fight now.

Round 7: Peterson taking a beating. Nothing left but heart.

After round seven, Barry Hunter (Peterson's trainer) stopped the fight.

"I didn't like what I was seeing," Hunter said afterward. "If you know Lamont, you know he wasn't going to give up. I had to stop it."

Hunter might have added that there's nothing dishonorable about a fighter giving his all and being outclassed by a better fighter.

Spence has an aura of honesty about him. When he talks about his skills, it comes across as candid self-appraisal rather than bragging.

"There's still a lot to prove," Errol says. "There are so many guys in the welterweight division. I want to clean them all out. Everybody wants to be that number-one guy. That's what we're all fighting for."

But as a practical matter, there are a limited number of competitive fights that can be made for Spence at 147 pounds. It won't be easy to get quality fighters to face him. Some lesser boxers will line up for a payday. But not many beltholders or high-level contenders will risk their standing against him.

Spence can do everything that most fighters do, only he does it better. The fact that he's a southpaw makes him more difficult to contend with. And in the ring, he's "Sugar Ray Leonard nasty." The one open question about him is his chin. For the most part, Errol has been steered clear of fighters who hit hard enough to test it. Beyond that, he's a complete fighter.

After Spence beat Kell Brook, Bart Barry wrote, "Spence is the first prizefighter to give one hope about PBC's prospects for survival as a promotional outfit, not merely a venture-capital black hole. Spence is PBC born and PBC raised. If Al Haymon's outfit gives us a unified champion in our sport's best division, the PBC and its model will deserve a second look and maybe even a bit less cynicism."

That unification is unlikely to happen in the near future. And because of the PBC model (as well as its apparently dwindling cash reserves), Spence has fought only once every eight months as of late. There has been no continuity in his promotion from fight to fight, and Errol still doesn't have an identity in the public mind. This shortchanges a fighter who might be great.

★ ★ ★

There was a time when boxing's best fought each other as a matter of course. That era peaked when HBO had the resolve and money to make super-fights and the landscape was graced by warriors like Ray Leonard,

Thomas Hearns, Marvin Hagler, and Roberto Duran. Too often in recent years, boxing fans have been reduced to imagining big fights rather than watching them.

Enter an ambitious undertaking known as the World Boxing Super Series (WBSS).

The WBSS is funded by Comosa AG (a European entertainment company). It began as a joint venture with Sauerland Promotions. Richard Schaefer was brought into the mix to promote WBSS fights that are contested in the United States and, more importantly, to negotiate a deal for WBSS television rights with an American network. It was also contemplated that Schaefer would be involved in dealing with third parties in other countries where he might have better connections than Sauerland.

It its inaugural year, the WBSS has featured eight-man elimination tournaments in boxing's cruiserweight and super-middleweight divisions. Schaefer outlined the premise behind the venture as follows: "Most sports have a signature event or events. Baseball, football, soccer, golf, tennis, NCAA basketball. The idea is to brand this as a signature event. Comosa thinks they'll lose money for the first two or three years while they're building their brand and then turn a corner."

There was a lot of pie-in-the-sky hype at the start. In March 2017, the WBSS announced that fighters in the first two tournaments would compete for $50 million in purses, although Schaefer soon conceded that $50 million was "just a number because we don't know yet who will enter the tournaments."

Comosa also entered into a long-term licensing deal with Authentic Brands Group (which controls commercial rights to the name, likeness, and image of Muhammad Ali). That enabled tournament organizers to declare hyperbolically that the fighters in each weight division would do battle for "The Greatest Prize in Boxing, the Muhammad Ali Trophy."

The participants and seedings in each weight division were determined last summer. No recognized world title-holders were entered in the 168-pound mix, although George Groves picked up a vacant WBA belt when he defeated Jamie Cox in the first round of the tournament.

The cruiserweights were another matter. All four major cruiserweight beltholders—Murat Gassiev (IBF), Yunier Dorticos (WBA), Oleksandr

Usyk (WBO), and Mairus Briedis (WBC)—entered the fray. They were joined by a credible supporting cast of Marco Huck, Krzyslof Wlodarczyk, Dmitry Kudryashov, and Mike Perez.

But there have been problems, the most significant of which is the absence of a deal with an American television network.

Multiple sources say that, at the start of the negotiating process, Schaefer asked Showtime for a $15 million licensing fee that he would then use to sign tournament participants. Showtime responded that Schaefer was dreaming and suggested that he try to work something out on a lesser scale with Al Haymon (Showtime's primary provider of content). Nothing came to fruition on that front.

Epix offered $500,000 for all fourteen fights in the first two tournaments and was prepared to go higher as negotiations progressed. But the WBSS felt that they were in different universes when it came to an appropriate license fee for the bouts.

Meanwhile, there are rumblings that all is not well between Comosa, Sauerland, and Schaefer. Feelings have been bruised, and there are questions as to whether Schaefer overstated what he could bring to the table in terms of American television money and whether Showtime backed away from a promise to support the tournaments.

The absence of a significant TV deal has made it impossible for the WBSS to catch on in the United States. That's a shame insofar as the cruiserweights are concerned.

The WBSS super-middleweight tournament has sparked interest in England, primarily because of the involvement of Groves and Chris Eubank Jr. But the cruiserweight tournament is special. The championship round will be contested between Murat Gassiev and Okelsandy Usyk on May 11. Two fighters who have earned the right to call themselves the best cruiserweights in the world will square off with the winner being legitimately acclaimed as #1.

The World Boxing Super Series cruiserweight tournament is what boxing should be about.

★ ★ ★

Some observations on the March 17, 2018, St. Patrick's Day fight card promoted by Top Rank in The Theater at Madison Square Garden.

Irish Olympian Michael Conlan (the only Irishman on the card) was the big ticket seller. Super-lightweight Jose Ramirez was the big winner. Four of the eight bouts were of consequence, and the first of these marked the fall from grace of Felix Verdejo.

Top Rank signed Verdejo out of the 2012 Olympics and at one time was touting him as Puerto Rico's next ring icon. Felix has charisma (which helps outside the ring) and fast hands (which help in it). He'd compiled a 23–0 (15 KOs) record but failed too often to close the show against pedestrian opposition.

Antonio Lozada Jr. (37–2, 31 KOs) was chosen as Verdejo's opponent on the theory that he was a beatable measuring stick. In other words, Verdejo-Lozada was made for Verdejo to win. And Felix couldn't do it.

Rather than engage, Verdejo prefers to move, potshot, and move some more, which usually succeeds against slow plodding opponents like Lozada. But after nine rounds of frustration, Lozada caught up to Felix in round ten, staggered him with left hook up top, battered him around the ring, and dropped him with another hook. Verdejo rose and was struggling to survive when, with 23 seconds left in the bout, New York State Athletic Commission chief medical officer Nitin Sethi mounted the ring apron and instructed referee Eddie Claudio to stop the fight.

Verdejo was leading on the judges' scorecards 87–84, 86–85, 85–86 at the time of the stoppage. But had the fight gone the distance with the final round scored 10–8 in Lozada's favorite, Antonio would have emerged victorious on a split-decision.

Light-heavyweight Oleksandr Gvozdyk (14–0, 12 KOs) also disappointed. Gvozdyk had looked good in previous outings and was regarded by some as on the same level as Sergey Kovalev, Dmitry Bivol, Artur Beterbiev, and Adonis Stevenson. He might be, but he didn't show it on Saturday night. Facing Mehdi Amar (34–5–2, 16 KOs) of France in a sloppily-contested World Boxing Council "interim" title bout, Oleksandr plodded to a winning 118–110, 117–111, 116–112 verdict.

The fight of greatest interest was Jose Ramirez (21–0, 16 KOs) vs Amir Imam (21–1, 18 KOs). Normally, that would have been the main event. But Top Rank saved Michael Conlan for last on the theory that it wouldn't look good if eighty percent of the 4,672 fans in attendance walked out of the arena before the main event.

The World Boxing Council trumpeted the fact that Ramirez-Imam was its 2,000th world championship fight. More specifically, Ramirez-Imam was for the vacant WBC world 140-pound title. Regis Prograis vs. Julius Indongo (contested on March 9) was for the vacant WBC "interim" world 140-pound title. And Adrien Broner was supposed to fight Omar Figueroa on April 21 to determine the "mandatory" challenger for the WBC world 140-pound champion (whoever that might be). All of this left open the question of what would happen to the "interim" WBC world champion when a "real" WBC 140-pound champion was crowned. Then Figueroa fell out of the Broner fight, Jessie Vargas was substituted as Broner's opponent at a catchweight of 144 pounds, and the issue got slightly less convoluted.

The WBC is celebrating its fifty-fifth anniversary this year. Perhaps it could adopt the motto: "Fifty-Five Years of Sanctioning Fees."

Ramirez has become a symbol of immigration rights and farmers' water rights in California's Central Valley. Against Imam, he fought at a brisk pace, and forced the action for every minute of every round.

Imam had faster hands and was reasonably effective when he jabbed but seemed less interested in jabbing than in staying away.

Ramirez committed to the body early and often. There were some good exchanges when Imam stood his ground and fired back out of necessity. But over time, Jose broke Amir down. Ramirez might not have wanted it more, but he fought like he did en route to winning a 120–108, 117–111, 115–113 decision.

That set the stage for the super-featherweight bout between Michael Conlan and David Berna.

Berna has fought virtually his entire career in Hungary and had cobbled together a manufactured 15-and-2 record. He fought seven times last year, winning five and losing twice. The losses were by knockout in the first and second round. The five wins were against fighters with a composite ring record of 6 wins in 35 fights. He was a safe opponent.

Conlan knocked Berna down with a straight left to the pit of the stomach in round one and a blow of questionable provenance in round two. Berna rose from the second "knockdown" showing no interest in further hostilities, and referee Eddie Claudio stopped the fight. ESPN replayed the first knockdown but not the second, perhaps because there was no punch of consequence to see.

Signing with Top Rank was the right move for Conlan (now 6–0, 5 KOs). His ring skills are more suited to the amateur than professional ranks. But Top Rank will give him exposure on ESPN and a diet of opponents he can beat while maneuvering him to a title opportunity against weak opposition.

And a closing note . . .

Amir Imam is the best of what's left in Don King's inventory of fighters. He was 18-and-0 and on a fast track until being knocked out in 2015 by Adrian Granados. Since then, Imam has had three wins in three fights, but the opponents had a total of 47 losses between them.

Ramirez-Imam was styled as a "co-promotion" between King and Top Rank, the first time that King and Bob Arum had co-promoted a fight since Miguel Cotto vs. Ricardo Mayorga in 2011. But on St. Patrick's Day, King was more of an appendage to the promotion than an integral part of it. He made some pre-fight promotional appearances with Arum. Just prior to the bout, he was in the ring wearing a faded "Only in America" jacket accessorized by a huge Donald Trump tribute button. But that was all.

It's about power. King no longer has it. He has gone from being the greatest ringmaster that the boxing circus ever had to just one of the clowns.

★ ★ ★

On June 9, 2018. Tyson Fury returned to the ring at the Manchester Arena in England after a 924-day absence.

Fury will go down in history as one of boxing's oddest heavyweight champions. He won the crown by decision over Wladimir Klitschko on November 28, 2015, in one of the dreariest heavyweight title bouts ever. Then psychiatric problems, drug issues, and other difficulties forced him from the ring. A proposed rematch with Klitschko was cancelled twice, the second time after Tyson acknowledged that he was psychologically unfit to fight. Fury also admitted to using cocaine after urine samples taken from him in September 2016 tested positive.

Compounding his troubles, Fury was justly pilloried in the media after making a series of misogynist, homophobic, anti-Semitic statements.

Speaking of himself, Fury told Oliver Holt of the *Daily Mail*, "Whatever is conventional, I am the opposite. So if you want to walk in a straight line, I am going to walk in zigzags. If you want to throw a one-two, I'll throw a two-one. I have always been not straightforward. Nothing has run smoothly with me throughout my life. Everything has had ups and downs and lefts and rights, and that's just the way it has panned out for me. Some people love it, some people hate it. Some people think I'm a barm cake. I don't really care what they think of me to be honest."

More alarmingly, Fury later acknowledged, "I think I'm a screw loose in the head sometimes. I'm not joking. I can wake up in the morning, everything's fine. The afternoon, I could commit suicide."

But Fury can fight. He has size, natural strength, reasonably fast hands, and a good boxing IQ (which at times, seems like the only IQ he has). Moreover, from a marketing point of view, there's a curiosity factor surrounding Tyson, even if it's akin to watching a beached whale that has washed ashore and is struggling to get back in the ocean.

The opponent chosen for Fury's comeback bout was Sefer Seferi, a 39-year-old Albanian club fighter who now lives in Switzerland. Seferi brought a 23–1 (21 KOs) record into the contest. But he has limited boxing skills and had fought most of his career as a cruiserweight against mediocre opposition. Nothing on his resume indicated that he'd be competitive against Tyson, which was why he was selected as the opponent.

Fury (25–0, 18 KOs) was a 50-to-1 betting favorite.

When fight night came, Tyson entered the ring looking like a man who'd won a pie eating at least once a week since his triumph over Klitschko. He's huge to begin with, a broad 6-feet-9-inches tall. And before he began training for his comeback, his weight had ballooned to almost 400 pounds.

He weighed in for Seferi at 276–½ pounds, thirty pounds more than for the Klitschko fight. And the extra thirty pounds were flab.

Seferi weighed in at 210.

Fury showed little interest in fighting in the opening stanza. In round two, referee Phil Edwards told him to stop fooling around and box, which had no effect whatsoever on the flow of the action. In fact, late in that round, Tyson stopped boxing altogether to watch a fight that had broken out at ringside. This was consistent with the theme of the evening, which was that, against Seferi, Fury could do pretty much what he wanted to do. Then, in round four, Tyson became a bit more serious about boxing. After that stanza, Seferi quit in his corner. He was brought in to lose, and he did.

One should be wary of criticizing a fighter for saying "that's enough." But the booing that followed the conclusion of the bout was justified.

"It was what it was," Fury said afterward. "He took a couple of hard punches and he told his corner not to send him out for round five. If I'm brutally honest, I could have knocked him out in ten seconds. I could have done him in the first round. But what would that have done me? I got four rounds instead of ten seconds."

Realistically speaking, this is the proper way to bring Fury back if he's to become a serious contender rather than just a vehicle for a cash grab. Tyson has a name. He can make a lot of money by fighting the likes of Tony Bellew, not to mention Anthony Joshua and Deontay Wilder. Whether he can regain his old ring skills and hold his fragile psyche together long enough to climb to the top of the mountain again is another matter.

Meanwhile, one should consider the thoughts of Terence Dooley, who earlier this year wrote, "Maybe it is time to extend a little understanding to Fury and wait to see what comes next. Mental illness is the most elusive opponent any of us will ever face. If Fury is fighting that fight, then he needs our understanding which may also lead to sympathy. But that's up to you."

★ ★ ★

Also on June 9, 2018, Terence Crawford, faced off against Jeff Horn at the MGM Grand Arena in Las Vegas.

Crawford (now 33–0, 24 KOs) is on the short list of fighters who are in the conversation for boxing's #1 pound-for-pound ranking. Last July, he consolidated the four major 140-pound belts with a third-round knockout of Julius Indongo. Then he moved up in weight.

Horn entered the Crawford bout with an 18–0 (12 KOs) record and was the WBO 147-pound beltholder by virtue of a misguided decision over an aging Manny Pacquiao in Horn's Australian homeland in July 2017.

The issue wasn't whether Crawford would beat Horn but the degree to which Horn would test him. Or phrased differently, not who would win but how many rounds?

Horn and his camp made a lot of silly statements during the build-up to the fight. At one point, Glenn Rushton (Jeff's trainer) likened his charge to Rocky Marciano. That had even less credibility than promoter Bob Arum's proclamations that the bout would be highly competitive.

More significant than the fight itself from a long-term point of view, Crawford-Horn was the first big exposure for boxing on ESPN+. An April 21, 2018, match-up between Amir Khan and Phil LoGreco had been a test run of sorts.

ESPN+ is a streaming subscription video service priced at $4.99 a month or $49.99 a year. When Top Rank and ESPN announced an exclusive boxing partnership last year, fight fans were told that the venture would bring massive exposure to Top Rank fighters with stars like Crawford fighting on ESPN and reaching an audience far beyond what HBO had brought them.

Crawford should be happy with the $3,000,000 purse that, according to ESPN, he was paid to fight Horn. But the other side of the coin is that Crawford—the 2016 Boxing Writers Association of America "Fighter of the Year"—fought on Saturday night in a half-empty arena at the MGM Grand in a bout that was televised on an app.

"When we revised our deal with ESPN to take into account the digital platform," Arum explained, "we wanted to really start with a blockbuster." Then the Hall of Fame promoter added, "You can't hold back the future, and the future is direct to consumer. In the next ten to twenty years, everyone will be watching their entertainment on direct to consumer platforms. Like Netflix in entertainment, ESPN+ will be the place for sports in abundance. To fans now in the United States and around the world, it is the future. Get used to it."

The entire Crawford-Horn undercard was also shown on ESPN+. There was more cheerleading than serious commentary from the announcing team of Todd Grisham and Jon Saraceno during a string of lopsided preliminary fights. Then the trio of Joe Tessitore, Tim Bradley, and Mark Kriegel came onboard for the two main bouts.

Jose Pedraza outpointed Antonio Moran 96–94 X 3 in a bloody encounter, after which it was time for Crawford-Horn.

Horn came to fight. But so did Crawford. And as expected, Terence was the better fighter.

Crawford makes adjustments well as a fight progresses. He usually takes a few rounds to figure out his opponent. Then he breaks his adversary down and dominates the action. He's equally comfortable fighting on the inside or at a distance. When he smells blood, he takes his assault to a new level.

By round four, Crawford-Horn had become a one-sided battle. By round seven, Horn was in survival mode. In round eight, he took a bad beating. After that stanza, his corner, the ring doctor, someone, should have stopped it. But no one did, so Horn went out for round nine to get knocked down and battered some more until referee Robert Byrd halted the carnage at the 2:33 mark.

The award for dumbest comment of the night went to Glenn Rushton, who complained afterward, "It was definitely a premature stoppage."

Horn is an ordinary fighter. Still, Crawford turned in a scintillating performance. It was sort of like watching Luciano Pavarotti sing in an ordinary opera. The libretto might not be that good, but it's still Pavarotti.

The one flaw on Terence's resume is the absence of an elite opponent.

"I want the other champions," Crawford told Arum in the ring immediately after the fight, "I want the big fights. Bob, make it happen."

Meanwhile, Arum said of the 30-year-old Crawford, "He reminds me of Sugar Ray Leonard. And that to me is a great, great compliment because I always thought that Leonard was the best. This guy is equal to if not better than Ray was. The future is unlimited."

But at age thirty, Leonard had beaten Marvin Hagler, Thomas Hearns, Roberto Duran, and Wilfred Benitez. Crawford has beaten Viktor Postol, Felix Diaz, Julius Indongo, and Jeff Horn.

★ ★ ★

Showtime televised a triple-header from Barclays Center on September 8, 2018, headlined by Shawn Porter versus Danny Garcia for the vacant WBC 147-pound title. That belt became available when Keith Thurman, who narrowly decisioned both Porter (2016) and Garcia (2017), was forced to relinquish his title due to injury-induced inactivity.

Porter, who will turn 31 on October 7, had amassed a 28–2 (17 KOs) ring record in ten years as a pro. He won the IBF 147-pound belt in 2014 with a fourth-round knockout of Paulie Malignaggi, but lost it by majority decision to Kell Brook in his next outing. Thereafter, he defeated Erick Bone, Adrien Broner, Andre Berto, and Adrain Granados but dropped a decision to Thurman.

Garcia (now 34–2 with 20 KOs) is seven months younger than Porter. He rose to prominence with an upset knockout of Amir Khan in 2012 that earned him the WBA and WBC 140-pound belts. One year later, he solidified his standing with a decision over Lucas Matthysse. His most formidable test came on March 3, 2017, when he lost a split decision to Thurman.

Porter and Garcia are trained by their fathers. But there's a significant difference in the way that plays out. Kenneth Porter maintains a dignified public profile, while Angel Garcia often comes across as a boorish provocateur. Neither trainer was onstage for the July 30 kick-off press conference in New York or the final pre-fight press conference on September 6. In part, that was because the promotion wanted to avoid the type of racist homophobic rant that Angel has engaged in under similar circumstances in the past.

Initially, Kenneth Porter sought to emphasize the similarities between the fighters' camps, noting, "All of us in the trenches in boxing come from the same place." Pressed for more, he then said of Angel, "He has a kid that can fight. He's a great fighter, but the father has never been on my radar. He never sat in on some of the courses that I took. He was never on the national teams I went up against or the international competitions. So that isn't something that I'm concerned with."

When asked about his relationship with Angel, Danny volunteered the tidbit, "Me and my dad go to strip clubs together. We throw money together." Later, he added, "We're not looking at it like your dad versus my dad. This is just Team Garcia versus his team."

As for the fight itself, Shawn declared, "It will be action-packed and exciting. It always is when I fight. This is what I do, and I love it."

"I just feel like I'm the better fighter," Danny countered. "And that's it."

The first televised bout of the evening on Showtime was a heavyweight match-up between Charles Martin (25–1, 23 KOs) and Adam Kownacki (17–0, 14 KOs).

Martin age 32, is on the short list of least impressive heavyweight beltholders ever. Two years ago, he fought Vyacheslav Glazkov for the vacant IBF title. Forty-eight seconds into round three, Martin stepped with his lead foot onto Glazkov's lead foot and Vyacheslav went down awkwardly. Seconds later, as Glazkov was throwing a right to the body, he tumbled to the canvas and rose, limping badly. At that point, without a meaningful punch having been landed, the fight was stopped. A subsequent examination revealed that Glazkov's anterior cruciate ligament (ACL) had been torn clean through. Twelve weeks later, Martin fought Anthony Joshua in London for a wheelbarrow full of money and was knocked out in the second round. Other than Joshua, he has never fought a world-class opponent.

Kownacki, age 29, is a big, tough, often-out-of-shape fighter whose management has cherry-picked opponents from the list of usual suspects. He seems most comfortable in the ring when brawling. While he isn't a big puncher, he takes a good punch. And the damage from his blows adds up. He wears down opponents over the course of a bout.

Kownacki weighed in to face Martin at 263–¼ pounds, his most ever for a fight. Martin tipped the scales at 246. The 7-to-5 odds in Adam's favor reflected the view that, while Martin might hit harder, Kownacki is mentally stronger and has the better chin.

It was a sloppy spirited action bout, entertaining and inartfully fought. Both men fought as though they didn't know much about defense. Or if they did, they couldn't put it into practice. Both fighters looked tired as early as round three, although Kownacki seemed ready to fight at the start of each stanza while Martin invariably looked as though he could use another thirty seconds of rest.

All three judges scored the contest 96–94 for Kownacki, which was a bit more generous to Martin that the action called for. Adam will now move toward a more lucrative fight while Martin slides further toward opponent status.

Kownacki-Martin was followed by a WBC welterweight "title elimination bout" between Yordenis Ugas and Cesar Barrionuevo. That encounter devolved into twelve rounds of boredom marked by jeers and boos from the crown and ended in a 120–108, 120–108, 119–109 decision for Ugas.

Then came Garcia-Porter.

Porter, a 3-to-2 underdog, looked sluggish in the early going. The swarming aggression that normally characterizes his ring style wasn't there. One reason for that might have been effective counterpunching from Garcia, who also managed to hold and tie Shawn up whenever Porter got inside. The action heated up in the second half of the fight when Shawn began fighting with more intensity.

It was a hard bout to score with the judges in agreement on only four of twelve rounds (round 1 for Garcia; rounds 4, 6, and 7 for Porter). That led to a 116–112, 115–113, 115–113 verdict in Porter's favor. This writer scored the fight even at 114–114.

★ ★ ★

Boxing returned to The Theater at Madison Square Garden on December 1, 2018. Vasyl Lomachenko vs. Jose Pedraza in the main event drew a sellout crowd of 5,312. The non-televised undercard was respectable. And the three-fight telecast that followed the Heisman Trophy presentation on ESPN had moments of drama.

The first televised bout of the evening showcased Teofimo Lopez (10–0, 8 KOs), a 21-year-old lightweight who's rapidly moving from prospect to contender status. Mason Menard (34–3, 24 KOs) was Lopez's designated victim. All three of Menard's losses had been by knockout and this was expected to be the fourth "KO by" on his record.

Lopez has all the confidence and arrogance of a young fighter with a big punch who's on the rise. It took him all of 44 seconds to blast Menard into oblivion.

Next up, 24-year-old Isaac Dogboe (20–0, 14 KOs) sought to defend his WBO 122-pound title against Emanuel Navarrete (25–1, 22 KOs) of Mexico. Dogboe was born in Ghana but grew up in England. He claimed his belt with an eleventh-round stoppage of Jesse Magdaleno in April of this year and was considered a fighter who doesn't need protecting.

Navarrete was fighting outside of Mexico for the first time, which is often a sign of a padded record.

Dogboe entered the bout as a 7-to-1 betting favorite and mounted a two-fisted assault to the head and body in the first stanza. But Navarrete had come to fight and began landing shots of his own in round two, at which point Isaac's chin seemed a bit suspect. As the bout wore on, Dogboe did his best work on the inside. When he gave Navarrete room to punch, Emanuel obliged him.

It was a spirited, back-and forth encounter that was even after eight rounds. Then Navarrete picked up the pace and won the final four frames going away. By the end, Dogboe's face was badly swollen; his left eye was almost shut; and he was trying simply to survive. He made it to the final bell but was dethroned by a 116–112, 116–112, 115–113 margin.

Good fight, good decision.

Lomachenko (11–1, 9 KOs) vs. Pedraza (25–1, 12 KOs) was promoted on the basis of both men having titles, which is a little like promoting a title-unification football game between the Big Ten and Ivy League champions.

Lomachenko's ring prowess has been amply catalogued. All but one of his professional bouts have been contested for world titles. He's an elite fighter while Pedraza is a good one. In match ups like that, the elite fighter almost always wins.

Top Rank had planned to match Lomachenko (the WBO 135-pound champion) against Raymundo Beltran (the WBA beltholder) as part of an "immigrant-from-Mexico-gets-citizenship" feel-good story. But Pedraza upset the applecart in August of this year by winning a unanimous-decision over Beltran.

Lomachenko was returning to the ring after surgery to repair a torn labrum suffered in his right shoulder during a May 12, 2018, victory over Jorge Linares. Still, Vasyl was an early 12-to-1 favorite over Pedraza and the odds moved as high as 20-to-1 reflecting the fighters' respective ring skills.

The crowd was highly-partisan in favor of Lomachenko. Fighters from Puerto Rico are rarely booed in New York during pre-fight introductions, but it happened here.

It was an interesting exercise for boxing purists. The early rounds were tactically fought. Then Lomachenko figured out what he had to do to beat Pedraza down and did it. Many of the early rounds were close enough that the judges could have given them to whichever fighter they wanted to. But Lomachenko pulled away late, putting an exclamation mark on his performance with two eleventh-round knockdowns that came close to ending matters short of the 119–107, 117–112, 117–112 judges' verdict in his favor

Lomachenko looked a bit less "high tech" against Pedraza than he has in the past. He didn't exploit angles as effectively and control the range as well as in some of his earlier fights. Part of that was because Pedraza is fast on his feet and spent long portions of the evening jabbing and moving away. Another reason might be that Lomachenko's best fighting weight by his own evaluation is 130 pounds. There were times when he had trouble with Jorge Linares's height and reach when they fought seven months ago. That was also true for stretches of time against the taller Pedraza. Mikey Garcia might be a bit too big for Lomachenko.

★ ★ ★

Barclays Center is becoming known for the aroma of weed that wafts through the arena on fight night. But there was a breath of fresh air on Saturday, December 22. His name was Dominic Breazeale.

Breazeale, age 33, comes across as one of the nicest people in boxing. He's outgoing, friendly, thoughtful, and articulate; has been married for eleven years ("happy wife, happy life," he says); and is the doting father of three sons.

"I'm a happy person," Dominic proclaims. "On a gloomy day, I'll find the sun."

At 6-feet-7-inches tall and fighting in the neighborhood of 255 pounds, Breazeale is a formidable physical presence. He played quarterback in college at the University of Northern Colorado and took up boxing at age 23.

"Boxing is a hundred times harder than football," he notes. "If you have a bad day in football, there's someone else to lean on."

Breazeale represented the United States in the super-heavyweight division at the 2012 Olympics but lost in an early round to Magomed Omarov of Russia. He turned pro later that year and arrived at Barclays Center sporting a 19–1 (17 KOs) ring record. He most notable fistic outing came on June 25, 2016, when he challenged newly crowned Anthony Joshua for the IBF heavyweight title. Dominic put up a courageous fight but was too unskilled to prevail. The bout was stopped in the seventh round. He fought twice the following year, stopping Izuagbe Ugonoh and Eric Molina. Breazeale vs. Carlos Negron at Barclays was his first fight in almost fourteen months.

Negron, age thirty, brought a 20–1 (16 KOs) record into the bout. At 6'6", 226 pounds, he matched up in size against Breazeale. But Carlos, who represented Puerto Rico at 178 pounds in the 2008 Olympics, had been knocked out as a pro by a shopworn Epifiano Mendoza (although that loss came in 2011). Like Breazeale, Negron had been inactive as of late, last fighting eighteen months ago.

All of Breazeale's strengths and weaknesses were on display against Negron. Words like ponderous, wooden, and slow come to mind when describing his ring style. But he moves inexorably forward and wears lesser opponents down. Negron landed more than he should have, but his punches lacked power. Midway through round nine, Dominic landed a big overhand right on the side of Negron's neck, dropping him to the canvas and ending the fight.

As for the future; Breazeale is the mandatory challenger for Deontay Wilder's WBC heavyweight title. But the assumption is that his challenge will be put on hold if Wilder can nail down a more lucrative bout against Tyson Fury or Anthony Joshua. That would trouble Breazeale. He wants to fight Wilder because of the challenge that Deontay represents, the money that would be involved, and because of an ugly incident that occurred in a hotel lobby in February 2017 when, in Dominic's words, "Wilder and a mob of about twenty people unprovokedly attacked my team and my family."

Meanwhile, reflecting on his role as a boxer, Breazeale says, "The best thing about being a fighter is that we're one-percenters. It's nice to know that you're special."

And what about the cruelty inherent in his trade? What goes through Dominic's mind when he's hurting someone; when he has stiffened an opponent with a jab, stunned him with a follow-up right, and then, as per the demands of his profession, is readying to hit him again?

"I've never sat back and analyzed punishing another man," Breazeale answers. "I'm not sure what I'd find if I did. It's brutal; I know that. We're modern-day gladiators. It's what we sign up for. It's the nature of the beast."

All fighters are entitled to respect. But in the minds of some, Curtis Harper squandered that entitlement.

Curtis Harper Goes Viral

For most of his eight-year career as a professional boxer, Curtis Harper labored in obscurity. But by now, most boxing fans have seen the video of Harper walking out of the ring seconds after the bell rang for the start of his scheduled August 24, 2018, fight against Efe Ajagba at the Minneapolis Armory.

More than one million viewers have watched Harper on YouTube during the past five days. Google "Curtis Harper" and 650,000 results will appear on your computer monitor. His exit from the ring was reported by most major news organizations and featured on CNN's home page. The commentary has been overwhelmingly derisive and centers on the demeaning storyline that Harper was terrified of his opponent.

But there are issues that go beyond the standard event coverage. Harper has been plagued by serious eye problems. Some medical experts, including doctors at the New York State Athletic Commission, have said that he shouldn't be in a boxing ring at all.

Harper is a 30-year-old, 250-pound journeyman heavyweight from Jacksonville, Florida. His ring record stands at 13 wins against 6 defeats with 9 knockouts and 3 KOs by. He has won one fight over the past four years, a third-round knockout of Andrew Greeley. To put that victory in perspective, in thirty fights since April 2008, Greeley has emerged victorious one time.

The high point of Harper's career came on March 13, 2015, when he went eight hard rounds against Chris Arreola on Premier Boxing Champions' inaugural telecast on Spike. Arreola entered the ring at a blubbery 262 pounds. Harper weighed 265. The assumption was that Curtis would get whacked out early. And that assumption was bolstered in round one when he was decked by a right hand and rose on wobbly legs, looking like 265 pounds of Jell-O.

But Arreola was woefully out of shape. And Harper evinced the mindset, if not the skills, of a professional fighter. The bout devolved into two huge guys staggering each other back and forth in what resembled a barroom brawl highlighted by a POP-CRASH-POW seventh round. Arreola won a 76–75, 77–74, 78–73 decision. 76–75 was the most accurate of the scorecards.

That brings us to Harper versus Efe Ajagba, a Nigerian heavyweight who now lives in Texas.

Ajagba is a Premier Boxing Champions fighter. Prior to entering the ring to face Harper, he had five knockout victories in five fights with four of these knockouts coming in the first round. The fight card was televised by FS1 and Fox Deportes with Warriors Boxing and TGB Promotions as co-promoters. Warriors Boxing president Leon Margules says that TGB put Ajagba on the card and arranged for Harper to be the opponent.

Everyone understood that Harper was overmatched. But boxing regularly sees fights that are more one-sided than Ajagba–Harper was expected to be.

Harper, his wife (Sandra Rosenberg), and trainer Nate Campbell flew out of Jacksonville on Wednesday, August 22. They changed planes in Charlotte and arrived in Minneapolis at 10:07 p.m.

Ajagba–Harper was one of eleven fights scheduled for Friday night. The fighters entered the ring as planned and were introduced to the crowd. Referee Celestino Ruiz gave his final in-ring instructions. The fighters returned to their respective corners. The bell rang.

And then it happened. Harper turned his back on Ajagba, stepped between the ring ropes, and walked away from the ring, down an elevated ramp, across the stage, to his dressing room. Whatever thoughts were racing through his mind didn't show. His outward appearance was calm, cool, and collected.

It can't be written that Harper said "no mas" because there was nothing to be "mas" of.

Harper's flight left Minneapolis at 8:12 a.m. the following morning. He and his wife arrived back in Jacksonville on Saturday afternoon.

Rick Glaser, who has represented Harper in past dealings and been in touch with the Minnesota Office of Combative Sports on the fighter's behalf, says that Curtis is "a martyr under protest."

Asked to explain, Glaser elaborates, "What happened here was, on August 12, Curtis was given a contract to fight Ajagba for six thousand dollars. He specifically asked the person who gave him the contract whether the fight would be on TV and was told no. He signed the contract on August 13 and sent it back that day. After that, he was treated like garbage. He and his wife didn't get their plane tickets until August 22 [the day of their flight]. They flew into Minneapolis and waited at the airport for an hour and forty-five minutes before they were picked up. Then, at the weigh-in on Thursday, Curtis learned that, contrary to what he'd been told before, his fight was going to be on TV. And he still hadn't been given a countersigned contract. So he wanted more money."

Harper struggles when asked to explain his motivation for leaving the ring on August 24.

"I'm still upset," he says before adding, "I signed the contract but they never gave me a signed contract back. They told me that there was no TV, and then it was a TV fight. I kept asking for the signed contract and they wouldn't give it to me."

Asked when he decided that he wasn't going to fight, Harper answers, "I pretty much made up my mind in the dressing room, but I wasn't sure. Then, when we touched gloves and I saw one of the people who hadn't done right by me in the other corner, that was it."

"I was shocked when Curt walked out," Sandra says. "But we've talked and I understand why he did it. For Curt to be insulted by all these people who don't know him is very hurtful to Curt and to me."

It's a dicey proposition for an outsider to speculate on Harper's motives. He has been a sparring partner for WBC heavyweight champion Deontay Wilder on multiple occasions, which is no easy task. And he showed courage on a national stage in his 2015 fight against Chris Arreola.

That said; Harper didn't have much of a chance to beat Ajagba. The question in most people's minds was how—and how badly—he would be beaten up.

Fans have the tendency to view fighters as video-game action figures. But the reality of boxing is very different from that.

Teddy Atlas has been in boxing as a trainer and television commentator for decades. He understands the psychology of fighters at all levels of the game, having been taught his initial lessons by Cus D'Amato.

Asked about Harper, Atlas opines, "Over the years, this guy has shown enough substance and character to get in the ring and face the risks of fighting regardless of what his other faults might be. So what happened? If you sign a contract, you should live up to it. But someone can sign a contract and then get to a desperate place."

"Once upon a time," Atlas continues, "this guy was a kid with aspirations. But his dreams didn't work out. I can understand his getting down. I can understand his saying that all these promoters and other leeches are sucking the blood out of him and no one cares. He's thinking now, I'm not getting much money for this fight. Maybe I'll have to spend part of what I get for medical expenses when the fight is over. Maybe the hopelessness of his situation hit him that day. Not the hopelessness of this one fight, but the overall hopelessness of his situation. He got angry and maybe a little scared and felt like the whole world was against him. Don't condemn him too quickly. It's more complicated than what most people think it is."

Don Turner trained Evander Holyfield and Larry Holmes, two of boxing's greatest warriors.

"Fighters quit all the time," Turner says. "This guy just did it honestly. He didn't take a dive. He didn't bite off part of someone's ear to get disqualified. I don't condone what he did but I understand it."

Harper didn't "run" in the literal sense. He turned and (in rather dignified fashion, actually) stepped through the ropes and walked slowly down the elevated runway leading back to the dressing room. He didn't respond to the booing and taunts from the crowd.

And what of the fans who were deprived of action that they'd paid for?

The fans in attendance got their money's worth. There were ten other fights on the card that night. And Ajagba vs. Harper was more memorable than any of them. Years from now, when the other fights have faded from memory, those fans will be telling people, "I saw the most amazing thing one night at the fights."

Still, there's a line that fighters shouldn't cross, and Harper crossed it. A fighter shouldn't walk to the ring for a televised fight and then walk out.

Leon Margules, who co-promoted the fight card, says, "I heard from someone who was in the locker room with Harper afterward that Harper said the bell for round one rang so he wanted to get paid."

"We're not the bad guys in this," Margulies continues. "There are promoters who would have thrown Harper and his wife out of their hotel and cancelled their return flights. I think he should explain himself and apologize. I think he should be suspended for a reasonable period of time with what's reasonable being determined by his explanation. And I think he should repay the direct out-of-pocket expenses that his doing this cost us."

Then Margules rattles off a list of direct out-of-pocket expenses: (1) roundtrip airfare for three people (Harper, Rosenberg, and Campbell) between Jacksonville and Minneapolis, $1,541); (2) hotel accommodations (two rooms for three nights, $1,002); meal money ($40 per day for three people for three days, $360). That comes to roughly $2,900. Now double that and then some when adding in expenses for Ajagba. Margules says that direct out-of-pocket expenses for Ajagba-Harper (not including the fighters' purses) came to $7,465.

But as noted above, there's another issue regarding Curtis Harper. It might be that he shouldn't be fighting at all.

Prior to Deontay Wilder's March 3, 2018, fight against Luis Ortiz at Barclays Center, there was an issue with regard to Ortiz's blood pressure and the promoters feared that Ortiz might be pulled off the card at the last minute by the New York State Athletic Commission. So as insurance, they brought in former IBF beltholder Charles Martin as a back-up opponent for Wilder. That left open the issue of what to do with Martin in the event that Wilder-Ortiz proceeded as planned. The decision was made to match him in an undercard fight against Curtis Harper.

But the NYSAC refused to grant Harper a license to fight because he'd undergone cataract surgery in 2017 and treatment for a retinal tear in 2015. The NYSAC was further advised of an outside medical opinion that, if Harper continued to fight without additional corrective surgery, it was "just a matter of time" before he went blind in one eye. The commission medical staff also believed that, even if Harper had the corrective surgery, it would be too dangerous for him to continue fighting.

Harper says that the necessary corrective surgery was a minor procedure that was performed in Jacksonville in early July of this year. Thereafter, on July 26, Dr. Robert Schnipper, an ophthalmologist, filled out an ocular examination form that was transmitted to the Minnesota Office of Combative Sports. In it, Schnipper referenced Harper's 2015 retinal tear and 2017 cataract surgery but found him fit to fight. The Minnesota Office of Combative Sports concurred with that assessment.

Harper has been given a pro forma suspension by the Minnesota Office of Combative Sports, which mandates that all fighters have a mandatory 14-day rest period after each scheduled fight. James Honerman (a spokesperson for the MOCS) says that his office is currently gathering information and will decide the status of Harper's license after a hearing on September 7.

Ironically, if Harper is allowed to fight again, he'll be more marketable than ever before as a fighter. Boxing fans now know who he is. He's a human-interest story. If he re-enters the ring, he'll be a name, not an opponent.

Don't judge Curtis Harper too harshly. But remember that boxers are held to a high standard because thousands of courageous fighters who boxed before them set that standard.

In boxing, the action outside the ring is sometimes more interesting than the action in it.

Jermell and Jermall Charlo on Fox

On December 22, 2018, the Charlo twins—Jermell and Jermall—fought Tony Harrison and Matt Korobov at Barclays Center in Brooklyn.

The Charlos are 28 years old and have been fighting professionally for ten years. Jermell entered the ring with a 31–0 (15 KOs) record and as the reigning WBC 154-pound beltholder. Jermall had compiled a 27–0, (21 KOs) record. He previously held the IBF 154-pound title and now campaigns as a middleweight.

Everything seems personal for the Charlos. It's hard to imagine either brother outsourcing revenge to the other (as Vitali and Wladimir Klitschko did on several occasions) and finding satisfaction in payback that wasn't beaten out with his own fists.

Jermell vs. Tony Harrison and Jermall vs. Matt Korobov were thought to be stay-busy Christmas presents for the Charlos. Jermell was a 10-to-1 betting favorite over Harrison while Jermall was listed at 20-to-1 over Korobov. Neither brother gives an opponent much to work with. They're good defensive fighters who strike swiftly when opportunity beckons.

Several disquieting themes underlay the promotion. The first of these revolved around the fact that, on November 1, both Charlos "missed" tests that were to be administered by the Voluntary Anti-Doping Association (VADA) pursuant to the WBC Clean Boxing Program. Initially, the New York State Athletic Commission sought to distance itself from the issue, saying that the WBC-VADA tests were "separate from the New York State Athletic Commission's Rules & Regulations." But that was an untenable position.

Piecing together from multiple sources what happened next, the NYSAC then asked the Charlos for a more detailed explanation of why they'd missed their tests and failed to answer their cellphones on November 1. Previously, Jermall had tweeted that the brothers had been doing "promotional stuff." But the commission didn't get an adequate response. Instead, it was suggested from above ("above" being the New York State Department of State, which oversees the NYSAC) that the commission back off on requiring the Charlos to document the reason why they'd missed the tests and, instead, administer new tests. In today's world of microdosing, this passes for a bad joke. And the joke became even less funny when the NYSAC had one brother's test administered by Quest Diagnostics and the other brother's test administered by Lab Corp.

Quest Diagnostics and Lab Corp can tell the difference between blood and urine. But they don't do state-of-the-art testing (such as carbon isotope ratio testing) for banned performance enhancing drugs.

On December 14, Greg Leon of Boxing Talk interviewed Tony Harrison and told him, "I've got to ask what you think about the Charlos, who have two different coaches, missing drug tests on the same day?"

Harrison gave a vague response.

"Allow me to ask the question in a different way," Leon pressed. "If you were the champion, would you ever defend your title against a challenger who missed a drug test?"

"No," Harrison answered. "Honestly, I would not. It leaves too much of a gray area. I wouldn't do it, but it's out of my hands. There's literally nothing I can do. I just have to take it for how it is, man, the life of being a B-side fighter."

Then, on December 15, it was revealed that Willie Monroe Jr, who'd been scheduled to fight Jermall Charlo at Barclays Center on December 22, had tested positive after taking a banned supplement called Nugenix (a testosterone booster). Monroe was removed from the card and replaced by Matt Korobov, which sent the message that, in New York, fighters who might be dirty should simply miss tests and they'll be allowed to fight.

Four years ago, the New York State Athletic Commission said that it wouldn't license Korobov to box because of what it termed a congenital brain condition. Some other jurisdictions don't consider this particular condition to be a potential danger and subsequently granted Korobov a license to box. To date, the NYSAC has refused to explain when it changed its own standard on this issue and the reason for the change.

Finally, when asked about Monroe at a December 19 media workout, Jermall and Jermell Charlo engaged in what one might consider an exercise in hypocrisy.

"Cheaters never win," Jermall offered.

Jermell was more expansive, proclaiming, "They should suspend him from boxing. Monroe shouldn't be allowed to come back. I'm glad they was able to catch this beforehand. It sucks that someone would cheat, and they know that they're cheating. We need the sport to be cleaned up. Take all his bread. Take them away from the sport. They shouldn't be allowed back. They should be banned for life and probably sentenced to a jail sentence or something. Yeah, send their ass to jail!"

Bottom line: Jermall Charlo vs. Matt Korobov at Barclays Center on December 22, 2018, matched a fighter who missed a PED test in November under questionable circumstances against a fighter who, four years ago, was unable to obtain a license to box in New York because of a congenital brain condition.

When fight night arrived, Jermell Charlo vs. Tony Harrison was a tedious tactical encounter. Harrison fought much of the bout like a man who would be happy to survive for twelve rounds, pick up his paycheck, and go home. The general consensus was that Jermell won nine of the twelve rounds. Jimmy Lennon Jr. announced that there was a unanimous decision and read the three judges' scorecards: 116–112 (Robin Taylor), 115–113 (Ron McNair), and 115–113 (Julie Lederman). That left people wondering how two judges could each have given Harrison five rounds. The wonderment then turned to disbelief when Lennon uttered the words "And the new WBC super-welterweight champion of the world . . ."

Ironically, the Charlo-Harrison decision went against the house fighter. This suggests that poor judging rather than corruption was at its core.

In the nightcap, Jermall Charlo pounded out a unanimous decision victory over Matt Korobov by a 119–108, 116–112, 116–112 margin. Jermall won the fight, but 119–108 was off the mark.

Perhaps the most notable thing about the December 22 fight card was that it marked the inaugural telecast of boxing under a recently-negotiated contract between Premier Boxing Champions and Fox.

On September 5, 2018, PBC and Fox announced a four-year-deal that calls for the Fox broadcast network to air ten "marquee" fight cards per year with an additional twelve cards being shown annually on FS1 and Fox Deportes. The announcement held out the promise of championship-caliber boxing on a free platform. Thus, a lot of fight fans were disappointed on November 13 when Fox announced its fight schedule through March 16, 2019.

The two Charlo fights were joined on December 22 with a 20-to-1 match-up between Dominic Breazeale and Carlos Negron. January 26, 2019, will feature Keith Thurman vs. Josesito Lopez with the odds currently favoring Thurman by 10-to-1. Virtually all of the PBC-Fox main events announced to date have what amounts to a designated winner vs. a designated loser.

Let's draw an analogy to another sport. Fox televises Big Ten college football. The schedule for the first four months of its boxing series is equivalent to televising Michigan vs. Rutgers and Ohio State vs. Minnesota again and again and never getting to Penn State vs. Wisconsin or Michigan vs. Ohio State.

The core of the Fox commentating team handled itself well during the first telecast. There were too many voices. But Kenny Albert conducted blow-by-blow chores smoothly. Joe Goossen and Ray Mancini have been in the trenches. And Lennox Lewis adds dignity and class to anything he touches.

The use of Larry Hazzard as Fox's "rules expert and unofficial scorer" raises an interesting issue. Harold Lederman resigned as a ring judge in New York when he took a commentating position with HBO. So did Steve Weisfeld when Weisfeld worked as a rules expert for HBO. Hazzard is commissioner of the New Jersey State Athletic Control Board. And his son, Larry Hazzard Jr, was the judge who scored Charlo-Korobov 119–108 in favor of Jermall.

But for boxing fans, the more important issue is this.

For all the money that's being put into the system now by Fox, ESPN, DAZN, and Showtime, we should be seeing better fights than we're seeing. Each of the networks maintains that quality control is built into its respective output deal with its favored promoter or promoters. But in today's world, when "quality control" is measured in terms of "championship" belts and top-ten rankings, it means nothing.

Championship belts are dispensed today like chocolates from a vending machine. There's a never-ending supply of bogus beltholders and undeserving "mandatory" challengers for elite fighters to fight.

Thus, 2018 is ending on a bittersweet note. There's more boxing on television and streaming video now than ever before. But sadly, there are fewer great fights. And that's unlikely to change in the near future. Every promoter, TV network, and sanctioning body of note has its own little kingdom that it's anxious to protect to the overall detriment of the sport. If baseball were run like boxing, there wouldn't have been a World Series this year. Instead, the Boston Red Sox would have been declared "American League World Champions," the Los Angeles Dodgers would have been designated "National League World champions," and baseball would be a niche sport.

"I only live for today," Tyson Fury said shortly before fighting Deontay Wilder. "Whatever happens today is a blessing, and whatever happens in the past is gone forever. You can never recalculate it or get it back, not unless you find a time machine somewhere in the bushes."

Deontay Wilder vs. Tyson Fury in Perspective

Something good happened on December 1, 2018. A big fight lived up to its billing.

Two physically imposing men—one of them 6-feet-9-inches tall, the other two inches shorter—squared off in a boxing ring. There was a dramatic ebb and flow to the action with one of the men swinging for the fences with every punch.

Welcome to Deontay Wilder vs. Tyson Fury—a fight between two loud personalities, one of them the "lineal" heavyweight champion of the world and the other the World Boxing Council heavyweight champ. They're not great fighters but they're good ones.

Wilder won a bronze medal on behalf of the United States at the 2008 Olympics and, prior to facing Fury, had fashioned a 40-and-0 professional ledger with 39 knockouts. He isn't a "small" heavyweight. But at 6'7" and weighing in under 220 pounds, he's a "light" heavyweight.

After ten years as a pro, Wilder is still a project. His technique is flawed. His footwork is clumsy. Some of his overhand rights misfire so far off the mark that boxing aficionados are inclined to smile at his awkwardness.

People laughed at Rocky Marciano too. Marciano couldn't do this and he couldn't do that. But he could punch.

It's easy for an opponent to win rounds and look good against Wilder. Until the opponent gets knocked out. Deontay comes into fights in top condition. He lets his hands go. And he can punch.

"The killer instinct I have, it's natural born," Wilder says. "I deliver whether I'm mad at you or whether I'm happy. I can beat your ass and smile at the same time. There's nothing like showing people so they believe it. I show people each and every time."

Fury, despite his size (he fights in the neighborhood of 260 pounds), is not a big puncher. Nor is he particularly well-conditioned. But his boxing skills and 85-inch reach make him difficult to fight. On November 28, 2015, he decisioned an aging Wladimir Klitschko in a stultifyingly dull bout to claim the WBA, IBF, and WBO belts in addition to the "lineal" heavyweight crown. That brought Tyson's ring record to 25-and-0 with 18 knockouts. Then he self-destructed.

Fury's trials and tribulations have been well documented. He can be charming and has charisma. On good days, he can flip a switch in his head and transition back and forth between calm rational thinker and disturbed showman. On bad days, he has been psychotic.

At the post-fight press conference after beating Klitschko, Fury stated, "I am what I am. If people don't like it, change the channel. That's all I got to say. I will be dictated to by nobody. I'm the man. You don't like it, change the station. You don't like it, don't take photos. You don't like it, don't print in your newspaper. Do I care? Not really."

One week later, he sparked controversy by posting a video on YouTube in which he opined, "I believe a woman's best place is in the kitchen and on her back."

Then Fury sat for an interview with Oliver Holt of the *Daily Mail* in which he equated homosexuality with pedophilia and proclaimed, "Every time I stray away from the Lord's word, I find emptiness and darkness. The world is very evil out there and people may think I am a lunatic or whatever, but it's very, very true. And if you believe in the word, then you believe what I am saying. The devil is very strong at the minute. Very strong. I believe the end is near. Just a little short few years, I reckon, away from being finished. I have been praying to God from being as small as I can remember. Always said my prayers at nighttime and that sort of stuff. I did believe in God. I believed in Jesus the Son, I believed in the Father and the Holy Spirit. All that sort of stuff. It's okay believing. There are people out there who tell me that the Devil doesn't exit and demons don't exist. But there's also people who practice exorcisms and casting demons out of people. That's what they do for a living. Are they getting paid for something that's totally ludicrous? Do they go to school and educate their selves all their lives to do this for nothing? Why are there so many priests and people of God and celibicism and all that sort of stuff and Buddhist monks who don't talk forever. It can't just be baloney, can it? I may sound daft but I'm actually not daft when it comes to it. I know what's going on out there."

On December 9, 2015, the British Sports Journalists Association issued a statement condemning Fury's equating homosexuality with pedophilia. The following day, in an interview with Sky Sports News, Fury denied that he was homophobic and proclaimed, "I wouldn't be a very good Christian if I hated anybody, would I? If Jesus loves the world, I love the world. I can actually say that I have no hate for anybody. I haven't any enemies, I don't hate any race, color, creed, generation, nobody. My team is one of the most diverse teams amongst religions in the world of boxing. Tyson Fury is uniting the world. Uniting Christians and Muslims in a time when everything is up in the air. We don't hear about that, do we? We just hear about the comments that people want to twist and want to make me sound like I hate people and that I hate the world. I love all of God's children."

On April 27, 2016, Fury attended a kick-off press conference in Manchester for a scheduled July 9 rematch against Wladimir Klitschko. Then, on May 13, he sparked new controversy with a foul-mouthed 57-minute video rant filmed in training camp and shown on SportsView in which he suggested that rape and bestiality would one day be legalized and also included anti-Semitic remarks:

★ "It's like you're a freak of nature if you're normal. You're the odd one out. I'll just get myself changed into a woman. That's normal, isn't it today? Call myself Tysina or something like that, put a wig on. I don't think it's normal. I think they're freaks of nature. Everyone just do what you can; listen to the government; follow everybody like sheep; be brainwashed by all the Zionist Jewish people who own all the banks, all the papers, all the TV stations. Be brainwashed by them all."

★ "I think it'll be perfectly normal in the next ten years to have sexual relationships with your animals at home. You know; your pets, your cats and dogs and all that. That will be legal. You are already allowed to marry your animals and stuff. It is going to happen, isn't it? Whatever you can think of that's bad will be made legal because that's what the devil wants. They might start making it legal so that four or five men can grab a granny and rape her in public in front of kids and all that. Or grab an old man and rape him. In the schools now, they're asking the little kids at five and six, do they want to be a boy or girl when they get older. What the fuck is that?"

One might add here that, shortly after the April 27, 2016, kick-off press conference for the Klitschko rematch, Fury was asked about Anthony Joshua by a reporter for IFL-TV and answered, "I don't hate Joshua. I don't dislike him. I like the guy. He's doing well. He's got a good body. I bet he's got a big cock. I wish I had it." And during a May 30 interview with IFL-TV, when asked about the possibility of fighting Deontay Wilder and Anthony Joshua, Fury responded, "I'll let 'em fight me. I'll bend 'em over and boom—split them down the middle with this long dick. I'll rape Wilder over Joshua. Wilder's my man."

On May 16, 2016, Fury apologized for his May 13 homophobic, anti-Semitic rant. "I apologise to anyone who may have taken offence at any of my comments," a written statement issued in his name read. "I said some things which may have hurt some people, which as a Christian man is not something I would ever want to do. I mean no harm or disrespect to anyone and I know more is expected of me as an ambassador of British boxing and I promise in future to hold myself up to the highest possible standard. Anyone who knows me personally knows that I am in no way a racist or bigot, and I hope the public accept this apology."

Thereafter, Wladimir Klitschko criticized Fury's comments, saying, "His statements about women, gay-community men and women, and then when he got to Jewish people; he sounded like Hitler. The man is an imbecile. I'm fighting an imbecile. We have an imbecile champion. In this crazy world, with everything that's going on, we don't need somebody having the stage and bringing the hate to Jewish people. I cannot accept it. I won't accept it. Friction creates friction. The more hate you bring out there—with women, the gay community and Jewish people—what next is he going to say? It's just something we don't need in this world, it's beyond boxing."

On June 24, 2016, referencing his own Gypsy roots, Fury responded to Klitschko's reference to Adolf Hitler with the declaration, "Hitler killed hundreds of thousands of gypsies. A lot of my ancestors were mass-murdered by Hitler. To call me that is a very, very bad insult. Let's not forget; your people, the Ukrainians, were the guards in the death camps where my people were slaughtered. You stupid fucking Ukrainian prick."

That same day, citing an "ankle injury" sustained in training, Fury announced that his July 9, 2016, rematch against Klitschko was postponed. The fight was rescheduled for October 29. But on September 13, Tyson failed to attend the kick-off press conference, saying that his car had broken down.

Then, on September 23, Mick Hennessy (Fury's promoter at the time) announced that Fury had been found "medically unfit to fight" and that "medical specialists have advised that the condition is too severe to allow him to participate in the rematch and that he will require treatment before going back into the ring."

By now, it was clear that Fury's medical problems were psychological in nature. That was confirmed in an interview posted on October 4, 2016, on *Rolling Stone*.

"I've not been in a gym for months," Fury acknowledged. "I've not been training. I've been going through depression. I just don't want to live anymore, if you know what I'm saying. I've had total enough of it. I've been pushed to the brink. I can't take no more. I'm in a hospital at the moment. I'm seeing psychiatrists. They say I've got a version of bipolar. I'm a manic depressive. All from what they've done to me. All this shit through boxing, through taking titles. I beat the best man but I'm still shit. I used to love boxing when I was a kid. It was my life. All the way through, it was my life. You finally get to where you need to be and it becomes a big mess. I hate boxing now. I wouldn't even go across the road to watch a world title fight. That's what it's done to me. I don't even want to wake up. I hope I die every day. And that's a bad thing to say when I've got three children and a lovely wife, isn't it? But I don't want to live anymore. If I could take me own life and I wasn't a Christian, I'd take it in a second. I just hope someone kills me before I kill meself or I'll have to spend eternity in hell. I'm in a very bad place at the moment. I don't know whether I'm coming or going. I don't know what's going to happen to me. I don't know if I'm going to see the year out to be honest. I am seeing help, but they can't do nothing for me. What I've got is incurable. I don't see a way out, I don't even see a way of living for me,

I don't want to live anymore. It has brought me to the brink of death. That's where I'm at at the moment."

The spotlight hasn't always been kind to Deontay Wilder either. There are times when he comes across as a decent man with an admirable work ethic. "My first job was working at Burger King," Deontay reminisced earlier this year. "It was a low-paying job, but I made sure I was the best worker there. Anything I do, I want to be the best. It's not about all those things that people get so wrapped up in their minds. Everyone got themselves so wrapped up into who making the most money and who got the most followers. It ain't about that to me."

But Wilder has had several run-ins with the law, the most serious of which came in 2013 when he was arrested and charged with domestic battery by strangulation after an incident in a Las Vegas hotel room. According to the police report, the woman in question had a possible broken nose, swelling around her eyes, a cut lip, and red marks on her neck. Wilder's attorney later said that Deontay was apologetic and had mistakenly thought the woman was planning to rob him. The matter was settled out of court.

Then, on February 3, 2017, heavyweight contender Dominic Breazeale posted a statement on Instagram that read, "I want to address the fact that Deontay Wilder and a mob of about 20 people unprovokedly attacked my team and my family in the [hotel] lobby last night [after a fight card in Birmingham, Alabama]. My coach and I were blindsided by sucker-punches and my team was assaulted as well, all in front my wife and kids. This cowardly attack has no place in boxing and, believe me, it will not go unpunished."

Also, part of the Deontay Wilder feel-good story was his image as a loving husband and father. Deontay and his wife, Jessica Scales Wilder, had four children together. But in 2014, Wilder started dating TV-reality-star Telli Smith, who he met at Los Angeles International Airport. Smith became pregnant in 2017 and, in December of that year, told *People* magazine, "It's been a crazy journey. Deontay had baby fever, but I don't want to be a typical baby mama. I want to get married."

Smith gave birth to a daughter on March 7, 2018. Deontay and Jessica are now divorced, but Deontay has not yet remarried.

When it was time to set up the business end of Wilder-Fury, the fight was one of the easier high-profile matches to make. Both fighters wanted the bout. Wilder is an Al Haymon fighter with ties to Showtime in the United States. Fury is promoted by Frank Warren, who has a deal in the United Kingdom with BT Sport.

But first, Fury had to be rehabilitated in the ring and in the public mind. During a 30-month absence from boxing, his weight had ballooned to almost four hundred pounds.

Thus, it was decided that Fury's first fight back would be on the under-card of Terry Flanagan vs. Maurice Hooker in Manchester on June 9, 2018, against Sefer Seferi (a 39-year-old Macedonian who Tyson outweighed by 66 pounds). After four sluggish rounds, Seferi quit on his stool.

Next, on August 18, Fury lumbered to a ten-round decision over Francesco Pianeta on the undercard of Carl Frampton vs. Luke Jackson in Belfast. In Pianeta's three most recent fights, he'd beaten Daso Simeunovic (a novice with one professional fight on his resume) and lost to Petar Milas and Kevin Johnson.

Fury looked more fluid against Pianeta than he had against Seferi and he weighed eighteen pounds less (258 vs 276). But the flesh around his waist was jiggling. And while he won every minute of every round, he never noticeably hurt Pianeta.

Tyson wasn't fully back. But given his proclivity for going off the rails, it made sense from a business point of view for him to fight Wilder sooner rather than later because "later" might mean "never." On September 21, it was announced that Wilder-Fury was a done deal and that the fight would be contested on December 1 at a soon-to-be-chosen venue, later designated as Staples Center in Los Angeles.

The kick-off press tour was a traveling circus with stops in London, New York, and Los Angeles. There was a lot of profanity (both men), simulated masturbation onstage (Wilder), and in-your-face jawing.

British boxing writer Tris Dixon summed up the promotion with the observation, "Wilder-Fury is unpredictable. It is wild. It is bonkers. It is loud and in your face. It is the Vegas hooker under the neon lights. It is a smash and grab, a heist. The go-slow on the Fury comeback roller coaster has broken, the accelerator has come off in someone's hand, and the ride is headed for the precipice. Will he hit the summit again or will he plummet at the Alabama man's rock-like fists? We are passengers on this wild ride. Some will watch through their fingers. Some will wave their hands in the air, flying along with happy screams while promotional and broadcasting competitors might be reaching for the sick bags. But they're still watching. We all are. We all will be."

Fury's persona drove the promotion. It was odd that Wilder—a fighter who'd been WBC heavyweight champion for three years and successfully defended his title seven times—needed an opponent to raise his own profile. But that was the situation Deontay found himself in.

"This fight means everything to me," Wilder acknowledged. "This is my coming-out party."

Early numbers suggested that the pay-per-view telecast would do well in the United Kingdom but poorly in the United States. Staples Center can accommodate 20,000 fans for boxing. Ultimately, there was an announced attendance of 17,698, but that included a lot of freebies.

The fight shaped up as boxer (Fury) versus puncher (Wilder). Deontay opened as a 6-to-5 betting favorite. As fight night approached, the odds moved to 8-to-5.

The case for a Wilder victory was obvious

Fury has boxing skills. But his handlers had kept him away from punchers throughout his career. The exception to that was his fight against Wladimir Klitschko. But Klitschko, by that point, was a tentative puncher who was having trouble pulling the trigger.

Wilder is not a tentative puncher. He pulls the trigger quickly and is dangerous at all times

Fury, by his own acknowledgment, is mentally fragile. That's never good in a fighter.

Also, Tyson was being trained for the Wilder fight by a 26-year-old novice named Ben Davison whose primary contribution, some said, was bringing his fighter down in weight to a respectable number.

And most significantly, Fury's years of self-destruction had been marked by drug abuse, alcohol abuse, and a weight gain of more than one hundred pounds. Could he sustain a championship-caliber effort against Wilder over the course of twelve hard rounds?

People knew what to expect from Wilder. The unknown variable was Fury.

"I am no challenger for no man," Fury proclaimed at the October 1 kick-off press conference in London. "I am the lineal heavyweight champion of the world. Nobody forced me to fight Deontay Wilder, I picked him because I believe he's an easy touch. I will stand right in front of him and prove what I will do. I will punch his face seven days a week and twice on a Sunday. If we fought thirty times, I'd win thirty times."

Thereafter, Fury elaborated on that theme, saying, Wilder has only one style: come forward and knock you out. If he doesn't do that, he's lost. He's got one way, one path. It's all he knows. But he doesn't have the ability to set up the knockout against me, doesn't have the schooling. He's inexperienced at the championship level. He can't figure me out. I'm a man of many, many faces."

"You're known for being clever, aren't you?" Tyson was asked during a November 14 media conference call.

"I don't know about clever," Fury answered. "If I was clever, I'd be a rocket scientist and not a boxer. But I have got the ability to see punches [and avoid them], which is a very good skill. I'll be looking to avoid the knockout punches and land mine. Boxing is about hitting your opponent and not taking any in return. I don't look at boxing like I'm going to hit you in the face and you're going to hit me back because then I'd be a fool. It's my business to get out of the way."

Fury weighed in for the fight at a relatively soft 256 pounds; Wilder at 212–½ (the lightest Deontay had been since tipping the scales at 207–¼ for his pro debut in 2008).

Bart Barry summed up the proceedings as follows: "Wilder is a professional athlete who fights like he's insane. Fury is an insane man who boxes conventionally. For 36 minutes, absolutely nothing might happen. Fury is a good boxer but not much of a fight-night entertainer. Wilder is an entertainer but not much of a boxer. Each man has the best chance of besting the other man by being himself. Wilder would be a fool to try boxing Fury, and Fury would be a greater fool if he tried to slug with Wilder. How much fun it will be, how wickedly suspenseful, when the opening bell rings and you get to cheer for one loon or the other without much idea of what comes next."

When fight night arrived, the pay-per-view undercard consisted of three dreary mismatches. Then Wilder-Fury began. Slowly

Fury's flesh jiggled a bit as he moved around the ring. He put his hands behind his back and struck his tongue out at Wilder from time to time. Other than that, he didn't do much for the first five rounds. He made Deontay miss but didn't make him pay.

There were times when Tyson held his hands low and shook them in a herky-jerky motion that made him look like a character in a flickering old silent movie. Effective feints are one thing. A fighter jerking his hands around like they're attached to a vibrator is another. It means the fighter's hands are not in position to punch. A boxer more skilled than Wilder could have timed Tyson's hand movement and taken advantage of it.

Wilder went for the knockout with every punch. That's the way he fights and it's all he can do. The most noticeable punch missing from his arsenal was an effective jab to set up his right hand. The absence of that jab enabled Fury to keep the fight in the center of the ring where he wanted it for most of the night.

By the midway point, the fight was clearly moving in Fury's favor. The area around Wilder's left eye was swelling. Deontay was starting to look tentative. Tyson was landing authoritative right hands. And when Deontay landed, Fury took the punches well. Also, it appeared as though Wilder rather than Fury was the fighter who was tiring.

In round nine, the tension escalated when Wilder dropped Fury with a right hand behind the ear. But in terms of the flow of the fight, it was an isolated moment. Fury rallied to win rounds ten and eleven on each judge's scorecard.

Round twelve, was a time-capsule round. Less than a minute into the stanza, a right-hand-left-hook combination decked Fury for the second time in the bout. This time, unlike in round nine, the fight appeared to be over.

Fury lay on his back, seemingly only barely conscious.

Wilder shimmied to a neutral corner.

"Credit to him," Tyson said afterward. "He caught me flush. But I got a good fighting spirit and I never say die. I ain't gonna lay down just because I got punched in the face and knocked down. I'm gonna get back up and fight. I'm not the lineal champion for nothing. You can make two decisions on that floor: stay down or get up. As long as there's life left in this body, I'll continue to fight."

Fury rose to his feet just before the count of ten, a heroic effort that evoked images of a barely conscious Larry Holmes climbing off the canvas against Earnie Shavers and Renaldo Snipes.

Referee Jack Reiss let the fight continue.

And Wilder couldn't finish. Indeed, a minute later, Fury shook him with a clubbing right hand that had Deontay holding on.

The general consensus was that the fight was close with Fury having a slight edge. Alejandro Rochin of Mexico was off the mark with a 115–111 scorecard in Wilder's favor. Robert Tapper (Canada) saw the contest 114–112 in favor of Fury. That left the deciding vote to Phil Edwards (United Kingdom) who scored the bout a 113–113 draw.

All three judges awarded Fury rounds five, ten and eleven and Wilder rounds one, nine and twelve (the latter two by 10–8 margins). That gave Wilder a two-point cushion and left rounds two, three, four, six, seven, and eight up for grabs. Rochin scored four of those six rounds for Wilder. Tapper scored five of the six for Fury. Edwards scored four of the six for Fury.

Asked about the decision at the post-fight press conference, Fury responded, "I should have won the fight but I'm not gonna complain. It was what it was." One day later, he was more voluble, saying, "Wilder got a gift decision in his home country. To be honest with you, I've never seen a worse decision in my life. I don't know what fight them judges were watching. But it's boxing. It ain't the first time this has happened. You win some; you lose some; and in my case, you draw some."

Meanwhile, December 1 confirmed several often-repeated theories about Wilder: (1) he has excellent power, (2) his ring skills are limited, and (3) he has heart. Again and again, boxing fans have seen a fighter go into the twelfth round needing a big round to win and not going for it. Wilder never stopped trying. He never gave up. He went for it.

Fury is also a fighter. "I was suffering from mental health problems," Tyson said the day after Wilder-Fury. "When you give up the passion to live anymore, you're in a bad place. I'm a well man now. Everything is good. I'm happy to be alive and healthy and well."

When told that tickets for Canelo Alvarez vs. Rocky Fielding at Madison Square Garden were going well, Eddie Hearn (Fielding's promoter) quipped, "It doesn't surprise me. Rocky has always been a big ticket-seller." But Alvarez-Fielding was all about Canelo.

Saul "Canelo" Alvarez Comes to Madison Square Garden

It's a long journey to Madison Square Garden from the Arena Chololo Larios in Tonala, Mexico, where 15-year-old Saul "Canelo" Alvarez made his debut as a professional fighter thirteen years ago.

Canelo is now boxing royalty. At age 28, he has crafted a 51–1-2 (35 KOs) ring record and shown a willingness to go in tough. His financial ledger is equally imposing. Canelo puts people in seats and engenders more pay-per-view buys than any other boxer today. On December 15, 2018, his fistic and financial might were on display against Rocky Fielding at Madison Square Garden.

Boxing is in MSG's DNA. And vice versa. The first Madison Square Garden—located at Madison Square on Madison Avenue and 26th Street in Manhattan—was built in 1876. Three later incarnations followed, each of them synonymous with elite indoor sports. The current Madison Square Garden opened fifty years ago. Muhammad Ali and Joe Frazier did battle twice within its walls.

Canelo's 53 previous bouts had been contested in Mexico (35 times), Nevada (11), Texas (3), California (3), and Florida (1). His decision to fight in New York was part of a larger branding effort and marked the start of a lucrative contract with DAZN.

On October 17, it was announced that DAZN, Canelo, and Golden Boy (Alvarez's promoter) had entered into an agreement to stream Canelo's next eleven fights on DAZN platforms throughout the world with DAZN paying a minimum of $365 million for the honor. DAZN will also stream an unspecified number of less prominent Golden Boy fight cards during the five-year contract term and otherwise dispose of rights to Alvarez's fights in countries where it doesn't have a streaming platform.

Canelo's purse for fighting Fielding was $15 million. His pay for future outings will depend upon the opponent and various benchmarks regarding DAZN's performance. The minimum purse for each of these fights (likely to be contested on Cinco de Mayo and Mexican Independence Day weekends) will be $35 million.

Michael "Rocky" Fielding, age 31, is from England and sported a 27–1 (15 KOs) record. He isn't a quality super-middleweight. But he'd knocked out someone named Tyron Zeuge on July 14, after which, in the la-la land known as the World Boxing Association, he became the "regular" WBA 168-pound world champion. That placed him behind Callum Smith, who destroyed Fielding in one round three years ago and is the real WBA 168-pound world champion.

Fielding brought two things to the Canelo-Rocky promotion: his belt and his nickname. Beyond that, he could have been any fighter. He was the B-side in a promotion in which only the A-side mattered.

Rocky comes across as an amiable man (the Brits might call him a "chap" or "bloke") who'd be pleasant to sit with while watching a soccer game on television. By all accounts, he's a decent man. The general sentiment among the media was the hope that he'd be well-paid for his effort and not get too badly beaten up.

Alvarez had a huge edge over Fielding in terms of natural athletic ability. Canelo also has better ring skills, hits harder, is faster, and takes a better punch. Against all that, Fielding (6-feet-1-inch tall) could claim a five-inch height advantage and three-inch edge in reach over Canelo.

Jamie Moore, who trains Fielding, put an optimistic spin on things. During a December 3 media conference call, Moore declared, "A lot of fighters, especially the ones who he spars, say you don't realize how good Rocky is or how unorthodox he is. I don't think Rocky's record really tells the tale of how hard he punches. A lot of the guys he boxed early on, you saw go in there to survive so they were able to fiddle their way through. And there's a lot of unanswered questions regarding Alvarez moving up to super-middleweight. The height and reach advantage what Rocky's got is huge."

Canelo played along with that theme, saying, "It's not a secret that I'm a better fighter and that I'm more experienced. But I'm taking a risk by entering into the comfort zone of a champion at his weight. Boxing is the sport where you should be least overconfident. One punch can change everything."

But reality and fantasy are two different things. Great Britain has produced some remarkably good fighters over the years. Fielding fit into a different category: the plucky, give-it-everything-he-has, sacrificial lamb. He's tall and thin and looked as though a well-placed body shot from Canelo might break him in two. He's an arm-puncher who doesn't get much leverage on his punches. When asked about his power and build at a media sit-down two days before the fight, Rocky conceded "I'm not like Hulk Hogan," before adding, "I'm going to give it everything I have to get the victory."

Canelo-Fielding was the equivalent of entering an off-the-lot car in the Indianapolis 500. At the end of the day, it's one car with one driver against one car with one driver. But the car off the lot isn't going to win.

At the final pre-fight press conference, Chepo Reynoso (who manages Alvarez) proclaimed, "Madison Square Garden, be prepared. Canelo is coming to conquer you."

On fight night, Canelo Alvarez arrived at his dressing room at Madison Square Garden at 7:50 PM. As an elite fighter, he'd been given the New York Knicks changing room—part of a complex that includes a players' lounge, video room, head coach's office, trainer's room, and multiple shower stalls.

The dressing room was round, twenty feet in diameter with recessed lighting above. Two imitation leather sofas and fourteen black cushioned folding metal-framed chairs ringed a plush blue carpet with a large blue-orange-and-white Knicks logo emblazoned in the center. Backdrops with logos for Golden Boy, Tecate, and Alvarez stretched from just above the floor to the ceiling, blocking off the Knicks cubicles and wood-paneled walls. Two large Mexican flags had been hung facing each other.

Canelo's team included Chepo Reynoso, physical conditioner Munir Somoya, several videographers, and myriad camp aides, relatives, and friends. Those on the immediate team wore maroon track suits with gold trim. Trainer Eddy Reynoso was in another room readying Ryan Garcia for an undercard fight and would join them later.

Canelo lay down on one of the sofas with a towel beneath his head, took out his smart phone, and checked for messages. One of the backdrops was moved aside so he could watch the undercard fights on a large flat-screen television attached to the wall, but there was no DAZN signal.

Ramiro Gonzalez (Canelo's publicist and friend) handed Alvarez a smartphone with the DAZN app already downloaded so he could watch the action. Katie Taylor was en route to winning every round on each judge's scorecard against Eva Wahlstrom.

Chris Mannix came in to conduct an interview with Canelo for the DAZN stream.

"Do you want to do this in English?" Mannix asked.

"I understand," Canelo told him. "But I answer in Spanish. Is okay?" It was okay.

When the interview was done, Canelo checked again for messages on his smartphone.

Few people in the room were talking. Those who did conversed in quiet tones.

Golden Boy president Eric Gomez came in and shook hands with everyone.

Five minutes later, Dr. Gerard Varlotta entered to administer the standard New York State Athletic Commission fight-night physical examination. Canelo had a bit of swelling and a small scab beneath his right eye, the result of a recent sparring session. A more severe cut suffered above his left eye in a rematch against Gennady Golovkin three months earlier had healed.

"I had hair your color when I was young," Dr. Varlotta (whose nickname is Rusty) informed the fighter.

Canelo smiled.

The mood was far more relaxed than it had been in the dressing room prior to Canelo's most recent two fights against Golovkin.

At 8:40 p.m., Edith Marquez (a singer and actress who would sing the Mexican national anthem later in the evening) came in to wish Canelo well. Her gown accentuated her figure and demanded attention. And she got it. Chepo rose from his chair and sang a love song for her. Then, one by one, the members of Team Alvarez posed for pictures with her.

Canelo picked up Ramiro Gonzalez's smart phone again. Ryan Garcia vs. Braulio Rodriguez had begun. At nine o'clock, the DAZN stream appeared on the flat screen television.

More relatives, some with toddlers, came and went. Canelo hugged each of the arrivals, paying special attention to his daughter, Maria

Fernanda. Three months earlier, an hour before his rematch against Gennady Golovkin, Canelo had walked Maria around his dressing room at the T-Mobile Arena, holding her arms above her head to steady her legs. Now she could take several steps on her own before losing her balance.

Garcia knocked Rodriguiz out in round five. That was followed by Sadam Ali vs. Mauricio Herrera.

Referee Ricky Gonzalez entered and gave Alvarez his pre-fight instructions.

More well-wishers and sponsor representatives came and went.

Mexican legend Julio Cesar Chavez came in to conduct an interview with Canelo for Spanish-language television.

At 9:25 p.m., Eddy Reynoso began taping Canelo's hands. Nigel Travis, who was in the room as Rocky Fielding's representative, objected to what he argued was illegal stacking (layering gauze and tape in a forbidden way). The issue had been discussed (and presumably resolved) at a meeting with New York State Athletic Commission director of boxing Matt Delaglio the previous day. Now executive director Kim Sumbler and deputy commissioner George Ward were called in to further resolve it. There was a slight adjustment to Canelo's handwraps and Travis left grumbling.

Canelo lay down on a rubdown table. Soft Latin music sounded in the background. Munir Somoya stretched him out for fifteen minutes. Then Canelo rose from the table and danced briefly with Chepo in his arms to laughter all around.

Oscar de La Hoya and Bernard Hopkins came in to wish Canelo well.

Canelo gloved up, then pounded a round black leather cushion that Eddy Reynoso was holding. By 10:40 p.m., he was ready for battle. But Tevin Farmer vs. Francisco Fonseca (the next-to-last fight of the evening) was only in round five.

Now Canelo was marking time. He paced and shadow-boxed. There was some padwork. Farmer-Fonseca ended with Farmer winning a unanimous decision.

Three national anthems were next up on the DAZN stream. Canelo paced back and forth, rotating his arms during the singing of God Save the Queen and The Star-Spangled Banner. But he stood at attention as Edith Marquez sang the Mexican anthem.

Earlier in the evening, as many as forty people had been in the room. Now only Canelo, his cornermen, and two New York State Athletic Commission inspectors remained.

At 11:30 p.m., three hours and forty minutes after entering his dressing room, Canelo left for the ring. It was a fight he was expected to dominate. But once the bell rings, there are no guarantees in boxing.

There's a huge fan base for Puerto Rican boxers in New York. Not so for Mexican fighters. But the sell-out crowd of 20,113 stood testament to Canelo's drawing power. In the next hour, he would earn more money than Joe Louis made in his entire ring career and more than all but a few elite fighters have made for a single fight.

Fielding entered the ring to Neil Diamond's Sweet Caroline. This was his time on a world stage. Canelo was next, walking down the aisle to a thunderous roar and chants of "Mexico! Mexico!"

The "key to victory" was that Fielding didn't belong in the ring with Canelo. Rocky had enjoyed the build-up to the fight. "It was a great week," he said afterward. "Met some great people. I lived a dream."

Then savage reality intervened and the dream turned into a nightmare.

Once the bell rang, it was clear that Rocky had no chance. His jab was ineffective; he simply couldn't land it. At times, he traded power punches. But it was as though he had a sling-shot and Canelo was armed with a Magnum .357.

Canelo attacked with a brutal body assault, dropping Fielding with hooks to the liver in rounds one and two. Two minutes 15 seconds into round three, when Rocky brought his elbows down to protect his body, a thudding right hand up top dropped him for the third time. Twenty seconds later, another crushing hook to the body put him on the canvas for the fourth time, and referee Ricky Gonzalez appropriately stopped the slaughter.

"He's strong," Fielding said afterward. "The body shots were really tough. He placed his shots well, and he caught me. I gave it everything, and the better man won. Hats off to Canelo. I respect him."

Curiosities

It has become a tradition, as a reminder that there's a world outside of boxing, to include a bonus piece in each year's collection of boxing articles published by the University of Arkansas Press.

Albert Einstein:
Scientist, Humanist, Icon

★ "A ship is always safe at the shore. But that is not what it is built for."

★ "I prefer to make up my own quotes and attribute them to very smart people, so that I can use them to win arguments."

★ "If you don't have time to do it right, when will you have time to do it over?"

★ "Any man who can drive safely while kissing a pretty girl is simply not giving the kiss the attention it deserves."

★ "To punish me for my contempt for authority, fate made me an authority."

★ "Dancers are the athletes of God."

Sixty-three years after his death, the author of these quotes remains the world's most powerful symbol of scientific inquiry.

Albert Einstein's name is synonymous with genius. As Walter Isaacson wrote in a landmark 2007 biography, "The world has never seen before, and perhaps will never see again, such a scientific celebrity superstar, one who also happened to be a gentle icon of humanist values and a living patron saint for Jews."

The world fell in love with Einstein. He had a distinctive unconventional appearance that suggested a man preoccupied with weighty matters. With his casual attire, unruly hair, and expressive eyes, he looked like what we expect an eccentric genius to be.

At the close of the last millennium, *Time Magazine* hailed Einstein as the "Man of the Century."

Einstein was born in Ulm, Germany, on March 14, 1879. He was a genius, not a saint, unfaithful to two wives and often careless with the people who loved him.

"My passionate sense of social justice and social responsibility,"
Einstein acknowledged in his later years, "has always contrasted oddly
with my pronounced lack of need for direct contact with other human
beings. I am truly a lone traveler and have never belonged to my
country, my home, my friends, or even my immediate family with my
whole heart."

Einstein's early years in academia were difficult for him. He was
a free-thinker, which ran contrary to the rigid thought processes that
marked German scientific exploration at that time. Unable to secure
a university position after graduation, he took a job reviewing patent
applications at the Swiss Patent Office in Bern, a post he held from 1902
through 1909. That gave him the freedom to think creatively beyond the
structured academic norm.

In Einstein's youth, the study of physics was based on theories that
had been developed by Isaac Newton, who changed humanity's understanding of the physical world.

Newton offered a mechanical universe governed by gravity, mass,
force, and motion operating pursuant to rules that are predictable and
constant. The belief that time and space are absolute was central to his
teachings. Newton's findings were a mainstay of physics for more than
two centuries. Einstein challenged their validity.

Very few people understand Einstein's theory of relativity, and this
writer is not one of them. The theory defies easy description. Time and
again, Einstein was asked for a brief explanation and answered, "All my
life, I have been trying to get it into one book. And you want me to get
it into one sentence."

To draw an analogy: It was once inconceivable to the human mind
that the earth is a sphere spinning in space. Our forebearers' senses told
them that the earth is flat and that the sun orbits around it. Most of us
now take it on faith that the planet we live on is a sphere, not flat, and
that it orbits around the sun. We do so because our minds have been
patterned to think this way. It has been ingrained in our thoughts since
early childhood.

By contrast, it was—and still is—difficult to grasp Einstein's discov-
eries, most notably that time and space are not constant. His findings
defy common experience and common logic. Yet Einstein conceived of
these theories. And he did so, not through empirical observation but as

a consequence of "thought experiments" that were only later confirmed by physical data.

1905 will be forever known as Einstein's "annus mirabilis" (miraculous year). While still employed at the Swiss Patent Office in Bern, he published four papers.

The first, published in March, posited that light is not a wave but, rather, is comprised of packets (or particles). Decades later, this concept would serve as a crucial building block in the study of quantum mechanics.

The second paper, published in June, paved the way for future experiments confirming that matter is made of atoms.

Then, in June 1905, Einstein unveiled his special theory of relativity, positing that (1) Time is not absolute but, rather, moves at different speeds dependent upon the relationship between the forces of nature and the motion of the observer; and (2) Space, like time, is relative rather than absolute.

Or phrased differently; time and space are not constants that serve merely as a backdrop for other forces. They are active players in the drama of the cosmos.

Finally, in a fourth paper published in September 1905, Einstein theorized that, under certain circumstances, mass and energy are interchangeable and the energy contained in a system is equal to its mass times the speed of light squared . . . $E=MC^2$. That would have profound implications later on.

Einstein was redefining what physicists thought they knew about time, gravity, mass, and space. But there was a need for more. His special theory of relativity was incomplete in that it applied only to constant-velocity motion. And it was based on the premise that nothing can travel faster than the speed of light, which conflicted with the commonly held belief that gravity acts instantaneously between distant objects.

In the decade that followed, Einstein sought to resolve these issues. In November 1915, he published a new theory of time, space, and gravity entitled "The General Theory of Relativity" that posited warps and curves in space and time.

For most of mankind's existence, space had been thought of as the absence of matter, an otherwise empty enclosure for the universe. Then, in the mid-19th century, Michael Faraday and James Maxwell posited the existence of an omnipresent electromagnetic field in space that transports electromagnetic forces. Einstein took this theory a step further, positing the existence of an omnipresent gravitational field in space.

Einstein then sought to quantify mathematically how gravitational fields act on matter and how matter generates gravitational fields. Gravity, he concluded, was the curvature of spacetime. This spacetime wasn't a passive backdrop or empty container. Rather, he likened it to a trampoline that curves when a bowling ball and billiard balls roll across it. The curving of the trampoline, in turn, determines the path of the balls and causes the billiard balls to move toward the bowling ball. This curving of the fabric of spacetime, Einstein concluded, explained gravity, its relationship to acceleration, and the general relativity of all forms of motion.

Theoretical physicist Brian Greene summarized Einstein's description of the universe as follows: "Space and time come alive. Matter here causes space to warp there, which causes matter over here to move, which causes space way over there to warp even more, and so on. General relativity provides the choreography for an entwined cosmic dance of space, time, matter, and energy."

Now all Einstein had to do was demonstrate that his theory was correct.

"If my theory of relativity is proven successful," he stated, "Germany will claim me as a German, and France will declare me a citizen of the world. Should my theory prove untrue, France will say that I am a German, and Germany will declare that I am a Jew."

Validation came four years later.

Einstein had theorized that light bends when passing through a gravitational field. Thus, under certain circumstances, the deflection of light when passing by a massive object should be observable.

On May 29, 1919, an expedition to the west coast of Africa led by English astronomer and physicist Arthur Eddington observed a solar eclipse and determined that starlight passing by the sun bent, not in accordance with Newton's laws, but just as Einstein's theory of general relativity predicted it would. When word of this confirmation reached England, a headline in *The Times* of London proclaimed:

REVOLUTION IN SCIENCE
New Theory of the Universe
NEWTONIAN IDEAS OVERTHROWN

Albert Einstein had redefined the laws of physics and changed the way that scientists view the universe. His theory of general relativity would become a cornerstone of modern physics and influence all future exploration of the origin and evolution of the cosmos.

In the wake of his theory's validation, Einstein enjoyed renown that no scientist has known before or since.

"The newly discovered genius," Isaacson recounts, "was not a drab or reserved academic. He was a charming 40-year-old, just passing from handsome to distinctive, with a wild burst of hair, rumpled informality, twinkling eyes, and a willingness to dispense wisdom in bite-sized quips and quotes. Einstein performed. He gave interviews readily, peppered them with delightful aphorisms, and knew exactly what made for a good story."

"I am not a genius," Einstein maintained. "I am just curious. I ask many questions . . . It's not that I'm so smart. It's just that I stay with problems longer . . . The only sure way to avoid making mistakes is to have no new ideas."

But the adulation was muted in Einstein's homeland where the seeds of anti-Semitism were growing into strangling vines.

Einstein had been born into a family of Jewish heritage that had little interest in the rituals of religion. He never joined a synagogue and rejected common concepts of God.

"Religion should transcend a personal God and avoid dogmas and theology," he wrote. "If something is in me which can be called religious, it is the unbounded admiration for the structure of the world. Try and penetrate with our limited means the secrets of nature and you will find that, behind all the discernible laws and connections, there remains something subtle, intangible and inexplicable. Veneration for this force beyond anything that we can comprehend is my religion."

But as the 1920s progressed and talk of a Jewish conspiracy flourished in Germany, Einstein embraced his Jewish identity.

"There is nothing in me that can be described as a Jewish faith," he said. "However, I am happy to be a member of the Jewish people." Later, he would refer to the desire for assimilation as "a Jewish weakness, always trying to keep the Gentiles in good humor."

On January 30, 1933, Adolf Hitler became Chancellor of Germany. The February 27 Reichstag Fire led to the further consolidation of Nazi power.

It was time to go. Einstein emigrated to the United States, arriving in America on October 17, 1933. "If and when war comes," he prophesied, "Hitler will realize the harm he has done Germany by driving out the Jewish scientists."

Einstein lived in America for 22 years, teaching at Princeton University and continuing his exploration of the natural world. But his greatest work as a scientist was done.

In the 1930s, astronomers became aware of an unseen presence in the universe that seemed to exert a gravitational pull on visible stars. But for a variety of reasons, Einstein never accepted the concept of black holes as physically real objects. The irony of this, Isaacson notes, is that, "Black holes are the only places in the universe where Einstein's theory of relativity shows its full power and glory. Here, and nowhere else, space and time lose their individuality and merge together in a sharply curved four-dimensional structure precisely delineated by Einstein's equations."

Einstein also stubbornly resisted advances in quantum mechanics. His theory of relativity explored the cosmos on a grand scale. Quantum mechanics (also referred to as quantum physics or quantum theory) studies nature at the atomic and sub-atomic level.

Einstein's work in 1905 postulating a relationship between energy and mass had been influential in the origins of quantum mechanics, as was his belief that light comes in discrete units rather than waves. But in the 1920s, quantum theory moved in a new direction, propagating the view that unpredictable random behavior is an essential feature of the sub-atomic world. As science writer George Musser explained, "When a radioactive nucleus decays, it does so spontaneously. No rule will tell you when or why. When a particle of light strikes a half-silvered mirror, it either reflects off it or passes through. The outcome is open until the moment it occurs."

In other words, the outcome is left to chance.

This uncertainty principle was at odds with Einstein's faith in a predictable order of all things, large and small. He firmly believed that, if one knows all the physical variables in a system, the conduct of these variables can be predicted and that undiscovered fundamental forces of nature lay behind the apparently indeterministic nature of quantum mechanics.

"I cannot accept the view that events in nature are analogous to a game of chance," he wrote. "God does not play dice with the universe."

Thus, Einstein spent much of his later years searching for a "unified field theory" or "theory of everything" that would prove that all types of matter and energy, gravity and electromagnetism, are subject to strictly determinant physical causes and effects. While acknowledging that quantum mechanics "undoubtedly contains a part of the ultimate truth," he maintained that quantum theory was incomplete.

He was unsuccessful in this quest. For as Isaacson writes, "There is no reason other than a metaphysical faith or a habit ingrained in the mind to believe that nature must operate with absolute certainty. It is just as reasonable, though perhaps less satisfying, to believe that some things simply happen by chance."

Meanwhile, as Einstein settled into life as an American citizen, his image was becoming even more iconic and endearing.

"Why is it that no one understands me and everybody likes me?" he asked.

At the same time, Einstein was also becoming known for his social and political views.

Marian Anderson was one of the most celebrated singers of her era, an African-American woman with classical skills. In 1937, she performed in concert at Princeton but was refused accommodations at the Nassau Inn because of her color. Einstein invited her to spend the night as a guest in his home.

"There is separation of colored people from white people in the United States," he said. "That separation is not a disease of colored people. It is a disease of white people. I do not intend to be quiet about it."

Einstein also believed that "all people are "citizens of the world," "nationalism is the measles of mankind," and "a foolish faith in authority is the worst enemy of truth."

"He who joyfully marches to music rank and file has already earned my contempt," Einstein declared. "Heroism at command, senseless brutality, deplorable love-of-country stance, and all the loathsome nonsense that goes by the name of patriotism; how I hate all this. How despicable and ignoble war is. I would rather be torn to shreds than be part of so base an action."

In 1933, as Hitler consolidated power, Einstein abandoned his belief in absolute pacifism and resistance to military service. But he qualified this change in position, saying, "This does not mean that I am surrendering the principle for which I have stood heretofore. I have no greater hope than that the time may not be far off when refusal of military service will once again be an effective method of serving the cause of human progress."

In keeping with his opposition to nationalism, Einstein initially opposed the creation of a Jewish state, although he visited Palestine for twelve days in 1923 and supported the idea of Jewish settlements there. He never visited Israel after statehood was achieved, but spoke out later in favor of Israel's right to exist. His standing among worldwide Jewry was such that, when the nation's first president, Chaim Weizmann, died in 1952, Einstein was asked to serve in the largely ceremonial position as Weizmann's successor. He declined, saying that he was "deeply moved" by the offer but lacked "the natural aptitude and the experience to deal properly with people and to exercise official function."

Given Einstein's opposition to nationalism and war, there's sad irony in the fact that he's intricately linked in the historical record to the development of nuclear weapons.

In 1905, Einstein had postulated that inert mass contained large amounts of latent energy which could, if fundamental building blocks were broken apart, be released. He further postulated that, during this process, a certain amount of matter would be converted to energy and that the amount of energy created would equal the amount of mass lost times the speed of light squared.

On August 2, 1939, fearful that Hitler's Germany had begun a concerted effort to unlock the secrets of the atom, Einstein drafted a letter that was delivered to Franklin Roosevelt and led to the Manhattan Project. Six years later, on August 6, 1945, one gram of mass (half the weight of a butterscotch Lifesaver) was converted to energy to destroy the city of Hiroshima and end 200,000 lives.

Thereafter, Einstein declared:

* "It has become appallingly obvious that our technology has exceeded our humanity. The unleashed power of the atom has changed everything except our thinking."
* "I know not with what weapons World War III will be fought. But World War IV will be fought with sticks and stones."
* "We are drifting toward catastrophe beyond conception. If only I had known, I should have become a watchmaker."

Yet through it all, Einstein retained a fundamental faith in science. "Politics is for the present," he said. "Our equations are for eternity."

He died on April 18, 1955, at Princeton Hospital after a ruptured aortic aneurysm. He knew the end was near but faced death bravely, saying, "It is tasteless to prolong life artificially. I have done my share. It is time to go. I will do it elegantly."

The vastness of the universe is hard to conceptualize. Our sun is one of 100 billion stars in a galaxy known as The Milky Way. When Einstein published his general theory of relativity in 1915, it was thought that the Milky Way was surrounded by an infinite void. We now know that there are hundreds of billions more galaxies, many of them as large or larger than our own. Albert Einstein laid the cornerstone for the modern study of it all.

Trainer Don Turner recently opined, "The ring walk is when a fighter should be concentrating on his opponent and what he's going to do in the fight, not worrying about his costume and the music."

The Ring Walk

"I've covered sports for a half-century," Jerry Izenberg (the dean of American sportswriters) reminisced not long ago. "I've been to every kind of championship and seen every great athlete of the past fifty years. And no moment I've ever seen had the electricity of Muhammad Ali and Joe Frazier coming down the aisle and entering the ring the first time they fought. The sound of the crowd changed. It had been a low buzz during the break before the main event. Then it became something different. First, it got louder in the back of the arena. Heads turned. The buzz spread. And it kept getting louder and louder until it was a roar that told everyone that there were two champions in the house."

Once upon a time, even for boxing's biggest fights, ring walks were a straightforward matter. There was no entourage, no one pushing and shoving to get in front of a TV camera. The trainer led the way. The fighter put his hands on the trainer's shoulders, and they walked to the ring with the other cornermen behind them.

The ring walks preceding big fights were dramatic because of the stakes involved. And club fights had their moments too.

Longtime promoter Don Elbaum recalls, "I had a fighter named Manny Quinney. He was a light-heavyweight out of Buffalo who turned pro in the 1960s and started his career with five straight first-round knockouts. He could punch like you wouldn't believe. He looked like a killer. And he had the scariest ring walk I've ever seen. He'd walk to the ring waving his arms like a crazy man and grunting like a monster."

"So I'm promoting a fight with him in Erie, Pennsylvania," Elbaum continues. "I've got him on track to beat Young Otto's record of seven straight first-round knockouts. I've got the right opponent, a guy making his pro debut who was scared stiff and never fought again after that night. The opponent is in the ring. Manny comes down the aisle, waving his arms and grunting like a savage animal. He gets in the ring. And the opponent faints. I'm not making this up. Sometimes I exaggerate for the sake of a good story, but this is absolutely true. The opponent fainted dead away and Manny won by disqualification which broke his first-round knockout streak."

It used to be that the ring walk was simply how a fighter got to the ring. Then music was added to the ritual.

Ralph Dupas, a world-class welterweight from New Orleans who fought in the 1950s and '60s, entered the ring to blues music from time to time. Late in Muhammad Ali's storied career, The Greatest broke new ground by entering the ring to face Earnie Shavers to the majestic sound of the theme from *Star Wars*. As Oscar De La Hoya evolved as a Hispanic-American icon, he took to entering the ring accompanied by a mariachi band to build his brand within the Latino community.

Ring-walk music is now common. In recent years, it has run the gamut from Ricky Hatton's rousing entrance with a rock version of "Blue Moon" pulsating through the arena to Dmitriy Salita being led into battle by an Orthodox Jewish rapper.

Gangsta rap is a different matter. "We get complaints from time to time about the language in some of the music," Greg Sirb (executive director of the Pennsylvania State Athletic Commission) acknowledges. "People screaming the N word and bitch this and F that. You can argue that it is, or isn't, a free speech issue. I don't like some of the lyrics. But so far, we've let it go. It's not worth the hassle to test it."

Initially, Premier Boxing Champions sought to standardize ring walks to the accompaniment of a theme written by Academy-Award-winning composer Hans Zimmer. But the practice was abandoned after criticism that the music was too sterile and deprived fighters of their individuality.

Meanwhile, over the years, theatrical visuals have been added to the mix.

Jorge Paez entered the ring in costumes ranging from a Batman outfit to a wedding gown. Suffice it to say that Rocky Marciano would not have worn a wedding gown into a boxing ring.

Floyd Mayweather was carried to the ring on a throne borne by four musclemen clad as Roman centurions for his fight against Arturo Gatti. Not to be outdone, Jorge Arce rode a horse to ringside for his battle against Julio Ler. Naseem Hamed upped the ante when he fought Kevin Kelley at Madison Square Garden. More on that later.

Bernard Hopkins often walked to the ring to the sound of Frank Sinatra singing "My Way."

"I had two characters when I was fighting," Hopkins recounts. "The first was The Executioner. The second was The Alien. They came to the ring in different ways. The Executioner was angry. The Executioner had a boulder on his shoulder. The Executioner was all about inflicting pain and destruction. Two big guys came out with me wearing masks and boots and carrying swords. The Alien came later in my career and was about, 'Look at me. I'm as old as the hills and beating guys half my age.' Both ways, I was making a statement."

"There's two ring walks that stand out for me," Hopkins reminisces. "The ring walk for Felix Trinidad at Madison Square Garden was especially intense because of how important that fight was to my career and the situation with 9/11 [the Twin Towers had been destroyed eighteen days earlier]. And the other one that stands out for me was against Kelly Pavlik in Atlantic City. I had a lot to prove that night. Pavlik was favored to beat me. I was an old man, and Pavlik had beaten Jermain Taylor, who the judges said beat me."

Six years after beating Pavlik, Hopkins returned to Atlantic City and, at age 49, lost a unanimous decision to Sergey Kovalev. It had been planned that two entourage members would accompany The Alien on his ring walk that night and throw tiny alien figures encased in hard plastic eggs into the crowd. But before Bernard left the dressing room, it was pointed out to his marketing team that this was the equivalent of throwing rocks into a crowd of people in a dark room. Wiser heads prevailed and the plan was abandoned.

In some instances, ring walks today are choreographed as elaborately as a Broadway show.

Late in Wladimir Klitschko's career, his ring entrances were staged like a Wagnerian opera with smoke, flashing lights, dramatic music, multiple video screens, and whatever pyrotechnics the venue allowed.

Anthony Joshua enters the ring as part of a sound-and-light production that rivals Cirque du Soleil.

Ring walks like Joshua's don't just happen. They require a massive amount of planning and coordination between Sky TV, the venue, and Team Joshua (which includes management, marketing, and promotional personnel). Anthony is particular about his ring walk music but often doesn't decide which song will be played until the day before a fight. He's well-briefed on how his ring walk will unfold but generally doesn't do an advance walk-through. Instead, he trusts promoter Eddie Hearn, Sky, and the venue to ensure that things will be executed properly.

Elaborate ring walks are now so much a part of major fights that, in some instances, the ring announcer introduces the fighters twice. First before they walk ("now making his way to the ring") and then just before the referee's final instructions.

Michael Buffer, who has seen thousands of ring walks, declares, "Anthony Joshua's ring walk when he fought Wladimir Klitschko was the most spectacular entrance I've ever seen. You had ninety thousand screaming fans, an elevated platform, music, rockets, flames, flashing lights. It was awesome. No one who was there that night will forget the drama of that moment."

Trying to evaluate a fighter's state of mind during his ring walk is speculative at best. Al Bernstein, who has called fights from ringside for decades, says "I don't think you can tell much about how a fighter will perform based on his ring walk. The one time I deviated from that rule in my own mind was when Evander Holyfield fought Mike Tyson the first time. I was one of those people who didn't give Evander a chance. But there he was, walking to the ring, singing [a religious hymn]. My first reaction was, 'You're kidding me.' But he looked confident and completely at peace with himself. And I said to myself, 'Maybe Evander has a better chance to win this fight than I thought.'"

There are times when a well-planned ring walk can motivate a fighter. But walking to the ring can also be a scary experience.

When Naseem Hamed fought Paul Ingle in Manchester, Ingle was contractually obligated to enter the ring first. But he warned that he'd leave and go back to his dressing room if Hamed wasn't in the ring within a specified period of time. Hamed wasn't and Ingle did, leading George Foreman (who worked the fight as an HBO commentator) to observe that it was hard enough to walk to the ring once, let alone twice.

Asked to elaborate on that sentiment, Foreman says, "The moments before the fight, the killer quietness of the dressing room and that deadly walk through the crowd into the ring, were always like an out-of-body experience for me. It was like putting my life on ice for a moment. No way to prepare for that walk. Each one was life changing for me."

Larry Holmes had similar emotions and acknowledges, "I always felt jitters before a fight. I expected to get hit, and I expected it to hurt. The first time I fought, I was scared as hell. Over time, I got confidence. But I was still always scared that I might hurt somebody and scared that I might get hurt. When I walked down the aisle to fight guys like Ken Norton, Earnie Shavers, Mike Tyson, my heart was jumping. I asked myself, 'What are you doing this for?'"

Over time, Holmes learned to rev himself up for a fight by walking to the ring to the accompaniment of McFadden & Whitehead singing "Ain't No Stopping Us Now." Lennox Lewis employed a similar strategy when he entered the ring for his rematch against Hasim Rahman to the sound of James Brown's *The Payback*.

Mike Tyson's no-frills ring walks were designed to intimidate his opponents as much as to bolster his own confidence.

And of course, a well-designed ring walk excites the crowd.

The night that Naseem Hamed fought Kevin Kelley at Madison Square Garden, a sixteen-year-old fan named Paulie Mailgnaggi was in the cheap seats attending his first pro fight.

"I was interested in boxing but I hadn't had any amateur fights yet," Malignaggi recalls. "Ricky Hatton was on the undercard that night and Junior Jones fought Kennedy McKinney in the first TV fight. Then it was time for the main event. Hamed danced behind a screen until people were almost begging for him to come out. Then he danced down a ramp and down an aisle to the ring. There was smoke and lights. He had the crowd eating out of the palm of his hand. I loved it. I told myself, 'Someday I want that kind of aura around me.'"

That said, what the ring walk shouldn't do is distract the fighter.

"By the time you get to the ring walk," Teddy Atlas observes, "the fighters and the fight should be everyone's top priority. But things today sometimes run contrary to that. It's get your fighter ready. And wait. And wait. It's a problem for the guy who's waiting in the ring. And it can be a problem for the other guy too. They're all warmed up. They're ready to go. And then the Broadway show starts. It's not putting the fighters or the fight first."

Also, an ill-chosen ring walk can adversely affect a fighter's state of mind.

Naseem Hamed took ring walks in the United States to a new level when he fought Kevin Kelley. But four years later, Hamed went too far for his own good when he battled Marco Antonio Barrera in Las Vegas. That night, Naseem was strapped into a rig and "flew" down to the ring from the upper reaches of the MGM Grand Garden Arena with a backdrop of smoke, flashing lights, flame-throwers, and a virtual waterfall made of sparklers. The flight took almost three minutes and diverted Hamed's concentration from the task at hand. Adding insult to injury, someone threw a plastic glass filled with beer at him and landed on target as the rig neared ring level.

For most undercard fighters and fights at small venues, the ring walk is still fairly traditional with fighters walking in quiet anonymity. But the brighter the spotlight, the gaudier the walk is likely to be. Like roundcard girls, the ring walk for a big fight has become part of the show.

Is that good or bad for boxing?

"It makes no difference to me one way or the other," HBO's unofficial ringside judge Harold Lederman answers. "All I'm there for is the fight."

Other responses seem to be generational and are influenced by what people saw when they were young. Let the old guard have its say:

★ Hall-of-Fame promoter Russell Peltz: "I think the ring walks today are outrageous. I hate them. I'm old school; I know that. But boxing today is too much sizzle and not enough steak, and the ring walks are part of the problem. I want to be entertained by the fight, not the ring walk. It demeans what boxing is about. What's next? A choreographed walk from the ring after the fight is over?"

★ Jerry Izenberg: "Football teams run onto the field while the band plays and the crowd cheers. Fifty players from each team get onto the field in less time than it takes one fighter to do his ring walk. Very few fighters today have earned the right to that sort of fanfare. It reminds me of the time I was standing in the tunnel at Madison Square Garden with Lou Duva and one of his fighters. The music starts. It's time for the fighter to walk. And the fighter says, 'I ain't going.' Lou says, 'What do you mean, you ain't going?' And the fighter tells him, 'It's the wrong music.' Lou turned to me, shook his head, and said, 'Can you imagine Joe Louis saying, *I ain't going. It's the wrong music.*'"

★ Teddy Atlas: "The ring walk in boxing is part of a tradition, two fighters taking a short but long journey to a place that's dangerous and dark. That's lost now. It's not about introspection or history or tradition anymore. It's about self-celebration and how sensational can we make it. Ring walks today look like a Grammy Awards show because the people who run things have decided that's the way to generate more money. That's the economic reality of the situation, and it doesn't matter whether I like it or not."

Times change. The end of one tradition marks the beginning of another. So let's end where we began. With Muhammad Ali.

"I don't care how much money you have," Ali once said. "I don't care who your friends are. There's nothing like the sound of the crowd when you come down that aisle and they're yelling, 'Ali!, Ali!' You'd give your life to hear it."

But even the indomitable Muhammad Ali wasn't immune to jitters. Years ago, he was in Seattle to attend a dinner where he was honored as "The Fighter of the Century." The festivities included a fight card at The Kingdome. Meeting Ali, the undercard fighters were in awe. One of them, a lightweight with a losing record, addressed The Greatest and confessed, "Mr. Ali, when I'm going to the ring for a fight, I get real nervous. So I say to myself, 'I'm Muhammad Ali. I'm the greatest fighter of all time and no one can beat me.'"

Ali leaned toward the fighter and whispered, "When I was boxing and got nervous before a fight, I said the same thing."

Dave Wolf deserves to be remembered for what he accomplished and who he was.

Dave Wolf at 75

This week marks a bittersweet milestone. Dave Wolf would have been 75 years old on August 24, 2018.

Dave died ten years ago, on December 23, 2008. As I wrote at the time, he was passive-aggressive, anti-social, and one of the smartest people I've ever met. He also did as good a job of managing Ray Mancini as any manager ever did for a fighter and performed managerial magic on other occasions for the likes of Donny Lalonde, Duane Bobick, Lonnie Bradley, Ed "Too Tall" Jones, and Donnie Poole.

The legendary Jimmy Cannon once wrote, "The fight manager wouldn't defend his mother. He has been a coward in all the important matters of his life. He has cheated many people but he describes himself as a legitimate guy at every opportunity."

Dave was the antithesis of that. His first question was always "What's best for the fighter?" rather than "What's best for me?"

He had as full an appreciation of boxing and its traditions as any person I've known. Beneath his gruff exterior, there was a warmth about him that led to his being embraced by those who knew him best. And he's assured a slice of immortality because of his accomplishments in the sweet science and as the author of *Foul: The Connie Hawkins Story*, one of the best books ever written about basketball.

Recently, I asked some people who knew Dave what comes to mind when they think about him today.

Jon Wolf was Dave's brother.

Gina Andriolo met Dave in the 1970s while she was working for a small newspaper in Brooklyn. Later, she represented Dave as his attorney. Eight years after they met, they were married. They separated after four years of marriage.

Toby Falk and Dave were high school sweethearts. Decades later, they reunited and lived together in Dave's apartment on the upper west side of Manhattan from 1989 until his death in 2008.

Teddy Atlas trained two of Dave's fighters, Donny Lalonde and Donnie Poole.

Ray Mancini was Dave's signature fighter.

Ray Leonard fought Donny Lalonde, another of Dave's fighters.

Seth Abraham and Lou DiBella knew Dave in their capacity as executives at HBO.

Bruce Trampler was a matchmaker for Bob Arum during Ray Mancini's glory years with the promoter.

Promoters Russell Peltz and Artie Pelullo worked with Dave on several fights.

Ron Katz and Don Majeski have been matchmakers, advisers, and jacks-of-all trades in boxing for decades.

Al Bernstein, Larry Merchant and Jerry Izenberg knew Dave through their roles in the media.

Harold Lederman was a licensed ring judge when Dave was in his prime as a manager.

Randy Gordon was editor of *The Ring* when Ray Mancini was at his peak as a fighter.

Mark Kriegel wrote what is widely regarded as the definitive biography of Ray Mancini.

Craig Hamilton managed several fighters and is the foremost boxing memorabilia dealer in the United States. He dealt extensively with Dave in the latter capacity and helped Dave's family liquidate his memorabilia collection after Dave's death.

Some of their memories follow:

Jon Wolf: "My father had severe back problems that limited his mobility. Dave was six years older than I was, so when I was a boy, he played the role of father in teaching me to do things like riding a bike and playing baseball. He took me to the NFL championship game between the New York Giants and Green Bay Packers at Yankee Stadium when I was twelve years old. It was freezing cold, and Dave kept missing parts of the game to get up from our seats and go get hot chocolate for me to keep me warm. I played basketball in high school. Dave was in journalism school at Columbia by then and came to all my games. He'd sit in the stands and shout instructions. There were times when it was like he was coaching the game."

Gina Andriolo: "I was young when I met Dave, and I was very impressed. Right away, I could see he was one of the smartest people I'd ever known. He was very intense in his interaction with people. He could be brusque and combative. He always let people know where they stood with him. He liked being alone. And he loved sports; all sports, not just boxing. Dave could watch curling on TV and be happy."

Toby Falk: "Dave was creative, intellectually curious, very intense, stubborn, determined. He was a private person, not at all social. He had no interest in talking with most people. Every now and then, he'd go to an opening at the Museum of Modern Art with me because he loved me, but it was a chore for him. If he bonded with you, he really liked you. But there weren't many people who fit into that category. He'd stay up into the wee small hours of the morning watching old fights on television. But it wasn't just boxing. It was all sports. His idea of a beautiful summer Sunday was to sit inside and watch a baseball game on television."

Jerry Izenberg: "He was a very good writer. That's what stands out in my mind. People remember that he wrote *Foul*, which was a very good book. But he also wrote some very good magazine articles."

Al Bernstein: "Dave wrote one of my favorite books and one of the best sports books ever written. It was about Connie Hawkins, who'd been banned from playing in the NBA, and it broke new ground for what a sports book should be. Beyond that, Dave did what managers are supposed to do. He worked hard and maximized every opportunity for his fighters. I liked him a lot."

Bruce Trampler: "I've never dealt with anyone who did his homework the way Dave did. He was one of the most conscientious, dedicated, well-prepared managers ever. I spent hours on the phone with him going through every detail of every fight again and again. Every conversation turned into a cross-examination. He was always asking questions and taking notes. He was painstaking in his preparation at every level. I give him the highest marks in every category that has anything to do with managing a fighter. He could be an annoying bastard and he was a complete pain-in-the-ass to deal with. But he was doing his job as he saw it, and he was one of the greatest managers ever."

Ray Mancini: "Nobody—I mean, nobody—paid more attention to details than Dave. When I fought Alexis Arguello, Dave got Top Rank to agree that I'm going to leave the dressing room after the national anthem ends. If Arguello isn't in the ring and the fight doesn't start seven minutes after I'm in the ring, I'm leaving and Arguello has to wait for me to come back. That's fine with me because, as a fighter, I don't want to stand in the ring and get cold waiting for the fight to start. And everyone knew that Dave was crazy enough to take me out of the ring if Arguello was late. I loved it. I fought Ernesto Espana outdoors in a football stadium in Warren, Ohio. The day before the fight, Dave went to the stadium and stood in the ring at the same time of day the fight would start. Then he said, "Okay, this will be Ray's corner and this will be Espana's corner.' He was making sure I had as much shade in my corner as possible and Espana was facing the sun. As a fighter, you love stuff like that."

Lou DiBella: "He was a stand-up guy. For a guy without much charm, he was colorful in his own way. He was a guy who knew how to sit back and watch and figure out what was going on. He understood the strengths and weaknesses of his fighters. And unlike too many managers in this miserable business, he recognized that he had a fiduciary duty to his fighters and acted like it. There were never any side deals that the fighter didn't know about."

Mark Kriegel: "Dave was trained as a journalist. He was a story-teller, and that's part of what a great manager does. He understood why Ray Mancini mattered, and he was able to tell the story in a way that people understood. He went from being a journalist to a producer, and he was great at it. I never met him, but I can't think of another manager I would have liked to have met more."

Randy Gordon: "Dave would come up to my office at *The Ring* to look at old *Ring* magazines. This was before the Internet and eBay, so it wasn't easy to find them. He'd sit there and read, and then we'd talk about what he'd read. I learned a lot of my boxing history from those conversations. Some people thought Dave was on the weird side, different, strange, whatever word you want to use. But I enjoyed him as a fight guy, and I knew how much he cared about his fighters. He poured his heart into them."

Don Majeski: "It's easy to move a great fighter. Some fighters are so great that you don't really have to manage. You just point them in the right direction and ask for more money. A great manager gets the most out of the least. Dave got people to treat .200 hitters like they were .300 hitters and .300 hitters like they hit .350. He made Ray Mancini, who was good but not great, into an iconic fighter. Bob [Arum] gave Ray the exposure, but it was Dave who gave Bob the product. He made millions of dollars for Donny Lalonde, who was an okay fighter. He got Ed "Too Tall" Jones onto CBS. He always looked after his guys. He never wanted one of his fighters to be an opponent. He was one hundred percent for his fighters. He was a great boxing guy."

Craig Hamilton: "Ray Mancini was a likable white Italian-American fighter with a crowd-pleasing style. Any competent manager could have made good money with Ray, although probably not as much as Dave did. But look at the job Dave did for Lonnie Bradley. Lonnie was a black kid out of Harlem who was a competent fighter with a quiet personality. Dave maneuvered him to a winnable title fight [for the WBO middle-weight belt against 13-and-6 David Mendez] and then got him a half-dozen title defenses against guys who weren't very good."

Teddy Atlas: "There were some things Dave did that I took issue with in terms of our relationship. But I recognized his gifts and his ability to move a fighter. He was a smart guy. He knew how to play the game with the sanctioning organizations and was willing to play it. He loved playing the game. I think he enjoyed the maneuvering and getting to the kill more than the success of it. And he made money for his fighters. A fighter can be successful in the ring and not make a lot of money. Dave made good money for the fighters he managed. His talent was to take a fighter who was okay and make it appear to the world that the fighter was better than he was, maybe even great. He knew how to build a fighter and capitalize on it when the fighter won. He was a master at developing a storyline for his fighters and having it resonate with the press. He was difficult; some would say crazy. But he did the job for his fighters."

Ray Mancini: "Dave was a control freak. That was his thing. He was doing it for me, but he wanted total control and we had our battles. Sometimes I had to tell him, 'You work for me. I'm the fighter.' Then he'd get hurt and sulk and say things like, 'I guess you don't need me anymore.' If he got a bug up his ass about something, he wouldn't talk to me for a while and he wouldn't return phone calls. He was a complicated guy."

Gina Andriolo: "Dave approached boxing like a three-dimensional chess game. Regardless of the immediate issue he was dealing with, he was always looking three moves down the road. He had an amazing capacity for detail and kept meticulous records on everything. Every detail mattered. Most fight managers go to their fighters' weigh-ins. Dave would find out when the scales were being calibrated and send me to make sure they were calibrated right."

Harold Lederman: "Dave knew boxing; no question about it. He was a great boxing guy. But he was a tough guy to deal with when it came to officials. He was always arguing he didn't want this referee or that judge to work his fighter's fight. He never argued that he didn't want me, but there were a lot of guys he didn't want. And he argued long enough and hard enough that he was usually able to get rid of the guys he didn't want. That's one of the things that made him a great manager."

Jon Wolf: "Before one of Ray Mancini's fights in Las Vegas, Dave told everyone in the entourage, 'No one is to gamble until the fight is over.' He didn't want anyone leaving whatever good luck we might have on the casino floor or bringing any kind of bad luck in. That same trip, Dave sent me downstairs to buy copies of all the newspapers they had so he could read what was being written about the fight. I had four nickels left over after I bought the papers. So I put a nickel in a slot machine, and five dollars' worth of nickels came out. I played a few more nickels with similar results and went back upstairs with the newspapers and a bucket full of nickels. Dave took one look and asked, 'What the fuck is that?' I explained, and he told me, 'Get rid of them.' So I took the nickels downstairs, found an old lady who was playing the nickel slots, and said to her, "Excuse me, ma'am. I just won these and God told me to give them away.'"

Artie Pelullo: "Dave was a strange quirky guy, very opinionated. A lot of people thought he was a pain-in-the-ass to deal with, but I never had a problem with him. He came to me with Lonnie Bradley, and we did a couple of fights together. He wasn't the kind of guy you went to a bar with for a couple of drinks and light conversation. But you could make a deal with him and his word was good. I liked him."

Seth Abraham: "Dave didn't care much about pleasantries and what I would call conventional business practices. Several times, he came to meetings at HBO wearing shorts. It wasn't important but it was unconventional and it sticks in my mind. He was very perceptive and very bright. He always presented his case well. And as best I could tell, he was always honest with me. If you're in boxing, you have to learn who the honest people are and who are the dishonest people. As a TV executive, I did business with both. And I can honestly say, I never had any integrity issues with Dave."

Russell Peltz: "I didn't know Dave well, but I don't think he liked me very much. I say that because, one time, I wanted to make a match with one of his fighters and Dave told the fighter he didn't trust me. What had happened was, a few years earlier, Dave was managing Duane Bobick and wanted a comeback fight for Bobick after he'd been knocked out by John Tate. I offered him George Chaplin as an opponent and told Dave that Chaplin couldn't fight, which I believed was true. So Bobick and Chaplin fought in Atlantic City, Chaplin knocked him out, and Dave never trusted me again."

Gina Andriolo: "He loved his fighters. He believed in his fighters. And he looked after his fighters in every way. His philosophy was, a fighter should get in and out of boxing as quickly as possible with as little damage as possible and as much money as possible. God, he fought for his fighters. I remember, one time, Dave got particularly angry when a promoter who shall remain nameless sent him a contract he didn't like. It wasn't what Dave thought they'd agreed to. I was doing Dave's legal work at the time. He was shouting at me, 'Call that motherfucker up and tell him no fucking way. He can take his contract and shove it.' So I called the promoter up and—I was being tactful—I said, 'Dave has a slight problem with paragraph 4(B). Is there any way we can change it?' And Dave started screaming at me, 'That's not what I said. I said tell him he's a motherfucker and he can shove his contract up his ass.'"

Ray Mancini: "There were times when I said to myself, 'This guy is out of his mind.' Some of the things he asked for from promoters bordered on the ridiculous. Dave could take years off a promoter's life. Lots of managers threaten to call a fight off. When Dave threatened to call a fight off, the promoter knew he might."

Ray Leonard: "My best memories of Dave Wolf are from when I fought Donny Lalonde. He truly believed in Donny and the other fighters he worked with. We were cool with each other. What stands out most with me is that there was always respect between the two of us."

Gina Andriolo: "There were always enormous piles of old newspapers and boxing magazines all over the apartment. Sometimes, that was a source of conflict between us. I'm not talking about a reasonable number of papers. I'd ask, 'Why do we have to have ten-year-old newspapers stacked in the kitchen cabinets?' But Dave needed them there to be happy. And he knew where every piece of paper was. God forbid I should move a piece of paper and he couldn't find it."

Jon Wolf: "Dave and I shared a bedroom when we were young. One time—I was three or four years old—my parents came home and Dave had built a wall in the bedroom out of chairs and whatever other furniture he could move so I'd stay on my side of the room and leave his toys alone and not knock his blocks over or mess up whatever game he was playing."

Toby Falk: "There were piles of newspapers and magazines all over the apartment; thousands of magazines going back for years. In what I suspect was a major concession, he'd let Gina put flowery wallpaper in the kitchen when they were married. But he covered it over with fight posters as soon as she moved out."

Craig Hamilton: "Dave's main thing as a collector was fight programs, which a lot of people aren't interested in because they don't display that well. He had a solid fight program collection; Johnson-Jeffries and some other good ones. He wasn't much of an autograph guy. He had a few good on-site posters, including one from Ali-Frazier III in Manila, and a lot of Ray Mancini stuff that had some value because Ray has a following, particularly in Ohio. But for someone who was obsessed with collecting, Dave's collection wasn't that good. Most of the rest was garbage. Dave had thousands of magazines that were virtually worthless. I'm not talking about old *Ring* magazines from the 1920s and 30s that are worth something. I'm talking about magazines from the 1970s and later that you can't give away. Maybe a hospital will take them. They were stacked all over his apartment—in piles on the floor, on shelves, in closets, every place imaginable. There were piles and piles of magazines—three, four feet high—blocking access to bureau drawers and file cabinets. And they hadn't been dusted in years. You could see that from the cobwebs. Obviously, they had meaning to Dave. They were very personal for him. But it wasn't the place you'd bring a woman on a first date if you were trying to impress her. God bless Toby; I don't know how she put up with it."

Larry Merchant: "In a game that rewards individual initiative, Dave was a guy who jumped in, did his thing, and did it well. He was one of the more interesting characters in a business full of characters."

Toby Falk: "Both of us had been married and divorced twice, so we didn't feel the need to get married again. But we lived together for almost twenty years. He wasn't well for much of our time together. There were complications from diabetes and some other problems. When he was fifty-five, he was diagnosed with leukemia. He didn't fear death. He just didn't want to be incapacitated or linger. He was cremated, so I can't say he's turning over in his grave over what's happening now in America. But Dave was anti-authoritarian and very politically aware. And he hated injustice. Wherever he is now, I'm sure he's very upset by Donald Trump."

Ray Mancini: "Dave showed how the job should be done. He battled for everything for me. There were things other managers let happen to their fighters that Dave would never have let happen to me. What he did for my career, I can never thank him enough. I loved him. I loved him dearly."

And a note in closing . . .

Dave and I became friends in his later years. I don't use the term "friends" lightly. We had lunch together on a regular basis and talked often about people and events that had shaped us. As I wrote when he died, "Much of Dave's anger stemmed from the fact that he hadn't learned to read in a meaningful way until the age of twelve and thus had been labeled 'dumb.'"

When Dave was young, dyslexia and other reading disabilities weren't understood. The fact that he was able to surmount them to write *Foul* was remarkable in itself.

It was extraordinarily painful for a young boy with a high IQ who was sensitive in many ways to be labeled "dumb." One way Dave dealt with the pain was to construct a hard exterior that served as a protective shell. Explaining that to me over lunch one day, Dave told me a story.

Once, when Dave was in grade school and the teacher briefly left the classroom, one of the boys started teasing him in front of the other children, saying that Dave couldn't read.

"I can read," Dave said.

"Prove it," the boy countered. Then he went to the blackboard and wrote something in chalk. "Prove you can read. Read this."

So very laboriously, Dave read aloud: "Dave . . . Wolf . . . is . . . stupid."

More than a half-century later, Dave remembered that moment very clearly. And it still scarred him.

Rodney Dangerfield once told a stand-up comedy audience, "I went to a fight the other night and a hockey game broke out."

Club Fights on Ice

Unlike other major team sports, hockey has a tradition of fistfighting. Some hockey fights arise spontaneously. Others are premeditated assault. At times, the fights are instigated at a coach's instruction in an effort to halt the opposing team's momentum and change the flow of a game. Other times, they're in retaliation for an instance when a teammate has been physically abused.

Most teams had (and still have) an enforcer, often a player with limited all-around skills whose job is intimidation and retaliation. Historically, Bob Probert, Dave Schultz, and Marty McSorley were among the league's most imposing enforcers. In 1994, Probert and McSorley faced off against each other for a full two minutes while three officials looked passively on. Gordie Howe—the greatest player of his era—was sufficiently adept with his fists that most enforcers left him alone.

Fighting peaked in the 1970s and 1980s with season averages of at least one fight per game. The Philadelphia Flyers of the 1970s, who glamorized fighting en route to back-to-back Stanley Cup championships in 1974 and 1975, were known as the Broad Street Bullies.

"The goons were encouraged to create chaos," Larry Merchant (who covered hockey as a columnist and sports editor) recalls. "It was open season on the opposing team's stars which always seemed counterintuitive to me. I thought it marred a beautiful game. But that was the culture and that was how the league sold the game."

Fighting is a marketing tool. Hockey fights are still featured on sports highlights telecasts. The standard refrain has always been, "This is hockey, not figure-skating." There's a ritual throwing down of gloves, and the crowd goes wild. No one gets up to visit the concession stand and buy a hot dog while a hockey fight is underway.

Traditionalists say that fighting is part of the culture of hockey the same way that hitting a batter on the opposing team with a fastball after your teammate has been hit by a pitch is part of the culture of baseball. But in truth, hockey takes the hostilities further. Hockey "enforcers" even have their own position. No matter what the roster says, they aren't just defensemen or forwards. No other sport has a designated goon. A baseball team doesn't bring in a relief pitcher for the express purpose of throwing at an opposing batter.

Steve Albert, who served as the voice of Showtime Boxing for two decades, knows hockey well. His first professional sports play-by-play experience came in the early 1970s when he was a student at Kent State. Whenever the Springfield Kings of the American Hockey League journeyed to Ohio to play the Cleveland Barons, Steve called the game for WMAS radio in Springfield. After graduating from Kent State, he worked for three years as a play-by-play commentator for the Cleveland Crusaders of the newly-formed World Hockey Association. Later, he added play-by-play duties for New York Islanders telecasts to his resume.

"I never liked the fighting," Albert says. "I thought it was ridiculous. A few of the players know how to fight, but most of them fight as well as a boxer would play hockey. The just stand there, flailing away, trying to land anything. There's no technique. When did you ever see a hockey player throw a jab?"

That said; when a hockey fight did break out, Albert often treated his audience to blow-by-blow commentary.

"I recall a WHA game that I called on the radio around 1974," Steve reminisces. "It was between the Cleveland Crusaders and the Minnesota Fighting Saints at the Richfield Coliseum which, in case you're wondering, was also home to the Ali-Wepner fight. A fight broke out on the ice. Then another. And another. And another. Four fights going on at the same time, and I was trying to describe them all on the air as they were happening."

"But wait! There's more," Steve continues. "Suddenly, the coach of the Fighting Saints, Harry Neale, climbs up and over the glass behind the bench and gets into a slugfest with some Cleveland fans. So now I'm calling five fights at the same time. Then I look over to my right and see the Minnesota announcers embroiled in a fight with fans in the stands while they're on the air."

In recent decades, fighting has been all but eliminated from international hockey. Meanwhile, the National Hockey League has made an effort to cut down on fights although not do away with them entirely.

The NHL Rulebook now has more provisions governing the conduct of fights than many state athletic commissions. Fighting has long been a "major" infraction calling for a five-minutes banishment to the penalty box. And the league has instituted several additional rules to curtail fighting.

The "third-man-in rule" calls for the ejection of the first player who joins a fight that's already in progress. The first player from each team who leaves the bench to join a fight in progress is also automatically ejected from the game. And the player who starts a given fight receives an additional two-minute penalty.

The NHL rulebook also has separate provisions relating to the "instigator" of and "aggressor" in each fight. Head-butting, kicking, and kneeing an opponent are covered in categories separate and apart from "fighting."

Fights now occur on average in only one out of every three NHL games. But clearly, the league doesn't want to eliminate fights altogether. If it did, it could do what the NBA does. In the NBA, a player who throws a punch is ejected from the game. In hockey, he gets a five-minute rest in the penalty box.

Thus, when the New York Rangers acquired Cody McLeod earlier this year, much was made of the fact that McLeod had led the league in fights in two of the past three seasons. Rangers coach Alain Vigneault explained, "He brings a dimension that's different than what we have." And an article about McLeod in the *New York Post* was headlined, "Meet the Rangers' New Enforcer."

But as Steve Albert would say, "Wait! There's more."

In the mid-1980s, Teddy Atlas was called into service to train New York Rangers right wing Steve Patrick in the art of fighting. Patrick was 6-feet-4-inches tall, weighed 205 pounds, and wasn't "engaging" as often as the Rangers coaching staff would have liked.

Atlas worked with Patrick at Gleason's Gym, then located several blocks from Madison Square Garden.

"Back then, you had a couple of players with amateur boxing experience," Teddy recalls. "[New York Rangers enforcer] Nick Fotiu had been in some amateur fights which gave him a significant edge. With Steve Patrick, I explained to him, 'Basically, you're dealing with a four-foot-square area where the fight will take place. The other guy will be right in front of you, so you're talking about inside fighting, not throwing wild caveman punches. Use the other guy's mistakes against him. Most hockey players open themselves up before they throw, and that will give you opportunities. Take your time. Uppercuts will be your best weapon."

Paulie Malignaggi, another keen observer of the boxing scene, has his own take on the subject.

"When you're talking about a fight in hockey," Malignaggi notes, "obviously, it's a different technique. The fight might start with a punch. But then it becomes like judo, grappling, or street-fighting. You try to use the other guy's jersey to immobilize him by pulling it up over his arms so he can't punch or you pull it over his head so he can't see. Think of it as a boxer fighting with his robe on."

"As for the punching," Paulie continues, "a punch is a punch. And the guy who gets off first has an advantage. But hockey players can't really plant their feet to punch. Their feet aren't stable because they're gliding on ice, so it's all upper-body with very little leverage. The only thing that works in favor of the guy punching is that, from what I've seen, there's very little head movement in hockey fights."

Or as promoter Lou DiBella recently observed, "As far as technique is concerned, hockey players who are fighting make Butterbean look like Sugar Ray Robinson."

The Contender was big news when it debuted on NBC in 2004. Its return fourteen years later was far less celebrated.

The Contender: 2018

Hollywood has given us certain phrases that have become part of American culture: "Show me the money" (*Jerry Maguire*) . . . "Go ahead; make my day" (*Sudden Impact*) . . . "I'm going to make him an offer he can't refuse" (*The Godfather*) . . . And of course, "They're baaaack" (*Poltergeist II*).

On August 24, 2018, after a ten-year absence, *The Contender* will be back.

When *The Contender* made its debut on NBC in 2004, boxing fans were scouring the landscape for the few available fights to watch. Sylvester Stallone and Sugar Ray Leonard made headlines by co-hosting the new series. There was a huge production budget. *The Contender* was going to bring boxing back into the consciousness of mainstream sports fans. There was talk that it would become a dominant force and "take over boxing."

But that talk never became reality.

The original *Contender* series failed to live up to expectations. It lost sight of what boxing is about and devolved into a product-placement orgy with a game-show format.

Fighters were faced with "challenges" that included hauling Everlast medicine balls up the Sepulveda Dam and putting them in the back of a Toyota truck . . . Demolishing a cinderblock wall with sledgehammers and putting the blocks into the back of a Toyota Tundra . . . Navigating an "urban obstacle course" that required the fighters to "run through the Toyota traffic jam," jump over some hurdles with advertising on them, throw tires in a dumpster, empty the tires out of the dumpster, take the keys out of a Toyota, use the keys to unlock a lock, and climb to the top of a truck with advertising for Bally's on it . . . Running around an obstacle course while wearing Everlast boxing gloves, picking up Everlast medicine balls, and throwing the medicine balls in a basket . . . Pulling a 5,000-pound Toyota Tundra along a dry river bed, picking up Everlast heavy-bags with letters on them, and, at the finish line, assembling the bags so they spelled out the word "Contender."

American Idol outdrew the Season #1 finale of *The Contender* by 19,000,000 viewers. Worse, *The Contender* finished 2,000,000 viewers behind *Rob and Amber Get Married*.

But the producers kept persuading networks to give *The Contender* more chances. There were two seasons on ESPN and one on Versus. Then came a ten-year hiatus. That brings us to 2018 and the marketing of *The Contender* as the return of classic television.

Epix is a premium cable and satellite television network that was launched in 2009. It didn't exist when *The Contender* closed out its run on Versus. Epix is available to subscribers as a premium channel and, in some instances, as a component of larger cable packages. Its programming consists largely of theatrically released motion pictures, original series, documentaries, and entertainment specials.

Epix entered the world of live boxing programming in 2011 with a telecast of Vitali Klitschko's WBC heavyweight title defense against Odlanier Solis. A nice run followed with the network televising a string of Saturday afternoon fights that, for the most part, originated in Europe.

The Epix formula was simple. Pay a modest license fee for fights that HBO and Showtime had passed on, and supplement the foreign video feed with a commentating team calling the action from a studio in New York. The network did a good job on a small budget. But its boxing program ended in 2013 amidst allegations of financial impropriety.

Fast-forward to 2018. Epix was looking to get back into boxing and wanted to do something that would differentiate its programming from the current offerings of other networks. Thus, *The Contender*.

As described in recent promotional material, "*The Contender* follows sixteen promising professional boxers who have come to Los Angeles to compete in an elimination tournament with the final two facing off in Las Vegas for a $250,000 grand prize. These men will live together, train together, and eventually fight each other for the chance to change their lives."

Twelve episodes will air on consecutive Friday nights in this latest incarnation of *The Contender*. There will be fifteen fights, which means that, at some point, there will be more than one-fight per episode. The early fights will be contested under the auspices of the California State

Athletic Commission. Then the scene will shift to Las Vegas. All of the fights will be held before a live audience. First-round fights are scheduled for five rounds.

Freddie Roach and Naazim Richardson will coach the fighters and be in opposite corners for each bout. As in past seasons, the fighters will live and train on site.

Epix is paying roughly $1.5 million in licensing fees and marketing costs for each episode. Contrast that with its earlier live boxing program, where license fees ranged from $75,000 to $250,000 per telecast and production/marketing costs were generally under $100,000.

This season's *Contender* fights will be in the middleweight division.

All of the fighters have been assigned to either the "blue" or "gold" team for purposes of first-round competition. Each team decided internally who would represent it in the Episode #1 fight. Thereafter, throughout the first round, the team whose representative wins a given fight will choose who fights who in the following week's bout.

Andre Ward is the series host. He meets regularly with all of the fighters in a community room called The Loft and spars with the fighters from time to time.

As in past seasons, the skill level of the fighters is limited. For the most part, they're club fighters.

There's a different standard for evaluating *The Contender* now than there was a decade ago. The bar for success is set lower. Boxing is everywhere; on basic cable, premium cable, broadcast network television, OTT streaming video. *The Contender* is no longer regarded as a force that might someday dominate the sweet science. It's a niche reality-TV show.

That said; the current incarnation of *The Contender* is more respectful of boxing than was the case in earlier seasons. Fights will be shown in their entirety. In Episodes #1 and #2 (which have been available for media screening), the game show ambiance of earlier years is gone. The cinematography is excellent.

Those who loved *The Contender* in the past will find the revival satisfying. Think in terms of someone who likes McDonald's hamburgers. There might be a slight variation in the product from time to time, but the basic burger remains the same.

Still, there's room for improvement.

Much of *The Contender* is noticeably contrived.

In the real world of boxing, sixteen fighters don't live together in a beautiful training center and do everything that they're told to do when they're told to do it.

There are times when it seems as though almost every one of the fighters on *The Contender* comes from a broken home yet has managed to achieve an idyllic marriage and is a responsible loving father.

I've been in a lot of fighters' dressing rooms over the years. And I've never seen a fighter feel his pregnant wife's abdomen in the dressing room before a fight. Nor does a fighter's team leave him alone in the dressing room for dramatic purposes before and after a bout and make him walk to the ring alone.

Everything in *The Contender* is unrealistically pristine. The dressing rooms, corridors, and arena are squeaky-clean. There's too much talk and repetition. Andre Ward isn't Sylvester Stallone or Sugar Ray Leonard. And while Freddie Roach and Naazim Richardson are well-respected trainers, they're getting on in years. *The Contender* has an "old" feel to it.

There's no blow-by-blow commentary for the fights. The soundtrack is provided by Roach and Richardson shouting instructions combined with utterances from family and others in the crowd. That's not a problem in and of itself. But the formula fails when a hard punch lands, a fighter wobbles, and the video cuts to a family reaction shot. Rather than cut to shots of the trainers and others during a round, these images should be shown in a window so as to not interrupt the flow of the fight.

And most notably, one of the reasons that sports are exciting is that there's an immediacy to the moment. Things are happening NOW. The classic appeal of boxing is that a viewer can't turn away from the television because at any moment—BOOM!—something might happen. But with *The Contender*, whatever "booms" there are happened weeks ago.

I know Arne Lang as the very capable editor who oversees TheSweetScience. com. But there's a less literary entry on his resume.

Arne Lang: Ring Announcer

People in the boxing media have varied backgrounds. But there's only one I can think of who was a ring announcer.

Arne Lang is editor-in-chief of The Sweet Science.com. He was born in Brooklyn, grew up on Long Island, went to college and graduate school in Nebraska, and moved to Las Vegas in 1969 to take a teaching position at UNLV.

In the 1980s, Lang wrote for a weekly tabloid and co-hosted a weekend sports talk radio show called The Stardust Line that aired on Saturday and Sunday nights from 10:00 PM until midnight.

"On Saturdays, we followed the Dodgers baseball game," Arne recalls, "Vin Scully was my lead-in. You can't ask for better than that."

Lang attended his first fight as a credentialed member of the media in 1983. After the tabloid folded and he lost his radio gig, he took a hiatus from boxing. He returned to the sweet science in 2016 to take over the reins at TSS.

As editor-in-chief of The Sweet Science, Lang oversees fourteen writers. The job includes fact-checking ("some writers are more reliable than others"), ferreting out typographical errors ("spell-check helps"), rewriting where necessary ("I try to respect the intent and style of each writer"), having final say over headlines ("some writers suggest a headline; others don't"), and posting the articles. Lang is also responsible for variety in the rotation ("I try to coordinate things so we don't have too many articles on the same subject").

Now about that ring announcing . . .

In the early-1980s, Lang was working as a publicist for a Las Vegas jeweler named Alex Fried who promoted a handful of club fights. Chuck Hull was slated to work as the announcer for one of Fried's cards at the Union Plaza Hotel in downtown Las Vegas. But on the afternoon of the fights, Hull cancelled. Fried asked Lang, "Who can we get?" And Arne answered, "I don't know. I suppose I can do it."

Lang had no previous experience as a ring announcer. The only guidance he had came from an interview he'd conducted ten years earlier with Jimmy Lennon Sr. Arne was writing for a publication called *High Roller Sportsweek* at the time, and Lennon was in Las Vegas to work a wrestling show featuring Hulk Hogan.

"I asked Jimmy about the secrets of his trade," Lang recalls. "And he told me, 'You have to be as respectful to the four-round preliminary fighters as you are to the fighters in the main event. Talk to them in the dressing room before the fights so you get the pronunciation of their names right.'"

Lang's appearance as a last-minute substitute ring announcer at the Union Plaza Hotel came on August 21, 1992.

"I wasn't nervous," Arne remembers. "I'd taught sociology at the college level so I was used to being in front of people. I remember the main event pretty well. The fighters were Brian Lonon and Miguel Mercedes. They were fighting for some belt that no one took seriously, but it was a very good fight. I enjoyed myself. And I was serviceable, although I wouldn't say I was on the level of Lou Gehrig replacing Wally Pip."

It was a boxing fan's fantasy, everyman as ring announcer. And it didn't end that night. Lang was the ring announcer for forty to fifty fight cards after that.

"A guy named Al Rodrigues bought a place in North Las Vegas called the Silver Nugget and started promoting club fights," Arne recalls. "I was his publicist. The first show he did, the ring announcer was so bad that Al fired him in the middle of the show and asked me to take over for the rest of the night. From then on, I was his ring announcer and publicist. I also became the house announcer for fights at a place called Arizona Charlie's West. I never had a signature line like 'Let's get ready to rumble.' Basically, I was a ham-and-egger. But I enjoyed it."

Michael Buffer is the gold standard against whom all ring announcers are judged.

"I have this recurring anxiety dream," Buffer once told me. "I've had it for years. There are variations on the theme, but it's basically the same dream. I have a show to do and I can't find my tuxedo; or I can't get out of my hotel room; or the car breaks down on the way to the arena; or I'm up in the top seats looking down and everyone at ringside is looking for me but I can't find my way down; or I'm at ringside but I left my notes back at the hotel and I don't know who's fighting that night."

So . . . Did Lang have similar worries?

Sort of.

Dr. Margaret Goodman (who eventually became chief ringside physician for the Nevada State Athletic Commission and is now CEO of the Voluntary Anti-Doping Association) was just starting out as a ring doctor and worked quite a few shows at the Silver Nugget when Arne was announcing there.

"One afternoon," Lang reminisces, "I was talking with some fighters, and one of them referred to Margaret in an admiring way as 'Margaret Goodbody.'" Not long after that, I woke up in the middle of the night in a panic because I dreamed I'd introduced her as 'Dr. Margaret Goodbody.' I had occasion to introduce Margaret a number of times after that. Fortunately, I always got her name right."

A fighter's mouthpiece is as important as his gloves, maybe more so.

The Mouthpiece and Boxing

Long before fighters wore gloves as standard fare, boxers used makeshift protection ranging from a quartered orange to cotton to protect their teeth and lips. In the early-1890s, an English dentist named Woolf Krause fashioned a crude shield made from strips of gutta percha (a rubbery sap) that was placed in a fighter's mouth and held in place by the fighter clenching his teeth.

In 1902, Jack Marles, another London dentist, improved upon Krause's creation by using a more durable rubber to create a reusable gumshield for boxers to wear during training sessions.

That brings the narrative to Ted "Kid" Lewis, arguably the best pound-for-pound fighter to come out of England. Lewis was snaggle-toothed. When he fought, the edges of his teeth frequently cut his lips. Some sources say that Lewis wore a mouthpiece in combat for the first time in 1913. Others place the day of reckoning on August 31, 1915, when he dethroned world welterweight champion Jack Britton in Boston.

Lewis and Britton fought each other an extraordinary nineteen times between 1915 and 1921. Just prior to their final encounter, referee Dick Nugent was giving the fighters their instructions in ring center at Madison Square Garden when Britton's manager, Dan Morgan, objected to Lewis's use of a mouthpiece as an illegal foreign substance. The New York State Athletic Commission chief inspector concurred, and Lewis was forced to do battle without his mouthpiece en route to a 15-round unanimous-decision loss.

"It takes a while for these things to become accepted," boxing historian Mike Silver notes. "Initially, traditionalists opposed mouthpieces the same way they opposed the introduction of gloves."

As late as 1927, Jack Dempsey and Gene Tunney engaged in their historic "long count" bout with neither man wearing a mouthpiece. But by the 1930's, common sense had prevailed and mouthpieces were standard equipment in boxing.

A well-designed mouthpiece protects a fighter's teeth, lessens the danger to surrounding soft tissue, and helps guard against jaw fractures. Uppercuts, head butts, and elbows cause the most damage to a fighter's mouth. That's where the mouthpiece is of greatest service.

There's a school of thought that a well-fitted mouthpiece also guards against concussions by redistributing some of the force from a blow that would otherwise impact upon the brain. But that has yet to be proven by empirical data.

If a fighter breathes through his nose like he's supposed to and exhales through his mouth, the mouthpiece won't interfere with breathing. If the fighter's nose is broken, things get more complicated.

A good mouthpiece covers all of a fighter's upper teeth as well as a portion of the upper gum and cradles the upper teeth. Occasionally, a fighter prefers a mouthpiece that covers his lower teeth as well, but experts believe that these mouthpieces offer no added protection.

Pat Burns trained Jermain Taylor from his first pro fight through two victories over Bernard Hopkins and has had extensive experience at every level of amateur and professional boxing.

"Every mouth is different," Burns says. "You shouldn't buy a mouthpiece off the shelf. It's not one size fits all. Or ten sizes fit all. You go to a dentist who knows what he's doing and have him form-fit one to your teeth. First, he makes a mold like an orthodontist would when he's fitting you for braces. Then he pours a rubbery plastic into the mold, the fighter bites down on it, and it form-fits to the fighter's mouth. The dentist pulls it out, files away the rough edges, and cleans it up. The whole thing should cost under two hundred dollars, and you can get replacement mouthpieces for twenty dollars each. The fighter owns the mold so he should take it with him. I always tell my fighters to have at least three mouthpieces and they should never all be in the same bag.

"But some fighters, particularly amateurs, don't have the money to buy a good mouthpiece," Burns continues. "And it's like a lot of things that fighters and people in general do. They cut corners. So they buy a generic rubber mouthpiece off the shelf in a store for a couple of dollars, boil it, stick it in their mouth, and try to reshape it to fit. And then they pay a much bigger price."

Trainer Freddie Roach concurs, noting, "When I trained Marlon Starling, he insisted on fighting with an eighty-cent mouthpiece that he bought in some store. Probably, it would cost three dollars today. It was crazy. But Marlon was too cheap to go to a dentist and get it done right. One time, he fought a title fight against Lloyd Honeyghan [in Las Vegas in 1989] and got hit hard in the mouth in the first round. After the round, I took his mouthpiece out and a tooth came with it. But Marlon won the fight and he never did get a good mouthpiece."

"I had one mouthpiece that I loved," Roach adds. "A dentist in Boston made it for me, and it fit better than any mouthpiece I ever had. I lost it after a fight for the New England title in Boston Garden. First, I lost the fight to a kid from Rhode Island. And then the mouthpiece got lost in the post-fight shuffle of who had what. I felt like I'd lost my best friend."

There's virtually no state athletic commission regulation of mouth-pieces. At best, in the dressing room before a fight, an inspector asks if the trainer has his fighter's mouthpiece and a back-up. A well-made mouthpiece should last through a year of fights and sparring in the gym. Most fighters opt for flesh-colored mouthpieces. Some like black, green-white-and-orange, or whatever. The one thing a fighter shouldn't do is have a red mouthpiece because, subconsciously, the judges might think that he's bleeding from the mouth.

People rarely notice a fighter's mouthpiece except when it's knocked out of his mouth or something else goes awry.

In 2003, Diego Corrales went into a fight against Joel Casamayor with a mouthpiece that didn't fit properly. By the end of round six, the rough edges combined with Casamayor's punches had caused a deep laceration on Corrales's lower lip, another laceration that went almost completely through his right cheek, and more cuts inside his mouth. Swallowing blood was the least of his problems. That would have resulted in nothing more serious than vomiting. Inhaling the blood could have caused tem-porary choking. More ominously, if the laceration on Corrales's lip had worsened, it might have resulted in a permanent deformity. Ring doctor Margaret Goodman stopped the fight.

Two years later, on May 7, 2005, Corrales was involved in what Showtime commentator Al Bernstein calls "the ultimate mouthpiece story."

Corrales was fighting Jose Luis Castillo at the Mandalay Bay Events Center in Las Vegas. By the middle rounds, Diego's left eye was hideously swollen and he could no longer see right hands coming as the fight-ers traded horrific blows with abandon. Then, 25 seconds into round ten, Castillo decked Corrales with a left hook. Diego's mouthpiece was knocked out by the blow. Twenty-three seconds after he hit the canvas, it was back in and the action resumed. Another left hook put him down for the second time. At that point, Corrales looked like a thoroughly beaten fighter. He removed his mouthpiece and got to his feet very slowly. "The first time it came out, it came out by itself," he later acknowledged. "The second time, I took it out to breathe."

In days of old, when a fighter's mouthpiece came out during a round, the action continued until the bell rang. Now the referee bends over, throws the mouthpiece toward the fighter's corner, and waits for a lull in the action to instruct that it be reinserted.

Spitting out the mouthpiece as Corrales did has long been seen as a sign of surrender. But instead of ending the fight, referee Tony Weeks deducted a point from Diego and led him to his corner where trainer Joe Goossen reinserted the mouthpiece. Twenty-eight seconds after the knockdown, the action resumed.

Then everything changed.

"Castillo dropped his left hand to throw a right," Corrales said later, "and my right hand got there first. That set the whole thing off."

Corrales's right was followed by a barrage of punches. And suddenly, Castillo was back against the ropes, taking punches, glassy-eyed, his head wobbling like it was on a bobble-head doll. At 2:06 of the round, Weeks leapt between the fighters and stopped the fight.

Afterward, Bob Arum (Castillo's promoter) complained, "I never heard of a rule that, when you're knocked down and throw your mouthpiece away, the action stops. That's crazy. He pulled it out and threw it away to get more time. Either you disqualify him or you make him fight without the mouthpiece."

There are no optional time-outs in boxing. But Weeks let Corrales call one.

Two images of Muhammad Ali and mouthpieces linger in memory. One was very public. In round thirteen of Ali-Frazier III in Manila, a sharp right hand sent Joe Frazier's mouthpiece flying into the crowd. The other image was hidden from public view and dates to Ali's fight against Ken Norton in San Diego when Muhammad's jaw was broken in the second round.

Wali Muhammad (one of Ali's cornermen that afternoon) later recalled, "During fights, my job was, Angelo [Dundee] would take the mouthpiece out, hand it to me, and I'd wash the mouthpiece. That was particularly important if there was blood on it. A lot of fighters have their mouthpiece put back in without cleaning. Then if they get hit, they swallow their own blood. So I would always take the mouthpiece and wash it in good cold water, ice water. I'd leave a little water on it so it would be moist and then I'd give it back to Angelo. Against Norton, each round I was taking out the mouthpiece and there was more and more blood on it. I could see it was a lot of blood after each round because my bucket with the water and ice in it became red. In every other fight, between rounds I'd take the mouthpiece out and put it in the bucket and there was just slobber on it. But here, after each round, I had to shake the mouthpiece to get all the blood out of it into the water."

There are also two indelible images of Mike Tyson where mouthpieces are concerned. The first is part of boxing lore: Iron Mike on the canvas groping for his mouthpiece as he was counted out against Buster Douglas. Seven years later, Tyson's mouthpiece was the subject of a more sordid chapter in boxing history when he spit it out in order to bite off part of Evander Holyfield's ear.

Los Angeles Times columnist Jim Murray called that incident "boxing's lowest moment" and observed, "There are many things wrong with the manly art of self-defense, but we always thought those mouthpieces were in there to protect the teeth of the wearer, not the ear of an opponent."

Some thoughts on the light side of boxing.

Fistic Nuggets

Few people in boxing are as knowledgeable about performance enhancing drugs as Victor Conte and Margaret Goodman.

Conte is known to sports fans as the mastermind behind the BALCO scandal. But that was just one of many chapters in his remarkable life to date. In recent years, he has been a positive force for education and reform.

Goodman served for years as chief ringside physician and chair of the medical advisory board for the Nevada State Athletic Commission. In addition to maintaining a private practice as a neurologist, she is the founder and current CEO of the Voluntary Anti-Doping Association.

But before any of that, Conte and Goodman were musicians.

Conte was born in 1950 and began taking guitar lessons at age ten. One year later, while in fifth grade, he played guitar in a talent show at the Wishon Elementary School in Fresno, California.

"I played a surf song called *Pipeline,*" he remembers. "And it brought the house down. I thought it was the coolest thing."

At age 13, Conte and three of his cousins formed a band called Immediate Family. Victor played lead guitar while his cousins played bass guitar, saxophone, and drums. At age fifteen, one of his brothers joined the group as lead guitarist and Victor switched to bass. Then, at age nineteen, he founded a group called Common Ground with some family and friends. They played a neighborhood club in Fresno six nights a week for which each band member was paid $145.

In search of bigger and better things, Conte dropped out of Fresno City College and moved to Los Angeles where he joined another group prophetically called Pure Food and Drug Act. One of his mentors in Los Angeles was Ray Brown, the legendary bass player who had once been married to Ella Fitzgerald. Brown taught Victor the ins and outs of playing the upright bass. Then Pure Food and Drug Act signed a lucrative contract with Epic Records and, for the first time in his life, Conte had money. Lots of it. "I was on top of the world," he recalls.

Meanwhile, one of Conte's cousins had become part of the funky rhythm-and-blues band Tower of Power. In May 1977, Victor joined the group as its electric bass player. He stayed with Tower of Power until 1979, when he and his cousin started another group called Jump Street. Later, he toured as an electric bass player with Herbie Hancock's Monster Band, an experience he calls "the height of my musical career." One night, he experienced the joy of playing onstage with the band and legendary trumpeter Dizzy Gillespie.

"But it was getting harder and harder to keep going," Conte says. "I loved playing. But by then, I was married with three kids, and being on the road is difficult. You kiss your kids goodbye and say, 'I'll see you in six months.' So I left the band in 1983. And in 1984, I founded BALCO."

Margaret Goodman was born in Toronto. Her father played saxophone and clarinet, managed several rock groups, and ultimately became a record producer. When she was seven, the family moved to Beverly Hills.

"*Broadway Danny Rose* was the story of my father's life," Goodman said years later. "In the 1950s, he managed a group called The Diamonds that had hits with *Little Darlin'*, *Walking Along,* and *The Stroll*. He worked with Brook Benton and Dinah Washington. He started Sonny & Cher and the Righteous Brothers. But what always happened was, he'd take them to a certain point, and then somebody big with a recording studio and more clout in the industry would come along and take them away from him."

Goodman's father taught Margaret to read music and sing and introduced her to nightclubs and concerts. He wanted her to be a doctor, but music was the love of her life. Finally, father and daughter had a heart-to-heart talk.

'If you want to be a studio singer," he told Margaret, "you'll do fine. But if you have your heart set on becoming the next Barbra Streisand, go to medical school.'"

Goodman enrolled at Chicago Medical School. But it was expensive and she had to make ends meet. While some of her contemporaries were partying their way out of medicine, Margaret worked her way through school by singing on weekends at nightclubs in Chicago. Old standards: Cole Porter, Rodgers and Hart, Jerome Kern.

Conte still dabbles in music from time to time. In 2010, he wrote and recorded a song called *Balco Behop* on which he plays a *Take Me Out to the Ballgame* motif on bass guitar.

Does Conte miss being a fulltime musician?

"Not at all," he answers. "I was on the road for thirteen years as a traveling musician. I know what it takes to get to the top and stay at the top. And I reached a point long ago where I just didn't want to do it anymore."

As for Goodman, "I used to think I'd keep singing one way or another," Margaret acknowledges. "And I haven't. That's kind of sad. Sometimes I think I'd like to do it again. But it's been so long, I probably wouldn't be any good anymore."

★ ★ ★

On September 27, 2014, adult glamour model Jordan Carver and adult film star Melanie Muller entered a boxing ring in Dusseldorf, Germany, and did battle over four heated rounds. Their encounter could be dismissed as taking place beyond the outer fringe of boxing but for one notable fact.

The ring announcer was Michael Buffer.

Carver was born in Germany in 1986. According to Wikipedia, she worked as a hotel manager, beautician, and make-up artist before moving to Los Angeles to pursue a modeling career. In January 2010, she launched her own website featuring glamour photos, videos, and other content.

Wikipedia further notes, "Carver became successful due to the large size of her breasts paired with her otherwise slim figure." But in 2017, she posted a video on YouTube entitled "Why I Decided for a Breast Reduction" and a second video heralding her "new life as Ina Marie." She now says that she has left the adult industry behind. But memories remain. A recent Google search for "Jordan Carver" engendered more than 400,000 results.

Melanie Muller was born in Germany in 1988. Wikipedia reports that she worked as a "restaurant specialist and bartender" before turning to erotic modeling in 2010. She had a brief career in pornographic films and has been involved in a number of entertainment ventures including singing. In April 2014, Muller recorded and released a song in honor of the 2014 FIFA World Cup, the title of which translates into English as "Let's Go, Germany. Score!"

Carver vs. Muller (which can be found on YouTube) was honestly, albeit inartfully, fought. There were four two-minute rounds without headgear. The women didn't play-act or pose provocatively. They fought as best they could with Muller winning the decision.

As for Buffer's participation . . .

The Great One has longstanding commercial ties to Germany. He has been a spokesperson for Saturn, a large German electronics manufacturing company. And he was the ring announcer of choice for most of Vitali and Wladimir Klitschko's championship fights in Germany.

Where Carver vs. Muller was concerned, Buffer announced Carver as "The Queen of Fitness" and Muller as "The Queen of the Jungle, but tonight she wants to become Germany's first lady of fighting." He also intoned "Let's get ready to rumble!" at the appropriate time and, when the bout was over, announced the decision as he would after any big fight.

"It was part of a celebrity boxing series," Buffer recalls, looking back on that night. "And it was done on a pretty high level. They had a good crowd in a respectable venue. [Former heavyweight contender] Axel Schulz was one of the German television commentators, and the telecast got good ratings. I was brought in to give the event credibility. The fight was sloppy but totally for real. Both women tried hard to win. I did my job. They paid me well. And that was it."

★ ★ ★

It has long been said that a picture is worth a thousand words. So let's stop and gaze fondly at a recent Instagram post of a gentleman with outstretched arms standing amidst dozens of marijuana plants that are flourishing beneath indoor LED lights.

Shannon Briggs is 46 years old. He turned pro at age twenty and has compiled a 60–6–1 (53 KOs, 2 KOs by) ring record over the past quarter century. There have been high points: victories in his first 25 fights which made him a highly-touted prospect; a questionable verdict over George Foreman that brought him the "lineal" world heavyweight championship. And lows: a "KO by" against Darroll Wilson that raised questions about

Briggs's fortitude, and a loss to a 9-and-9 club fighter named Sedreck Fields when Shannon came in unprepared and out of shape.

There was also a 1998 defeat at the hands of Lennox Lewis, when Briggs gave Lewis all he could handle for five dramatic rounds. And a night in 2010 when Shannon displayed extraordinary courage as he endured a brutal beating from Vitali Klitschko but lasted a full twelve rounds.

Briggs is still hoping for another big payday in boxing. He's riding a nine-bout winning streak that includes seven first-round knockouts over opponents he was expected to knock out in the first round. But he last fought on May 21, 2016. And as a practical man, Shannon has been looking for other sources of income.

This brings us to Champ RX LLC—a Shannon Briggs venture that's producing an "alternative health and wellness" line of cannabidiol (CBD) products that are THC free.

Cannabidiol is a marijuana plant extract that, while not making users "high," has been prescribed to treat cases of post-traumatic stress disorder and has additional therapeutic properties. Its adherents claim that CBD can ease pain and shorten recovery time after heavy exercise and injury. It's sold in lotion, gel, cream, and oral spray form, and can also be applied under the tongue with a dropper. Many variants of CBD are legal under the World Anti-Doping Agency code.

Briggs is particularly fond of CBD isolate, which he describes as "cannabidiol in its purest form possible." He then explains, "CBD isolate crystals are a fine white powder that only contains the cannabidiol chemical compound. CBD isolate powder and CBD isolate crystals are the most powerful punch of CBD you can get your hands on."

CBD is a booming business. It's also often a cash business because many banks refuse to handle accounts for businesses that deal in marijuana products. It's expected to grow exponentially in the years ahead as more and more states relax their laws regarding the sale and use of marijuana.

Meanwhile, it would be interesting to know what Brigg does with the "waste product" (THC) from his horticultural venture.

★ ★ ★

Cus D'Amato used to tell his fighters to cut their hair short. He didn't want a spray of water shooting into the air when his fighter got hit because he was afraid it would make the impact of the punch seem greater than it actually was.

"Judges are supposed to score punches that land," D'Amato would say. "But some judges score blood. And others score water."

★ ★ ★

It happens often enough to require correction . . .

Time and again, I hear ring announcers, commentators, and others say Gennady Golovkin is "fighting out of Los Angeles by way of Kazakstan." Or Sergey Kovalev is "fighting out of Florida by way of Russia."

No! They have it backwards.

The Oxford English Dictionary defines "by way of" as "to pass through or across." For example, "He drove from New York to Massachusetts by way of Connecticut. . . . He flew from New York to San Francisco by way of Chicago."

If Gennady Golovkin fights in Las Vegas, he's coming "all the way from Kazakstan by way of Los Angeles." If Sergey Kovalev fights in New York, he's coming "all the way from Russia by way of Florida."

"By way of" means "via."

Get it right.

★ ★ ★

The recent death of evangelist Billy Graham conjures up memories of another Billy Graham, who epitomized what boxing was about in an earlier era.

Graham fought professionally from 1941 through 1955. He was undefeated in his first 58 pro fights and, during the course of his ring career, posted victories over Kid Gavilan, Carmen Basilio, and Joey Giardello. He was never knocked out and, more remarkably, was never knocked down. His final record stood at 102 wins, 15 losses, and nine draws with 27 knockouts. But boxing was different then. Graham never won a world title.

Graham is said to have been the model for Eddie Brown in *The Professional*, W.C. Heinz's novel about boxing. He also had a way with words and once observed, "If you watch *The Late Show* and it comes up a boxing movie, always bet on the guy who lost the first fourteen rounds. It's the price Hollywood makes him pay for knocking the other guy out in the fifteenth."

Asked by writer and critic Dorothy Parker for his definition of courage, Ernest Hemingway replied "guts." Pressed for more, he added "grace under pressure."

Ernest Hemingway, Boxing, and "Fifty Grand"

Ernest Hemingway referenced boxing from time to time in his writing. But one of his works was devoted entirely to the sweet science.

Hemingway's great novels were far in the future when he wrote "Fifty Grand." He was a 27-year-old journalist and short story writer. *The Atlantic Monthly* published the 8,000-word piece in 1927.

Fifty Grand is told in the first person by Jerry Doyle, the trainer for welterweight champion Jack Brennan. There was a time when Brennan was a very good fighter. "He certainly did used to make the fellows he fought hate boxing," Doyle notes. But Brennan is now tired and old. He has looked awful in training camp. In Doyle's words, "He just hasn't got anything inside anymore."

The odds are 2-to-1 against Brennan on the eve of his title defense at Madison Square Garden against challenger Jimmy Walcott. Two nights before the fight, Brennan tells Doyle that he has bet $50,000 on Walcott.

"It ain't crooked," Jack says to his trainer. "You know I can't win anyway. How can I beat him? I'm through after this fight. I got to take a beating. Why shouldn't I make money on it? I'll give them a good show. It's just business."

The fight itself is dramatically told, as one would expect. After all, this is Ernest Hemingway.

Brennan controls the early rounds with his jab.

"Walcott was after him," Hemingway writes, "going forward all the time with his chin on his chest. All he knows is to get in there and sock. But every time he gets in there close, Jack has the left hand in his face. That left-hand is just automatic. It's just like it was connected with Walcott's face. After about four rounds, Jack has him bleeding bad and his face all cut up. But every time Walcott's got in close, he's socked so hard he's [put] two big red patches on both sides just below Jack's ribs. Every time he gets in close, he socks Jack in the body so they can hear it outside in the street."

By the middle rounds, Walcott is dominating the fight. Jack's left arm is getting heavy. His strength is gone. His legs have deserted him. He's taking a terrible beating, especially to the body. All he wants now is to avoid the indignity of a knockout, finish on his feet, and collect his purse plus the $25,000 profit on his bet.

"It was going just the way he thought it would," Doyle recounts. "He knew he couldn't beat Walcott."

Round eleven.

"The gong rang and we pushed him out. He went out slow. Walcott came right out after him. Jack put the left in his face and Walcott took it, came in under it, and started working on Jack's body. Jack tried to tie him up and it was just like trying to hold on to a buzz-saw. Jack broke away from it and missed with the right. Walcott clipped him with a left-hook and Jack went down. He went down on his hands and knees and looked at us. The referee started counting. Jack was watching us and shaking his head. At eight, Jack got up. The referee had been holding Walcott back with one arm while he counted. When Jack was on his feet Walcott started toward him."

Then the plot becomes a bit contrived.

"Walcott came up to Jack looking at him. He backed Jack up against the ropes, measured him, and then hooked the left very light to the side of Jack's head and socked the right into the body as hard as he could sock, just as low as he could get it. He must have hit him five inches below the belt. I thought the eyes would come out of Jack's head. They stuck way out. His mouth come open. The referee grabbed Walcott. Jack stepped forward. If he went down, there went fifty thousand bucks. He walked as though all his insides were going to fall out."

Now the dilemma. If Jack collapses from the low blow, he'll win by disqualification and be $75,000 poorer than if he'd lost. He struggles to maintain his footing and assures the referee that he can continue.

"It wasn't low," Jack says. "It was a accident. I'm all right,"

"Come on and fight," Jack says to Walcott.

The referee waves Walcott in.

"Jack's face was the worst thing I ever saw, the look on it. He was holding himself and all his body together and it all showed on his face. All the time he was thinking and holding his body in where it was busted. Then he started to sock. Walcott covered up and Jack was swinging wild at Walcott's head. Then he swung the left and it hit Walcott in the groin and the right hit Walcott right bang where he'd hit Jack. Way low below the belt. Walcott went down and grabbed himself there and rolled and twisted around. The referee grabbed Jack and pushed him toward his corner. There was all this yelling going on. The referee was talking with the judges and then the announcer got into the ring with the megaphone and says, 'Walcott on a foul.'"

Walcott has been unable to rise and thus been declared the winner by disqualification. Did he have a fix of his own in mind when he deliberately went low on Jack? From Hemingway's point on view, that's secondary to the belief that Jack Brennan fought like a champion by continuing to fight after the low blow even though his goal was to deliberately lose.

But Hemingway didn't just write about boxing. He considered himself a boxer.

How good was he? Not very.

Hemingway's most notable ring encounter came at The American Club in Paris in 1925 when he sparred against a Canadian writer named Morley Callaghan. The two men had squared off on several previous occasions. Callaghan, in an account corroborated by third parties who were present, wrote about the experience in a book entitled *That Summer in Paris.*

"Ernest was big and heavy," Callaghan recalled. "Over six feet, and I was only five-foot-eight and fat. Whatever skill I had in boxing had to do with avoiding getting hit. I was a little afraid of Ernest. All of the lore and legend of the pros seemed to be in his stance and in the way he held his hands. His chin down a little to his shoulder, he made an impressive picture. Watching him warily, I could only think, 'Try and make him miss, then slip away from him.' All I did for the first three-minute round was slip away."

Then, between rounds, Callaghan realized, "I'm not trying to box with him. I'm trying to defend myself against the wild legends I've heard."

The Canadian was more competitive for the rest of that first sparring session.

Hemingway and Callaghan sparred together several times thereafter.

"The truth," Callaghan reminisced, "was that we were two amateur boxers. The difference between us was that he had given time and imagination to boxing. I had actually worked out a lot with good fast college boxers. He was a big rough tough clumsy unscientific man. In a small bar or in an alley where he could have cornered me in a rough-and-tumble brawl, he might have broken my back; he was so much bigger. But with gloves on and in a space big enough for me to move around, I could be confident. I could see that, while he may have thought about boxing, dreamed about it, consorted with old fighters and hung around gyms, I had done more actual boxing with men who could box a little and weren't just taking exercise or fooling around."

Their final sparring session was particularly intense.

"Ernest had become rougher," Callaghan recounted, "His heavy punches, if they had landed, would have stunned me. I had to punch faster and harder myself to keep away from him. It bothered me that he was taking the punches on the face like a man telling himself he only needed to land one punch himself. Then Ernest came leaping in at me. Stepping in, I beat him to the punch. The timing must have been just right. I caught him on the jaw. Spinning, he went down, sprawled out on his back."

The fly in the ointment was that F. Scott Fitzgerald, who was serving as timekeeper, had become so engrossed in the proceedings that he'd let the round run a minute long. Hemingway reportedly never spoke to Fitzgerald again.

Who else did Hemingway spar with? Well, at least one man wouldn't spar with him.

Jack Dempsey visited Paris while heavyweight champion and later recalled, "There were a lot of Americans in Paris, and I sparred with a couple, just to be obliging. But there was one fellow I wouldn't mix it with. That was Ernest Hemingway. He was about twenty-five or so and in good shape, and I was getting so I could read people, or anyway men, pretty well. I had this sense that Hemingway, who really thought he could box, would come out of the corner like a madman. To stop him, I would have to hurt him badly, I didn't want to do that to Hemingway. That's why I never sparred with him."

Then, years later, Hemingway engaged in a sparring session of sorts with Dempsey's conqueror, Gene Tunney. George Plimpton told the tale as follows:

"It happened at Hemingway's home outside Havana, where Hemingway was always trying to get Tunney, whenever he came to visit, to spar bare-fisted. Tunney would grumble and get up on occasion to do it, though mostly he looked up at Hemingway from his armchair and said no. On this occasion, the two men began shuffling around the big living room, and Hemingway did what Tunney half-expected. He threw a low punch, perhaps out of clumsiness, but it hurt. It outraged Tunney. He feinted his opponent's guard down and then threw a whistling punch, bringing it up just a millimeter short of Hemingway's face so that the fist and the ridge of bare knuckles completely filled the other's field of vision, the punch arriving there almost instantaneously so that immutable evidence was provided that, if Tunney had let it continue its course, Hemingway's facial structure—nose, cheekbones, front teeth, and the rest—would have snapped and collapsed inwardly. And Tunney looked down the length of his arm into Hemingway's eyes and said, 'Don't you ever do that again!'"

Katie Taylor once told me that she'd love to be able to go back in time, meet David, and discuss with him what it was like to fight Goliath.

David vs. Goliath

The Biblical battle of David vs. Goliath has endured for thousands of years as an inspiration for underdogs in one-on-one combat. But few people have written about that storied confrontation in more intriguing fashion than Malcolm Gladwell.

Gladwell authored a collection of essays published under the title *David and Goliath* (Little Brown and Company). The book examines nine individuals from various disciplines who battled powerful forces in contemporary times. The introduction to the book explores the original David vs. Goliath.

Three thousand years ago, the Bible tells us, an army of Philistines was seeking to militarily divide the Kingdom of Israel into two parts which would then be vulnerable to conquest. The warring armies faced each other from opposite sides of a ravine. Neither army dared attack since doing so would require descending into the ravine and being assaulted from above.

Finally, Gladwell writes, "The Philistines sent their greatest warrior down into the valley to resolve the deadlock one on one. He was a giant, six-foot nine at least [six cubits and a span] wearing a bronze helmet and full body armor. He carried a javelin, a spear, and a sword. An attendant preceded him, carrying a large shield. The giant faced the Israelites and shouted out, 'Choose you a man and let him come down to me. If he prevail in battle against me and strike me down, we shall be slaves to you. But if I prevail and strike him down, you will be slaves to us and serve us."

David, a shepherd boy who had come to the field of battle to bring food to his brothers, accepted the challenge. King Saul sought to dissuade him, warning, "Thou art not able to go against this Philistine to fight with him for thou art but a youth and he is a man of war."

But David was insistent.

You know the rest. At least, you think you do.

"We consistently get these kinds of conflicts wrong," Gladwell writes. "We misinterpret them. Giants are not what we think they are."

Or phrased differently, in Gladwell's eyes, David vs. Goliath wasn't an evenly-matched fight. David had several crucial advantages.

"Goliath was expecting a warrior like himself to come forward for hand-to-hand combat," Gladwell explains. "It never occurred to him that the battle would be fought on anything other than those terms. To protect himself against blows to the body, he wore an elaborate tunic made up of hundreds of overlapping bronze fishlike scales. He had bronze shin guards protecting his legs with attached bronze plates covering his feet. He wore a heavy metal helmet. He had three separate weapons, all optimized for close combat."

All David had was a shepherd's staff, a sling, and five smooth stones.

"Am I a dog that thou comest to me with sticks?" Goliath demanded of his young adversary. "Come to me and I will give thy flesh unto the fowls of the air and to the beasts of the field."

Not so fast, big guy.

As recounted in 1 *Samuel*, chapter 17, verses 49 and 50, "David put his hand in his bag and took thence a stone and slang it and smote the Philistine in his forehead that the stone sunk into his forehead and he fell upon his face to the earth. Therefore, David ran and stood upon the Philistine and took his sword and drew it out of the sheath and cut off his head."

Now for Gladwell's keys to victory.

"Ancient armies," he explains, "had three kinds of warriors. The first was cavalry: armed men on horseback or in chariots. The second was infantry: foot soldiers wearing armor and carrying swords and shields. The third were projectile warriors, or what today would be called artillery: archers and slingers. Slingers had a leather pouch attached on two sides by a long strand of rope. They would put a rock or a lead ball into the pouch, swing it around in increasingly wider and faster circles, and then release one end of the rope, hurling the rock forward. Slinging took an extraordinary amount of skill and practice. But in experienced hands, the sling was a devastating weapon. An experienced slinger could kill or seriously injure a target at a distance of up to two hundred yards. The Romans even had a special set of tongs made just to remove stones that had been embedded in some poor soldier's body by a sling. And projectile warriors were deadly against infantry because a big lumbering soldier weighed down with armor was a sitting duck for a slinger who was launching projectiles from a hundred yards away."

"Goliath is heavy infantry," Gladwell continues. "He thinks that he is going to be engaged in a duel with another heavy-infantryman. When he says 'Come to me,' he means come right up to me so that we can fight at close quarters. David without armor has speed and maneuverability. He puts a rock into his sling and whips it around and around, faster and faster, aiming his projectile at Goliath's forehead—the giant's only point of vulnerability. What could Goliath do? He was carrying over a hundred pounds of armor. He was prepared for a battle at close range where he could stand, immobile, warding off blows with his armor and delivering a mighty thrust of his spear."

"Goliath," Gladwell quotes historian Robert Dohrenwend as saying, "had as much chance against David as any Bronze Age warrior with a sword would have had against an opponent armed with a .45 automatic pistol."

Moreover, in many respects, Goliath seems to have been like an aging boxer past his prime.

"Goliath is supposed to be a mighty warrior," Gladwell notes. "But he's not acting like one. He comes down to the valley floor accompanied by an attendant—a servant walking before him, carrying a shield. Why does Goliath, a man calling for sword-on-sword single combat, need to be assisted by a third party carrying a shield? What's more, why does he say to David, 'Come to me'? Why can't Goliath go to David? The biblical account emphasizes how slowly Goliath moves, which is an odd thing to say about someone who is alleged to be a battle hero of infinite strength. Why doesn't Goliath respond much sooner to the sight of David coming down the hillside without any sword or shield or armor? When he first sees David, his first reaction is to be insulted. He seems oblivious of what's happening around him. There is even that strange comment after he finally spots David with his shepherd's staff: 'Am I a dog that you should come to me with sticks?' Sticks plural? David is holding only one stick."

"What many medical experts now believe," Gladwell continues, "is that Goliath had a serious medical condition. He looks and sounds like someone suffering from what is called acromegaly. One of the common side effects of acromegaly is vision problems. Why was Goliath led onto the valley floor by an attendant? Because the attendant was his visual guide. Why does he move so slowly? Because the world around him is a blur. Why does it take him so long to understand that David has changed the rules? Because he doesn't see David until David is up close."

"What the Israelites saw, from high on the ridge," Gladwell concludes, "was an intimidating giant. There is an important lesson in that for battles with all kinds of giants. The powerful and the strong are not always what they seem."

There are easier ways to make a living than fighting. Professional wrestling is one of them.

Ronda Rousey Rewrites the Script

Ronda Rousey was co-featured on a fight card at Madison Square Garden on Saturday night, July 7, 2018. But it wasn't what the combat sports world once envisioned it would be. Instead, the woman who was honored at the 2015 ESPY Awards as "Best Fighter" of the year wrestled a former plus-model named Nia Jax on the WWE LIVE SummerSlam Heatwave Tour.

Three years ago, Rousey was the UFC 135-pound women's champion. She'd been featured in mainstream publications ranging from *Time Magazine* to *The New Yorker*. Movie-goers had seen her in *Entourage* and *The Expendables 3*. *Sports Illustrated,* which featured Rousey in its annual swimsuit issue, called her the most dominant athlete in the world. She had an almost biological symbiosis with the spotlight and knew what to do when it was shining on her. Almost singlehandedly, she forced UFC to acknowledge and promote women's MMA.

Then came the fall. It turned out that Rousey, who won multiple gold medals as an amateur and a bronze medal at the 2008 Beijing Olympics, couldn't take a punch. She was knocked out by Holly Holm in the second round of their fight in Melbourne in November 2015. Thirteen months later, it took Amanda Nunez 48 seconds to accomplish the same end.

Cover-girl looks don't help once the bell rings.

Rousey, now 31 years old, has since found greener pastures, or at least safer waters. Earlier this year, she joined WWE (World Wrestling Entertainment) as an active combatant. The number of shows she will participate in this year has yet to be determined, as is the case with all WWE superstars. Suffice it to say for the moment that WWE won't be putting Ronda on the road for a dozen shows each month. She'll be reserved for spectaculars.

The scene at Madison Square Garden on July 7 was typical of big WWE events. There was a crowd of roughly 15,000, most of whom were in their seats when the first match began at 7:30 p.m. Jeans were the most common attire. There wasn't a tie in sight. It was a young crowd. Many in attendance were parents with grade-school-age children in tow. At 6-feet-11-inches tall, New York Knicks center Enes Kanter was the most visible celebrity in the audience. The action was magnified by four large video screens that hang from the rafters and also by another large screen that WWE erected at one end of the arena. Loud music blared between fights.

There were nine bouts including multiple tag-team and championship encounters with very little downtime in between. All of the matches pitted heroes against villains ("babyfaces" versus "heels" in WWE parlance).

Fans go to WWE events knowing that they'll get what they want. It's understood that there will be back-and-forth action in every bout. No tag-team match ends until each of the grapplers has seen at least some combat. And most important for those in attendance on Saturday night, it was expected that The Undertaker would score a dramatic match-ending pin. More on that later in this article.

The matches are scripted but not danger-free. The stunts require flexibility, agility, acrobatic skill, and strength. If the timing is wrong, particularly with a body-slam or leap from a turnbuckle, someone can get hurt. Think of it as synchronized gymnastics.

Many of the male combatants had body-builder physiques, although some looked as though they've been drinking a lot of beer lately.

There's a high level of audience participation at WWE events. Fans count punches aloud as they land, urge fighters to employ various strategies, and wave cell phones on cue in a suddenly-darkened arena. On occasion, they chant in unison, "This is awesome."

Rousey faced off against Jax in the eighth match of the evening.

Traditionally, professional wrestling was an end-of-the-line destination for former boxers who were no longer competitive in a boxing ring and were having trouble making ends meet.

In 1956, Joe Louis went on tour as a professional wrestler. The script for his matches was predictable. Louis was pitted against a villainous opponent who would engage in dirty tactics until rendered unconscious by The Brown Bomber's famed right hand. However, his wrestling career came to an abrupt end soon after it began when a 320-pound opponent named Rocky Lee timed a leap poorly and landed on Louis's chest, breaking two of his ribs and bruising the muscles around his heart.

Thereafter, Louis refereed occasional wrestling matches until 1972 when poor health intervened. That mirrored the journey Jack Dempsey traveled, beginning in 1931 when he refereed a wrestling match between Jim O'Dowd (good guy) and Billy Edwards (villain). Edward had the temerity to punch Dempsey, and The Manassa Mauler promptly knocked the heel unconscious. Dempsey continued to referee wrestling matches into his seventh decade when Walter "Killer" Kowalski accidentally kicked him in the stomach and sent him (for real) to the hospital.

Muhammad Ali was a "special guest referee" when Hulk Hogan and Mr. T battled Paul Orndorff and Rowdy Roddy Piper in WrestleMania I at Madison Square Garden in 1985. Ali also squared off against Japanese wrestler Antonio Inoki in Tokyo in 1976. But that confrontation was unscripted and stultifyingly boring as Inoki crab-walked around the ring on his butt for fifteen long rounds. Chuck Wepner was thrown out of the ring by Andre the Giant in an undercard bout that night.

More recently, Mike Tyson appeared as a "special outside enforcer" at WrestleMania XIV in 1998 and as a participant in a tag-team match on WWE Monday Night Raw in 2010. Floyd Mayweather was in the ring against Big Show at Wrestlemania 24 in 2008.

But those were all part-time ventures by boxers, and most of them were in non-combat roles. Rousey is now both a combatant and a regular on the WWE circuit. In that regard, her role model is Brock Lesnar, who won an NCAA heavyweight wrestling championship while at the University of Minnesota, was featured in the main event on five UFC pay-per-view telecasts, and has wrestled on and off for WWE for the past sixteen years.

One of the keys to a wrestler's success is the skill level of the partners and opponents that he or she performs with. In Rousey's first WWE outing (Wrestlemania 34 in New Orleans on April 8 of this year), she was paired with veteran Kurt Angle. Together, they defeated the tag-team duo of Triple H (known outside the ring as Paul Michael Levesque) and Stephanie McMahon when Rousey applied her famed arm-bar to McMahon.

Angle, McMahon, and Levesque are pros who go about their business exceedingly well. That said; Rousey surprised—and is continuing to surprise—a lot of people at WWE with how good she is.

A lot of hard work is involved in implementing a WWE script. Rousey is a natural. She has charisma. She has prodigious athletic gifts. And she plays to the crowd well. She's very much at home in live theater.

"Are you nervous?" Ellen DeGeneres asked Rousey shortly before her WWE debut.

"I'm nervous but not like Olympics nervous," Ronda answered. "The worst thing that can happen is that I'll look stupid."

As for Rousey vs. Nia Jax at "the world's most famous arena". . . Jax (whose real name is Savelina Fanene) is a 34-year-old native of Australia who WWE lists as being 6-feet-2-inches tall and weighing 272 pounds. Wikipedia says she's two inches shorter and 32 pounds lighter. Jax has been on the WWE circuit since 2015 and has engaged in various feuds as both a hero and villain.

Rousey is 5-feet-7-inches tall. When she fought on UFC cards, she weighed 135 pounds for a few hours before each weigh-in. She now weighs closer to 150.

I don't follow WWE storylines on a regular basis. But it appears as though Rousey challenged Jax for the WWE Raw Women's championship in Chicago on June 17 and was on the verge of dethroning Nia with her famed armbar. Then the villainous Alexa Bliss entered the ring.

Bliss (a/k/a Alexis Kaufman) is 28 years old and hails from Columbus, Ohio. She's at the opposite end of the size spectrum from Jax and is listed as being 5-feet-1-inch tall, 101 pounds. Alexa is the snarky blonde everyone in high school hated. She also reportedly has a deaf pet pig named Larry-Steve.

Bliss attacked Rousey from behind with a briefcase, thereby depriving Ronda of a championship victory over Jax. And to make matters worse, literally minutes later, the evil Ms. Bliss fought the now-impaired Jax in a bout that ended with the evildoer claiming the throne. Then, not content to simply wear the crown, Bliss taunted Rousey at a WWE show the following night. Ronda became so enraged that she punched Bliss in the stomach and threw her though a table, assaulted Kurt Angle (who doubles as WWE RAW's "general manager"), and attacked four referees who raced into the ring to restore order. This earned Rousey a 30-day suspension, placing her July 7 WWE appearance at Madison Square Garden in jeopardy. However, a loophole in the suspension allowed Ronda vs. Nia to proceed as planned.

Thus it was that Ronda Rousey and Nia Jax did battle in a ring pitched on the hallowed ground where Muhammad Ali fought Joe Frazier for the first time. As Rousey-Jax unfolded, WWE aficionados realized that the script was virtually identical to online accounts of the previous night's encounter between them at the Wells Fargo Center in Philadelphia.

On each occasion, Alexa Bliss and Alexa's sidekick (the not-quite-as-evil Mickie James) were guest referees. Rousey and Jax engaged in heated combat. But each time that Ronda was on the verge of a pin, Bliss and James conspired to deny her the victory. In one instance, James "slow counted." In another, Mickie claimed she had hurt her shoulder (or was it her wrist?) and hadn't been able to slap the matt for the final count. Eventually, Rousey and Jax grew disgusted with both referees and knocked them out, after which they returned to fighting each other. Then a third referee (who was honorable) charged into the ring to supervise the rest of the match which ended when Ronda submitted Nia with an arm bar.

By this time, the crowd at Madison Square Garden was in a proverbial frenzy. And the thunderous roars grew louder when 53-year-old Mark William Calaway (known to wrestling fans as "The Undertaker") strode to the ring for the final bout of the evening.

"The Undertaker" has moved back and forth between being a hero and a villain and is regarded as one of the greatest professional wrestlers of all time. He began his combat career in 1984 and has been with WWE since 1990, compiling a 24-and-2 record in Wrestlemania events. His victims have included Jimmy Snuka, King Kong Bundy, Diesel, Triple H, Rick Flair, Big Show, and Kane. At Wrestlemania 34 on April 8, 2018, (the same night that Rousey and Kurt Angle defeated Triple H and Stephanie McMahon), The Undertaker pinned John Cena after a mere 2 minutes 46 seconds of battle.

This was The Undertaker's first live performance at Madison Square Garden in eight years. Fans were treated to a tag-team affair that joined him with Braun Strowman and Roman Reigns against Kevin Owens, Baron Corbin, and Elias. It ended with The Undertaker scoring a crowd-pleasing pin against Owens.

And everyone went home happy.

Other Sports

In summer 2018, I began writing for Sporting News. *Most of my work for the venerable publication was about boxing and is included in other sections of this book. But I also explored other sports.*

The Sporting News Tradition

As Mick Jagger sang fifty years ago in *Sympathy for The Devil*, please allow me to introduce myself. I've just begun writing for *Sporting News* and would like to share what it means to me to tap into a treasured tradition.

The Sporting News was first published as a weekly newspaper on March 17, 1886. Its founder, Alfred H. Spink, was a director of the St. Louis Browns (the National League baseball team that would become the St. Louis Cardinals). The paper's first issue was 17-by-22-inches in size. In the century that followed, it evolved from a standard newsprint publication to a smaller glossier format.

Early issues of *The Sporting News* covered baseball, boxing, horse racing, and cycling. By the dawn of the twentieth century, it was devoted almost entirely to baseball and wielded considerable power. Indeed, its influence was such that *The Sporting News* helped broker a 1903 truce between the established National League and upstart American League that resulted in creation of the modern World Series.

During World War I, a joint venture between *The Sporting News* and American League led to weekly distribution of the paper to 150,000 American troops fighting overseas. The paper also pioneered advances in sports photo-journalism and the inauguration of post-season awards.

Jerry Izenberg, the dean of American sportswriters, recalls, "*The Sporting News* was called 'The Bible of Baseball' and for good reason. Baseball was a national religion in the first half of the twentieth century. It was America's national pastime. And *The Sporting News* was baseball's paper of record."

This was long before television and, in the early years, even before radio. Newspapers and magazines were how information was communicated in America. *The Sporting News* published complete box scores for every American and National League game. It had articles written by beat writers from every city with a big-league team. There was coverage of minor league baseball. And the minor leagues were important in those days, not just as a farm system for the big leagues but as an economic engine and source of civic pride for cities that had minor league teams.

"How important was *The Sporting News*?" Izenberg asks. "As late as the 1950s and even into the sixties, you could walk into any baseball clubhouse in America and the players would be reading it."

But competitors like *Sport Magazine* and *Sports Illustrated* were rising in popularity. Sports other than baseball grew more prominent. *The Sporting News* expanded its coverage into football and then more sports. However, the economics of a weekly magazine associated in the public mind primarily with baseball were becoming untenable.

In 2008, after 122 years as a weekly publication, *The Sporting News* transitioned to a biweekly schedule. In 2011, biweekly became once a month. In 2012, the print edition came to an end. Meanwhile, an online edition had been launched in 1996. That's the *Sporting News* that exists today (with "the" having been dropped from its title). Baseball is now one of many sports that *SN* covers extensively.

I've been writing professionally since 1977 on subjects ranging from United States foreign policy to Beethoven. Baseball was my first love in sports although I've achieved a certain amount of recognition as a boxing writer.

I remember reading *The Sporting News* as a boy when I devoured everything I could find on baseball. It's a privilege to become part of the *Sporting News* tradition. This is a publication that dates back to 1886. Let's put that year in perspective. In 1886, John L. Sullivan was heavyweight champion of the world. Ty Cobb and Babe Ruth hadn't been born. James Naismith had yet to invent basketball.

In the months ahead, I hope to share thoughts and provide insights to you, the readers of *Sporting News*, through a mix of fight reports, investigative journalism, portraits of boxing personalities, and the exploration of issues that make up the fabric of the contemporary boxing scene. There will also be forays into other sports.

There's more to come.

Let's have some fun.

It's remarkable how long-ago incidents resurface in memory from time to time.

A Conversation with Bear Bryant

Alabama kicked off its 2018 campaign with a 51–14 victory over Louisville on September 1, 2018. The Crimson Tide is ranked #1 in most pre-season polls and an early favorite to repeat as college football's national champion. Should that happen, it will be Nick Saban's seventh national title as a coach and his sixth at Alabama.

Saban's accomplishments have placed him in sports lore alongside the man who is regarded by many as the greatest college football coach of all time: Paul "Bear" Bryant. That, in turns, brings back memories of a long-ago conversation I had with Bryant.

The eleventh of twelve children, Bryant was born in Moro Bottom, Arkansas, on September 11, 1913. He was a large man, 6-feet-3-inches tall, whose nickname derived from his having wrestled a bear at a carnival when he was thirteen years old.

Bryant played football at Alabama from 1933 through 1935. He later reigned as head coach at Maryland (1945), Kentucky (1946–1953), Texas A&M (1954–1957), and his alma mater (1958–1982). During Bryant's years at the helm, the Crimson Tide won six national championships. At the time he retired, his 323 victories were the most for a coach in modern college football history. In 38 seasons as a head coach, he had one losing season (his first year at Texas A&M).

Bryant epitomized an era when college football coaches were regarded as gods. Men like Bud Wilkinson (Oklahoma), Woody Hayes (Ohio State), Bob Devaney (Nebraska), Darrell Royal (Texas), and Ara Parseghian (Notre Dame) were larger-than-life figures who could do no wrong in the eyes of their supporters. They were admired and adored the way military generals who led troops into battle were venerated by previous generations of Americans.

The thought that one of these men might be suspended as head coach or have his contract terminated because he failed to report inappropriate conduct by an assistant coach to the proper authorities was unheard of.

Woody Hayes, despite a long record of physically-abusive acts, wasn't relieved of his coaching duties until he was shown on national television sucker-punching a Clemson defensive lineman who intercepted a pass in the closing minutes of the 1978 Gator Bowl. And there was a school of thought that Hayes's dismissal was motivated, not by his anti-social conduct but by the fact that, the previous month, Ohio State had lost to Michigan for the third consecutive time.

As for a coach's contract being terminated because he evinced a lack of concern for the physical well-being of his players; the cornerstone of the Bear Bryant legend was his first year as head coach at Texas A&M. One hundred eleven players were on the Aggie squad when pre-season workouts began. After ten days of brutal workouts beneath the broiling Texas sun, there were 35 survivors.

The widespread assumption was that had Bryant chosen to run for governor of Alabama in the 1970s, he would have been elected.

Flashback now to the mid-1970s. Bryant had won four national championships at Alabama. I was a young lawyer working as a litigator for the Wall Street law firm Cravath Swaine & Moore. One of my responsibilities was defending against libel suits brought against the media conglomerate then known as Time Inc.

The Time Inc empire had its origins in 1923 when Henry Luce and Britten Hadden published the inaugural issue of *Time*. In later years, one hundred publications were added to the fold, including *Sports Illustrated*, *People*, and *Fortune*. In 1968, Little Brown & Company (a major book publisher) became part of Time Inc's expanding portfolio.

In 1974, Little Brown published Bear Bryant's autobiography, written with John Underwood. In the book, Bryant said some uncomplimentary things about a former player at Alabama. He didn't identify the player by name. Instead, he referred to him as "a cute little red-headed kid with freckles and big thick glasses . . . A tough little linebacker from Florida named—well, call him Danny."

That description narrowed the identification of "Danny" down to a field of one.

Sammy Gellerstedt was a 5-foot-8-inch, 196-pound noseguard (not linebacker) who played one season of varsity football (1968) at Alabama.

Despite his size, he earned first-team All-American honors and was named United Press International's "Lineman of the Week" after the Crimson Tide's victory over Mississippi State.

Gellerstedt left the University of Alabama after his sophomore season amidst rumors of lifestyle issues. More specifically, it was said that Bryant kicked him off the team because he believed that Gellerstedt was smoking marijuana (which Bryant strongly implied in his book).

In an earlier era, Joe Namath (who played quarterback at Alabama from 1962 through 1964) had clashed with Bryant over lifestyle issues. But those issues involved drinking, not drugs. Namath was suspended for two games and stayed the course. However, as the 1960s neared an end, recreational drugs were becoming more prevalent. Indeed, several years after Gellerstedt's departure, Bryant drew a line in the sand. On one occasion, as recounted in his autobiography, he ordered a search of every player's dorm room and found evidence of marijuana use by seven players. In his words, "We told the seven that they could withdraw from school or we would just let the law handle it. They all withdrew."

Bryant also made it clear in his autobiography that, to his way of thinking, one of the keys to a young man's character was whether he had a "good mama and papa." Then, after noting that "Danny's home life was sad," he offered the opinion, "The biggest mistake coaches make is taking borderline cases and trying to save them. I'm not talking about grades now. I'm talking about character."

Gellerstedt sued for libel. I was assigned to the defense team on the case.

Several years later, I would leave law to pursue a career as a freelance writer. I would work with Muhammad Ali and Arnold Palmer on biographies of their respective lives and interact with countless sports legends. But in 1974, that was in my future. I was excited then by the fact that I was about to talk with the great Bear Bryant to construct our defense against Gellerstedt's claim.

An appointment was set up. I was to call Bryant at his home telephone number, which I did at the appointed hour of 5:00 p.m.

The passage of more than four decades has dimmed my memory of the conversation. I remember making the call from my office on the 57th floor at One Chase Manhattan Plaza in Manhattan. Bryant answered the phone, and I introduced myself.

Bryant was no stranger to the law of libel. In 1962, he had sued *The Saturday Evening Post* for publishing an article that accused him of encouraging his players to play with intent to injure in a 1961 game against Georgia Tech. Thereafter, the magazine published a second article that accused Bryant and Georgia athletic director Wally Butts of conspiring to fix the 1962 Alabama-Georgia game in favor of the Crimson Tide. A second claim by Bryant followed. He settled with *The Saturday Evening Post* in 1964 for a total of $300,000.

Bryant confirmed to me on the telephone that he had, in fact, been talking about Gellerstedt in his book. "If I'd known it was gonna cause all this trouble," he said, "I never would have mentioned him."

But it was hard to get the factual underpinning for the passages in question out of Bryant; particularly his references to Gellerstedt's family life. His memory of details as well as larger issues seemed foggy. He broke off in mid-sentence again and again and kept repeating himself.

The 1970s were a more sheltered time for public figures than the world today. There was no prying social media. By and large, sports heroes were allowed to do as they pleased and remain untarnished.

In wasn't until 1995 that Keith Dunnavant, in a book entitled *Coach*, would write of Bryant, "His tendency to drink to excess was well known among his friends and among the news media, yet no one ever reported a word about this. Although he never drank at work or let it affect his job, the coach often overindulged in social situations. Whether he was an alcoholic depends on one's definition. But he liked to drink to have a good time, and it was difficult for him to stop before he got sloppy drunk."

Not long into our conversation, I realized that the The Great Bear Bryant was drunk. Or to use Dunnavant's phrase, "sloppy drunk."

There wasn't much of use that I could learn from him. I thanked him for his time and said good-bye.

Gellerstedt enrolled at the University of Tampa after his two years at Alabama and continued to enjoy gridiron success. He graduated from Tampa in 1971 and, thirteen years later, was inducted in that university's Hall of Fame. His lawsuit had been filed in Florida, where both he and Underwood were residents. After some preliminary motions, the case was settled.

In the spring of 1978, Bryant entered an alcohol rehabilitation program in a clinic located in Shelby County south of Birmingham. But he resumed drinking soon after his stay there ended. He retired from coaching following a December 29, 1982, victory over Illinois in the Liberty Bowl. Four weeks later, he died after suffering a massive heart attack.

Our sports gods aren't always what we think they are and want them to be.

Jim Brown was a great football player. His legacy gets complicated after that.

Dave Zirin, Jim Brown, and Muhammad Ali

Muhammad Ali and Jim Brown created a new template for athletes: competitors who were big, strong, and fast. They also heralded a more aggressive approach on the part of black athletes in confronting the status quo on racial issues.

Millions of pages have been written about Ali's excellence as a fighter and his impact on society. Brown has been less fully explored. *Jim Brown: Last Man Standing* by Dave Zirin (Blue Rider Press) gives Brown his due as a football player but keys on his social importance.

Brown is a symbol of things good and bad: personal pride, black empowerment, athletic supremacy, and the worst kind of misogyny. He has special credence and is more remarkable in some ways because he's regarded by many knowledgeable observers as the greatest football player of all time.

Brown played with the Cleveland Browns from 1957 through 1965. His career, Zirin writes, was "Homeric" and "marked by feats that still make grown men shudder with joy."

In nine seasons, Brown led the league in rushing eight times. He's the only player in NFL history to average one hundred yards rushing per game over the course of his career and the only running back to average more than five yards each time he carried the ball. Remarkably, despite the fact that he touched the ball on sixty percent of Cleveland's offensive plays, he never missed a game due to injury.

"To understand how Jim Brown was able to make such an enduring political impact," Zirin states, "we first have to understand the awe he inspired inside the lines. On offense, the all-time great skill players have inspired astonishment yet never physical fear. On that side of the line of scrimmage, the list of true intimidators begins and ends with Jim Brown."

As Brown's football-playing days wound down, he segued into acting with significant roles in films like *The Dirty Dozen, Rio Conchos,*

Ice Station Zebra, 100 Rifles, and a string of "blaxploitation" movies. He was a serviceable actor with a commanding screen presence and one of Hollywood's first black action heroes. That fit nicely with his standing as a forceful advocate for black empowerment.

Brown, Zirin writes, "represented the seedlings of 'Black Power' a decade before the phrase was popularly known."

In an era when sports unions were virtually non-existent, he led the movement for player rights within the Cleveland Browns organization. That led to complaints that Brown was a "locker room lawyer" and causing racial problems within the team.

"One man's racial problem is another man's equal rights," Brown responded.

He elaborated on that theme in a 1964 autobiography entitled *Off My Chest*, writing, "I do not crave the white man's approval. I crave only the rights I'm entitled to as a human being. The acceptance of the Negro in sports is really an insignificant development that warms the heart of the Negro less than it does of the white man who salves his troubled conscience by telling himself, 'Isn't it wonderful that Negroes and whites are out there playing together.'"

In 1965, Brown formed the Negro Industrial and Economic Union, later known as the Black Economic Union. Between 1965 and 1972, the BEU had offices in six cities and helped launch more than four hundred black-owned businesses. Brown's stated aim in forming the organization was "to make more black Americans rich and powerful. We wanted them spending their hours building their economics and to stop marching, singing, kneeling, and praying."

In that regard, Zirin notes, "Brown was not looking for a movement or to attach himself to anyone else's agenda. He was an organizer, not a movement builder. He worked to see the black community assert its economic independence and fight racism, but also looked at the existing manifestations of the 'fight against racism'—marching, demonstrating, even arming yourself for revolutionary ends—and saw a waste of everyone's time."

Thus, over the years, Brown has mocked the civil rights movement as "parades" and declared, "If I ever march, I'll march alone." He has declared his antipathy for the movement anthem—*We Shall Overcome*—with the observation, "I hated that song. It was about marching and singing. I didn't like marching. I didn't march. And I didn't like singing to get my freedom. To me, that was weak."

Even today, Brown reaffirms, "I didn't think much of Dr. King. If you think about a majority of the rhetoric, it's about what's being done to us. It doesn't have damn near anything that says what we're going to do for ourselves."

And how did Brown weigh the civil rights movement against dollars?

One of many interesting episodes in Zirin's book recounts how Olympic sprinter Tommie Smith planned to try his hand at pro football after the 1968 Olympics. Prior to the games, Brown agreed to represent Smith as his agent and loaned him $2,000 against future earnings. Smith won a gold medal in the 200-meter sprint in Mexico City and, with silver medalist John Carlos, raised his fist in a protest against racism during the medal ceremony. That made him persona non grata in the NFL. Brown demanded return of the $2,000 and refused to represent Smith.

The Black Economic Union lost steam in the early 1970s. Eventually it was supplanted by Amer-I-Can as the focal point of Brown's efforts to impact on society. Brown invested $400,000 of his own money to launch Amer-I-Can. Its stated mission is to foster individual improvement and combat gang violence. On numerous occasions, he has offered his California home as a site for negotiations among rival gangs.

No book about Brown would be honest or complete without an examination of his chronic mistreatment of women. Zirin doesn't shrink from the task of recounting what he calls his subject's "toxic violence" against women.

Brown had a badly fragmented home life during his formative years and was largely neglected by his mother. He was not a good family man during his first marriage, which lasted on paper from 1959 through 1972, and ignored his children from that marriage for much of their lives.

Again and again, Zirin makes the point that the central theme of Brown's life—from the way he played football to his struggle for black empowerment—has been about Brown's view of "manhood."

"Proving his manhood through fatherhood," Zirin explains, "was not nearly as enticing as doing it through sexual conquest."

Almost a decade after their divorce, Sue Jones Brown recalled, "Before we got married, he said there was always going to be other women. He said, 'I'm Jim Brown. I can marry anybody in the world, and there are always going to be other women. Can you deal with that?' I said I could, and I did."

Throughout his adult life, Brown has consistently stated a preference for sexual partners who are considerably younger than he is. At age 53, he wrote in *Out of Bounds* (his second autobiography), "Physically, between a young girl and an old one, there is no contest. I don't like being told what I'm supposed to want. I prefer girls who are young. My lady right now is nineteen." He also referenced his Hollywood home as a place for "creative orgies," acknowledging, "I've had up to eight girls in my room, maybe four on my couch and four on my bed. I might have sex in one night with four or five of them. But only if Jim Junior was feeling exceptional. Some people think that makes me a pervert. I think it makes me lucky."

But Brown's sexual conduct has extended beyond sleeping around.

Under Brown's "man code," Zirin writes, "Women were often his pastime, his distraction, his proving ground, and at times the repository for his frustrations, existing only as extensions of desire for either sex or violence."

In 1965, an 18-year-old woman named Brenda Ayers accused Brown of assault, claiming that he "forced an unnatural sex act" on her. He was tried and acquitted of the charges against him. The following year, Ayers filed a paternity suit. Brown, in Zirin's words, "hired a team of top attorneys that Ayers could not hope to match" and prevailed in court. Twenty-four years later, Brown publicly acknowledged that the child was his.

Also in 1965, an Ohio State coed filed a rape charge against Brown but withdrew the charge before the case came to trial.

In 1968, Brown was alleged to have thrown a 22-year-old model named Eva Bohn-Chin off a hotel balcony in Los Angeles to a concrete walk twenty feet below. The police found blood on the floor and walls of Brown's hotel room. Initially, he was charged with attempted murder. But the charges were dropped when Bohn-Chin refused to testify against him.

In 1971, he was accused of battery by two young women.

In 1985, a schoolteacher named Margot Tiff alleged that Brown beat and raped her when she refused to have sex in a ménage a trois with him and another woman. The district attorney in Los Angeles chose to not prosecute the case.

In 1986 (when Brown was fifty), his then-fiancée, 21-year-old Debra Clark, accused Brown of assaulting her.

Brown married for the second time in 1997 at age 61. Two years later, he was arrested after smashing the window of his 25-year-old wife's car in a fit of rage. He was convicted of vandalism and given the choice of spending six months in prison or accepting a three-part alternative package consisting of (1) four hundred hours of community service or forty hours of cleaning streets, (2) paying $1,700 to a domestic abuse charity, and (3) undergoing counseling for anger management. He chose prison rather than acknowledge that his conduct was related to domestic violence.

That was consistent with Brown's constant denial of the accusations that have been leveled against him by women. But as Zirin observes, "The cases against Brown are extensive. He has often said that he has never been convicted of violence against women, which is true. Yet the cases span the years from 1965 through 1999. It's a remarkable stretch that cannot be written off as just an endless series of law-and-order conspiracies, coincidences, or bad luck. Even without convictions of violence against women, there are enough 911 tapes and testimonials to see that this is not a fantasy created by those trying to destroy him."

There are also Brown's words from a 2014 interview, when he said, "All rejection is difficult to take, and who rejects you more than a fucking woman?"

"The history of accusations of violence against women," Zirin concludes, "has scarred Brown's legacy. Barack Obama—who as president took a particular joy from his regular interaction with black sports heroes of yesteryear—never dialogued with Brown. Donald Trump, however, rolled out the red carpet. In December 2016, the president-elect sat with Brown and former NFL player Ray Lewis [who, in 2000, pled guilty to obstruction of justice in conjunction with the police investigation of a double murder]. Brown left the meeting saying, 'I fell in love with [Trump] because he really talks about helping black people.'"

And now we come to Brown's relationship with Muhammad Ali.

Brown was never a member of the Nation of Islam, but he was comfortable with people who were. On February 25, 1964, hours after Cassius Clay dethroned Sonny Liston, the newly-crowned heavyweight champion sat in a room at a small black hotel called Hampton House with Malcolm X, singer Sam Cooke, and Brown. The four men talked for hours.

Brown later introduced Ali and Herbert Muhammad (Ali's manager and the son of Nation of Islam leader Elijah Muhammad) to Bob Arum. Thereafter, a company called Main Bout Inc was formed to promote Ali's fights. Herbert Muhammad and John Ali (Elijah Muhammad's top aide) controlled fifty percent of the stock. Brown had twenty percent. Closed-circuit guru Mike Malitz had twenty percent, and Arum had ten.

On April 29, 1967, Ali refused induction into the United States Army. Five weeks later, on June 4, Brown hosted a remarkable gathering.

"Ali had the opportunity to make a deal, to go into the service and not see combat," Brown later reminisced. "And Herbert asked me to talk to him about it. I'll tell you the truth. Herbert would not have minded Ali going into the Army because they were starting to make good money together, and I didn't think Herbert was necessarily wrong. If holding that meeting was a bad act, I wouldn't have done it. But when a man makes a decision of that magnitude, he needs friends to help him sort things out. We wanted Ali to understand all the implications of his acts and make sure he was given a choice. So I called some people into Cleveland. John Wooten, Walter Beach, and Sid Williams, from the Browns; Willie Davis, Curtis McClinton, Bill Russell, Kareem Abdul-Jabbar, Bobby Mitchell, Jim Shorter. We met at my office. They were beautiful guys, and some of them thought Ali should go into the service. But he was adamant. He said simply, 'I'm not going because it's against my religion.' And that was that. No one tried to convince him otherwise. We just wanted to discuss it with him, and I thought he showed tremendous courage."

There's an iconic photograph of that gathering. As described by Zirin, "Jim Brown, the greatest runner in NFL history and member of the 1964 champion Cleveland Browns, sits alongside the greatest winner in team sports history, Bill Russell of the Boston Celtics. Next to them is the linchpin of the most dominant team in college basketball history, twenty-year-old Lew Alcindor (later to be known as Kareem Abdul-Jabbar) of the UCLA Bruins. They are surrounded by a collection of black pro athletes. Also at the table is future Cleveland Mayor Carl Stokes. At the center of them all is Muhammad Ali."

Dave Zirin is currently sports editor for *The Nation* and a columnist for *The Progressive*. His writing has long focused on the politics of sports. He researches thoroughly, writes clearly, and thinks creatively.

Jim Brown: Last Man Standing is an honest, informative, and important book that lays bare what Zirin calls "the collision of Brown's greatness and his flaws."

Zirin's book also brought back memories for me of time that I spent talking with Brown. I was researching the book that ultimately became *Muhammad Ali: His Life and Times*. Brown was one of the people I wanted to talk with. Ali's best friend, Howard Bingham, gave me Brown's home telephone number and told Brown to expect my call. I called on the evening of May 11, 1989. Brown said he was busy but we could talk if I called back the following night.

He was true to his word. The next evening, we talked for almost two hours. Our conversation touched on a wide range of subjects: the night Cassius Clay won the heavyweight championship; the formation of Main Bout Inc; the meeting in Cleveland after Ali refused induction; and more.

Brown's thoughts that evening echoed themes that he has been passionate about for his entire life:

* ★ "The nature of the controversy was that white folks could not stand free black folks. White America could not stand to think that a sports hero that it was allowing to make big dollars would embrace something like the Nation of Islam. But this young man had the courage to stand up like no one else and risk, not only his life, but everything else that he had."

* ★ "Ali was a true warrior. It was unbelievable, the courage he had. He wasn't just a championship athlete. He was a champion who fought for his people. He was above sports; he was part of history. The man used his athletic ability as a platform to project himself right up there with world leaders, taking chances that absolutely no one else took, going after things that very few people have the courage to go after. Ali was involved in the Vietnam War. Ali was involved in the struggle for racial equality. The Boston Celtics weren't involved in the 1960s. The Montreal Canadiens, the Green Bay Packers, the New York Yankees; they weren't involved in that. From the standpoint of his ability to perform and his ability to be involved with the world, Ali was the most important sports figure in history. To do what he did, to achieve the pinnacle of

his profession, to fight for freedom for black people, to perform while being ostracized and still be a champion; Jackie Robinson died from that, and Ali was able to prevail.

★ "If you want to see man at his best, take a look at Ali in his prime. When Ali came back from exile, he became the darling of America, which was good for America because it brought black and white together. But the Ali that America ended up loving was not the Ali I loved most. I didn't feel the same about him anymore because the warrior I loved was gone. In a way, he became part of the establishment. And I suppose, in a sense, there's nothing wrong with that, because if you can come to a point where you make all people feel good, maybe that's greater than being a fighter for black people. But I didn't like it."

Fast-forward to April 14, 1991. I was with Ali at a hotel in Philadelphia for a banquet commemorating the twentieth anniversary of the first Ali-Frazier fight. Late that afternoon, I went to the dining room to look around. The hotel staff was setting up. Howard Bingham was there, sitting on the edge of a table, talking with a man who was wearing a tuxedo and a green-black-and-red kufi.

"This is someone you should meet," Howard told me.

Because the man was sitting, I didn't realize how big he was.

"I'm Jim," the man said.

He stood up and extended his hand.

And the realization hit.

"Jim Brown," I blurted out.

"No," he corrected. "Just Jim."

I've thought about that moment many times since then, most notably on June 9, 2015, just before Game 3 of the NBA Championship Finals between the Cleveland Cavaliers and Golden State Warriors.

Dave Zirin sets that scene: "The Cavs are at home in Cleveland after two games in Oakland, attempting to finally remove the 'God hates Cleveland' curse from the city. No Cleveland sports team has won a title since that day in 1964 when the Browns shut out the Baltimore Colts 27–0. The current star of Cleveland, LeBron "King" James, a person so physically imposing he looks like a twenty-first century incarnation of a

Greek god in African skin, took a moment before the start of the game to turn to a man sitting courtside. In front of the raucous packed house and a national television audience, the King bowed."

Jim Brown is now 82 years old. Mundane acts such as turning a doorknob are difficult for him. He walks with the assistance of two canes. But on this day, with both teams on the court just prior to the tip-off for one of the biggest games in Cleveland history, LeBron James turned toward Brown and bowed.

Just Jim.

Congratulations to Dave Zirin on a job well done. He has put us on the road to better understanding this complex formidable man.

Arnold Palmer was a staunch Republican. But there were limits to his party loyalty.

What Would Arnold Palmer Think of Donald Trump Today?

On September 25, 2016, Donald Trump (then the Republican presidential nominee) tweeted, "Really sad news: The great Arnold Palmer, 'the King,' has died. There was no-one like him—a true champion! He will truly be missed."

Many people knew Palmer better than I did. But I knew him. We worked together on a biography of his life a quarter-century ago. It was a nice relationship that became part of my own ongoing life journey. A year later, he asked me collaborate with him again; this time on an essay to commemorate the one hundredth anniversary of the United States Golf Association.

Arnold was politically conservative. He was also widely regarded as a symbol of decency and The Quintessential American. Meanwhile, Trump's fondness for golf is well-known. He crossed paths with Palmer on multiple occasions and they co-hosted the opening of the Arnold Palmer Villa at the Trump National Doral Miami golf resort in 2015.

I asked myself recently: What would Arnold Palmer think of Donald Trump today?

There was a time when playing golf with Palmer was as much a part of being president as inviting Billy Graham to the White House. The first president Arnold met was Dwight Eisenhower, who later became a family friend. They were introduced at the Laurel Valley Country Club in Ligonier, Pennsylvania, five months after Palmer's breakthrough triumph at the 1958 Masters in Augusta. Arnold was so quiet and unpretentious that Eisenhower didn't know who he was.

In the years that followed, the two men developed a fondness akin to a father-son relationship. But on October 2, 1958, the chagrined President wrote:

Dear Mr. Palmer,

Because of the general confusion the other day, I failed to realize when Ben Fairless [Chairman of the Board of U.S. Steel] introduced us that you were the Arnold Palmer of 1958 Masters fame. I hope you will forgive my lack of reaction and accept, even this belatedly, my warm congratulations on your splendid victory.

Ben suggests that some time we might have an opportunity to play at Augusta. This I should very much like though, judging from the brand of golf I have recently been displaying, I would be more than embarrassed.

Sincerely,
Dwight D. Eisenhower

In later years, one of Palmer's most prized possessions was a painting given to him at a surprise birthday party in 1966 by the artist, Dwight Eisenhower. It's a pastoral scene that graced the living room in the Palmer home in Latrobe, Pennsylvania, for years.

Professional golfers are a fairly conservative lot. A survey published in the October 2018 issue of *Golf* magazine asked PGA Tour players whether they had voted for Donald Trump in the 2016 presidential election. 56% said "Yes," 14% didn't bother to vote, and 18% were ineligible to vote. Only 12% answered "No."

Asked if they would vote for Trump if he ran again in 2020, 42% said "Yes" and 14% were undecided. 19% said that they would be ineligible to vote, and 5% said that they wouldn't vote. 20% said "No."

Palmer was comfortable in that political environment.

"My father was a Democrat," Arnold told me during one of our conversations. "He thought Franklin Roosevelt hung the moon, but I'm the opposite. I think you solve problems through family and personal charity. The less that big government and big-name outsiders get involved, the better it is for us all."

"I have strong opinions," Arnold elaborated. "But I've made a conscious decision not to make a big issue of them publicly. I voice my opinions to my friends and family, generally in a conservative way. There are times when I'm tempted to be more outspoken. But usually

I think about it for a day or two and pull in because I don't want to be like a lot of people who I hear voicing opinions publicly. So when I'm outraged about something, politically or whatever, I express myself in the office and at home. Then I hear from the people who've heard me. And it's rare that I get a hundred percent agreement on what I've said, so I drop it."

While writing *Arnold Palmer: A Personal Journey*, I spent time with Arnold in Latrobe and at the Bay Hill Club & Lodge in Orlando, Florida, where he maintained a winter home. Each morning, we'd sit in his office. I'd turn on my tape recorder and we'd talk. Then Arnold would have a bowl of soup and go out to play eighteen holes of golf. I'm not a golfer, but I'd walk the course with him.

One morning at Bay Hill, I asked Palmer to critique the golf game of each president he'd played with.

"General Eisenhower was certainly a better player than the average American who played golf," Arnold told me. "He hit the ball pretty well, but the strongest part of his game was his desire. He had other hobbies, but I don't think any of them meant as much to him as golf. Richard Nixon wasn't really a golfer. Gerald Ford had an eighteen handicap and deserved every bit of it. But he hit the ball hard and at times played very well. Ford's problem was, he had the yips putting."

Palmer also called Ford "more of an Ohio State guy." Ford, of course, had attended college at Michigan, but it wasn't hard to figure out what Arnold meant. His arch-rival, Jack Nicklaus, had gone to Ohio State.

The critique of presidential golf games continued. Then Arnold had a bowl of soup and went out to play golf. I walked with him.

Palmer was 63 years old at the time. He played brilliantly that day. Through twelve holes, he was four strokes under par on the course where the Bay Hill Invitational (now known as the Arnold Palmer Invitational) would be played the following week.

Arnold's drive off the thirteenth-tee split the fairway. Then, as we walked two hundred yards toward his ball, I asked about the man who'd been elected president of the United States one month earlier.

"Apropos of what we were talking about this morning, would you like to play golf with Bill Clinton?"

Six months later, Palmer and Clinton would, in fact, play golf together. And Arnold would tell me, "Bill Clinton has the potential to be a very good golfer. He putts the ball very well. He's strong and has a keen interest in the game. His swing is pretty good and he has a lot of determination to be a good player."

But that was in the future. On this particular day, Arnold answered, "I suppose so. I'd be interested in seeing what kind of game he played and what he was like as a person. Of course, if you want my opinion, I don't think Bill Clinton cares one bit about the average person. I think Bill Clinton is nothing but a phony. Bill Clinton . . ."

Arnold was getting madder and madder.

Then he hit his next shot into the pond that fronted the thirteenth green.

"Uh oh," I told myself. "I've got a big problem."

Arnold turned toward me with a look that was a combination of grimace, glare, and forced smile.

"Why did I lose my concentration like that?" he asked rhetorically.

Then he took a penalty drop and wound up with a double-bogey six. Later, he rallied to finish the round with a four-under-par 68.

So . . . That brings us to Palmer and Donald Trump.

It would presumptuous for me to speculate regarding what Palmer would think about the man who currently occupies the White House. So I asked someone who knew Arnold as well as anyone still alive: his older daughter, Peg.

"My dad was a complicated person," Peg told me when I asked the question last week. "He grew up poor and became rich. He was a Goldwater Republican and believed in the Republican party. He and I learned not to discuss politics together. We saw things very differently, and there was no sense in fighting about it. Apart from our general political differences, he felt I didn't understand how hard it had been for him to make his fortune and the compromises he'd had to make to be successful and stay successful, not just in golf but in the business world. It wasn't as easy as it looked."

As for Trump, Peg recalled, "My dad had dealings with him over the years at some charity fundraisers and a few other events that had to do with Trump's golf courses. My dad cherished golf and he appreciated Trump's support for the game. Trump looked up to my dad, so I suspect he was on his best behavior when they were together. But in the campaign, my dad saw a different side of him."

"My dad didn't like people who act like they're better than other people," Peg continued. "He didn't like it when people were nasty and rude. He didn't like it when someone was disrespectful to someone else. My dad had no patience for people who demean other people in public. He had no patience for people who are dishonest and cheat. My dad was disciplined. He wanted to be a good role model. He was appalled by Trump's lack of civility and what he began to see as Trump's lack of character."

"One moment stands out in my mind," Peg recounted. "My dad and I were at home in Latrobe. He died in September, so this was before the election. The television was on. Trump was talking. And my dad made a sound of disgust—like 'uck' or 'ugg'—like he couldn't believe the arrogance and crudeness of this man who was the nominee of the political party that he believed in. Then he said, 'He's not as smart as we thought he was,' and walked out of the room. What would my dad think of Donald Trump today? I think he'd cringe."

William Wordsworth wrote, "The Child is father of the Man." My love of reading began when I was young.

A Boy Learns to Love Books

When I was eight years old, there was a book fair in the library at Murray Avenue Elementary School. My parents gave me money to buy a book. An enthusiastic baseball fan, I came home with a copy of *Mystery at the Ball Park*.

I didn't know it, but my life was about to change.

Mystery at the Ball Park was the first of six "Mel Martin baseball stories" written by John R. Cooper and published between 1947 and 1953. Each of the books combined baseball with amateur detective work. Subsequent titles in the series included *The Southpaw's Secret, The Phantom Homer, First Base Jinx, The Fighting Shortstop*, and *The College League Mystery*.

The books were originally published in hardcover. I read them all in paperback. They were the first books that I recall reading on my own initiative and marked the start of reading on my own for pleasure. They led me from *The Taxi That Hurried* and *Horton Hatches the Egg* to young adult reading.

A year or two later, I turned to Chip Hilton.

The Chip Hilton series includes 23 books written by Clair Bee that were published between 1948 and 1966. Bee died in 1983 at age 87. A twenty-fourth book based on a partial manuscript he left behind was published in 2002.

In the early Chip Hilton books, Chip stars in baseball, football, and basketball for Valley Falls High School. Then he goes to college. One of the books—*Hoop Crazy*, published in 1950—was forward-looking for its time in that it centered on the issue of a black player who wants to join the school's all-white basketball team.

An article written by Jack McCallum for *Sports Illustrated* in 1980 celebrated Chip Hilton with the observation, "The Hilton series was the last of its kind, the final representative of what might be called the Frank

Merriwell genre. Gilbert Patten began writing Merriwell stories in 1896 for a publisher of dime novels and nickel magazines. During the first twenty years of [the twentieth] century, his stories were more widely read than any others for boys, and 'Merriwell finish' entered the language as a stock description for a dramatic ending to a game."

I have a clear recollection of giving an oral book report on *Pitchers' Duel* (the sixth book in the Chip Hilton series) to my class in sixth grade.

Here I should add that Chip Hilton was so popular that the NCAA created and, from 1997 through 2011, gave out a "Chip Hilton Player of the Year Award" to the Division I men's basketball player who best demonstrated outstanding personal character on and off the court. The first recipient of the award was Tim Duncan. Think about that for a moment. A major award named after—not John Wooden, Vince Lombardi, or Walter Payton, but—a literary creation.

Recently, I decided to revisit Mel Martin and Chip Hilton. As a first step, I thought I should learn a bit about the authors.

Surprise! There was no "John R. Cooper." That author credit was one of many pseudonyms used by Andrew Svenson, who wrote the first two books in the Mel Martin series and then turned writing duties over to a successor. The reason for Svenson's departure was that he received an offer from the Stratemeyer Syndicate (which packaged the Hardy Boys, Nancy Drew, and Bobbsey Twins) to become one of several authors writing Hardy Boys mysteries under the pen-name Franklin W. Dixon. Svenson also wrote all of the books in *The Happy Hollisters* series under the pseudonym Jerry West.

I still have my original copy *of Mystery at the Ball Park*. When I took it off a shelf and opened the brittle yellowing pages, I was surprised by its length: 208 pages. I began to read.

Mel Martin is sixteen years old and a junior at Westwood High School, located in a little town situated along a peaceful river. Mel's father died several years earlier, so Mel and his younger brother live with their mother and paternal grandmother. Robbie Smith, Mel's uncle, was a big-league pitcher in his younger days and is now a sport-ing goods salesman.

Mel is Westwood High School's best pitcher. Other characters include the Wright twins (first baseman Lefty Wright and catcher Righty Wright), outfielder Hobart "Speed" Ball, and coach Frederick "Pop" Korn.

As the plot unfolds, Coach Korn is ill with an undisclosed ailment. A mystery man named Mister McCloud filters in and out of the story and seems like a really bad guy. Mister McCloud has a sallow complexion and a scar that cuts across his brow above unfriendly close-set eyes. There's another bad guy who's "a greasy looking fellow with a big bulb-like nose." Then Coach Korn is hospitalized, and Mr. Wilbur (the school principal) announces that the mysterious Mr. McCloud will coach the team.

McCloud is openly hostile toward Mel and seeks to undermine the team through blatantly poor strategic decisions. At one point, Mel gets an anonymous threatening telephone call as he seeks to unravel the mystery of what turns out to be a series of home robberies and a real estate swindle. The call is particularly troubling since, soon after Mel receives it, he and his dog are knocked unconscious by a club-wielding thug. The book's climactic moment comes in the championship game with Westwood trailing 4-to-3 with two outs in the bottom of the eighth inning, a man on base, and Mel Martin at the plate.

"He rubbed his sweaty hands with dust and looked toward the pitcher," Svenson a/k/a Cooper wrote. "The deep shadow from his cap covered the intense expression on his face. He waited out the pitches. Two balls and then a strike. The next pitch came perfectly. The ball spun fast but the curve broke too late. Mel lashed out. When the bat connected, the boy snapped with his wrists and followed through with tremendous power. Over the leftfield wall sailed the ball."

Unlike Svenson, Clair Bee wrote under his own name. And for good reason. From 1931 through 1951, Bee was head basketball coach at Long Island University. During that time, his teams won two National Invitational Tournament championships (at a time when the NIT was a big deal) and once reeled off 43 victories in a row. He later coached the Baltimore Bullets in the fledgling National Basketball Association for two seasons.

The Chip Hilton books are written at a more sophisticated level than the Mel Martin series. In *Pitchers' Duel*, William "Chip" Hilton is the star pitcher and best hitter for Valley Falls High School. Mary Hilton is Chip's mother. Chip's father died a long time ago under circumstances that I assume were explained earlier in the series (this is book #7).

Chip and first baseman Biggie Cohen have big league potential. Coach Hank Rockwell is a wise steadying influence, but unscrupulous forces are trying to force him out of his job. The team also includes Chip's best friends: shortstop Speed Morris, catcher Soapy Smith, and outfielder Red Schwartz. Mayor Mark Condon, chief of police Boiler Cowles, and Sheriff Early Birks are corrupt local politicians. Peck Weaver and Buck Adams are illicit gamblers in league with the corrupt politicians. Muddy Waters is an ill-intentioned sportswriter for the local newspaper and frequently attacks both Chip and Coach Rockwell in his columns.

Led by Hilton, the Big Reds of Valley High School battle back from mid-season adversity to qualify for the state championship tournament. Then, shortly before the championship game, Chip signs an autograph for a man who says it's for his sick son. However, in reality, the folded-over piece of paper Chip has signed is a contract that purports to bind him to a minor league baseball team. It's a dastardly plot concocted by the gamblers to render Chip ineligible for the big game.

Chip misses the first 8–½ innings of the championship game while things are being sorted out. During that time, Valley Falls falls behind by seven runs but rallies with four runs in the top of the ninth to tie the score at nine runs apiece. Salem High loads the bases in the bottom of the ninth. There are two outs with a 3-balls-2-strikes count on the batter when the newly-vindicated Chip races onto the field, takes over on the mound, and picks the runner off second base to send the game into extra innings.

Now the pitchers' duel begins. Neither team scores again through the eighteenth inning. Then, in the bottom of the nineteenth, a wind-blown pop-up puts a Salem runner on third base. But that quirk of fate is nothing compared to the tragedy that follows.

Spoiler Alert: One of the things that separated Chip Hilton from most young-adult literary sports stars of his era was that Chip's team sometimes lost the big game. With a runner on third, Salem opts for a squeeze play that succeeds when the bunt goes into foul territory, hits a pebble, careens crazily into fair territory, and spins slowly to a stop allowing the winning run to score.

After the game, Coach Rockwell consoles his team with the words, "It's all right, kids. You were great. You can't win all the time. Someone has to lose. And since it had to be us, let's be good sports about it and take it with our heads and our chins up. Right now, I want to shake hands with every one of you. I'm proud to have been your coach."

And Chip's mother tells him, "It was just a game, Chip. One of many you've been through and one of many more you'll go through when you go to college. You can't expect to win all the time. The other team likes to win a championship too once in a while."

In truth, there were times when I got a bit bored rereading *Mystery at the Ball Park* and *Pitchers' Duel*. Some passions of our youth—like Hostess Sno Balls and Twinkies—seem less attractive as we age. After finishing the books, I had no desire to immerse myself in all of the other Mel Martin and Chip Hilton epics as I'd done decades ago. What was once high drama seems simplistic to me now.

But as I reread *Mystery at the Ball Park* and *Pitchers' Duel*, literary characters who had been lost for decades emerged from the shadows of my mind. Plot twists brought back fond memories as I read them. And I gave thanks to Andrew Svenson and Clair Bee for bringing Mel Martin and Chip Hilton into my life and inspiring a young boy's love of reading.

Issues and Answers

Hamilton Nolan has written, "Boxing is an ongoing skirmish between petty little businessmen willing to do anything to protect their fiefdoms." In 2018, the skirmishes were between big businessmen.

The New Order and the Future of Boxing

Part One

The September 27, 2018, announcement from HBO Sports that the network will discontinue live boxing programming at the close of this year marks the end of an era.

Gillette's fabled *Friday Night Fights* were on television for a little more than a decade. HBO's boxing programming spanned 45 years.

No one did it as well as HBO when HBO Boxing was at its best. Given the difficulty in making truly big fights today, it's unlikely that anyone will do it as well in the near future either.

There was a time when HBO—as its slogan heralded—was "the heart and soul of boxing." It served as a de facto commissioner for the sport and was the most powerful force in the sweet science. HBO made the mega-fights that fans wanted to see happen. At its best, it was wired into the brain of virtually every boxing fan in America.

At the turn of the millennium, the annual budget for HBO Sports was just under $150 million. Ninety million of that was allocated to boxing. Adjusted for inflation, $150 million in 2000 would equal $225 million today. In recent years, due to budget cuts, HBO Sports has spent roughly ten percent of that amount on license fees for fights.

Boxing was a key factor in building HBO's subscriber base in the 1980s and 1990s. But sports was never HBO's core product. By and large, viewers subscribed to the network for movies and other scripted entertainment.

HBO built its reputation on unique programming. Shows like *The Sopranos, Sex and the City*, and *Game of Thrones* went where no network had gone before. So did HBO's once-innovative brand of boxing coverage. But as HBO Sports executive vice president Peter Nelson observed this week, there's very little that's unique about boxing programming on any network today. In some cases, it's very good. But it's no longer unique.

Also, the world of boxing no longer lends itself to the level of excellence that HBO Sports achieved in the past. Boxing's current economic model works against giving the public competitive fights at the elite level. The days when superstars like Ray Leonard, Marvin Hagler, Thomas Hearns, and Roberto Duran went in tough fight after fight against one another are gone. The fights that boxing fans most want to see simply don't happen anymore. There's more boxing on television and streaming video today than ever. But very few of these fights will be remembered as legendary nights years from now.

We're living in an age of vertical integration and corporate consolidation. The path to power in today's economy lies through the merger of powerful economic interests.

The value of a sports entity as a business today is driven in large part by its television contract. ESPN closed a five-year deal this past May that will pay $1.5 billion to UFC over a five-year period beginning in January 2019. In the same stratospheric environment, NBC will pay $265 million a year for five years to WWE for Raw. Fox will pay WWE $205 million a year for five years for Smackdown. That's a total of $2.34 billion for WWE.

Content providers in boxing have long partnered with delivery systems. In the early years of ESPN (the delivery system), Top Rank was the network's exclusive provider of boxing content. To acquire the rights to televise Mike Tyson's fights, Showtime (the delivery system) agreed to buy boxing matches exclusively from Don King (the content provider).

The trend in media today is toward the consolidation of content providers and the deliverers of content. In boxing, content providers (e.g. Top Rank, Premier Boxing Champions, and Matchroom) are partnering with delivery systems (ESPN, Showtime/Fox, and DAZN).

These partnerships give the content providers (promoters) significant leverage in pursuing fighters because they guarantee that the promoters will have television dates to showcase fighters and the money to sign them.

There are two dominant alliances in boxing in the United States today: (1) ESPN-Top Rank and (2) PBS-Showtime-Fox. DAZN-Matchroom is bidding to become the third.

There's more money in boxing now than ever before, and much of it is tied to streaming video. In recent years, some small free-of-charge cards and niche pay-per-view fights that barely registered with boxing fans were distributed by streaming video. Streaming video was also a source of ancillary income for a handful of major pay-per-view events.

Now streaming video is a major component of ESPN's business plan. It's the sole means of distribution for all content on DAZN. PBC's alliance with Showtime and Fox relies heavily on more traditional delivery systems. But streaming video plays a role in PBC shoulder programming and is expected to rise in importance in the years ahead.

Relatively few boxing fans paid attention to streaming video in the past. They're paying attention now. It's ushering in a new era for the sweet science and, most likely, for all sports.

Each of the major alliances on the boxing scene has its own narrative. Let's start with ESPN and Top Rank.

On August 9, 2017, the Walt Disney Company unveiled plans for a direct-to-consumer ESPN subscription streaming video service to be called ESPN+. Thereafter, ESPN entered into an exclusive four-year contract with Top Rank to provide boxing content for various ESPN platforms including ESPN+.

ESPN+ is priced at $4.99 a month and debuted in April of this year. Four months later, ESPN and Top Rank announced that their 2017 contract had been replaced by a new agreement that runs through August 2025. This deal provides for 54 live boxing cards annually in addition to other boxing-related programming. The 54 live boxing cards will be broken down as follows: 18 on ESPN, 12 on ESPN+, and 24 "premium international events" on ESPN+. Undercard coverage for each event will be streamed on ESPN+.

Top Rank is sitting pretty. Manny Pacquiao carried the promotional company through what otherwise would have been some lean years. Now Top Rank has the weight of ESPN behind it. And it's no longer dependent on network programmers for dates. It can put individual fighters on the air as often as it likes.

Top Rank has an annual budget from ESPN. Top Rank president Todd duBoef says, "We'll give fans a range of fights from small fights to championship bouts on both ESPN and ESPN+. The content on one platform will not be better than the other. We'll balance the platforms."

Top Rank's boxing programming will also air on ESPN Deportes. Pay-per-view telecasts for mega-fights are likely down the road. And ABC (another Disney entity) could be drawn into the mix.

The ESPN deal has enabled Top Rank to move aggressively in the marketplace. On August 6, 2018, it announced that it had signed Terence Crawford to a new multi-year contract. It has put large numbers on the table to acquire rights to fights from other promoters such as the upcoming rematch between Eleider Alvarez and Sergey Kovalev. On September 11, Top Rank announced a multi-year licensing agreement with Frank Warren's Queensberry Promotions.

Premier Boxing Champions tried to reposition boxing to attract mainstream sports fans but has fallen short of expectations to date. Top Rank and ESPN are better positioned to succeed in this quest.

Combat sports is only a small part of what ESPN and ESPN+ offer. The network is the most powerful sports platform in the world and a direct pipeline to every sports fan in America. Top Rank's venture with ESPN will make boxing part of the daily conversation on ESPN. It will put boxing on multiple platforms that have the attention of general sports fans and use these platforms to broaden boxing's fan base while, at the same time, reaching those already in the choir.

In that regard, duBoef says, "We want a model for boxing that's more like the model for other live sports. We'll have enough boxing content in addition to live fights to keep the lights on all the time. That's what other major sports do, and that's what we should do in boxing."

The classic shoulder programming for boxing was HBO's *24/7*, which was designed to engender pay-per-view buys for big fights but became a viewing destination in its own right. Top Rank and ESPN are banking on the belief that they can have similar success including programming that revolves around the rebroadcast of classic fights. Very few people turn on the television to watch a rebroadcast of an old Super Bowl in its entirety. But they will watch historic encounters like Ali-Frazier III, Leonard-Duran I, and Hagler-Hearns.

ESPN sees streaming video as an important part of its business model for the future and a way to recapture some of the cord-cutters who have left the network in recent years. If it takes five or ten years for ESPN+ to become profitable, so be it.

Part Two

On May 10, 2018, Matchroom Boxing and Perform Group announced what was touted as a one-billion-dollar, eight-year joint venture.

Perform Group owns DAZN, an over-the-top subscription streaming video service that has launched sports-dedicated sites in Germany, Austria, Switzerland, Japan, and Canada. The Matchroom-Perform agreement calls for Matchroom to stage sixteen fight cards annually for eight years in the United States. DAZN will be the exclusive distributor in the United States for these events and also for twenty-two Matchroom "fight nights" that originate in the United Kingdom.

Of the sixteen shows that originate in the United States, Matchroom promises that four will be what it calls "gigantic events" or "tent-pole shows" while the other twelve will be "premium cable quality."

Sky-TV has rights to televise the fights in the United Kingdom.

Eddie Hearn (managing director of Matchroom Boxing) and Simon Denyer (CEO of Perform Group) announced the joint venture at a press conference in New York. Former ESPN president John Skipper, who joined Perform Group as executive chairman on May 7, 2018, was also in attendance.

One billion dollars spread over eight years equals $125 million a year. That led Hearn to proclaim, "We have bigger rights fees than HBO and Showtime put together."

Hearn also compared his new venture to Al Haymon's launch of Premier Boxing Champions three years ago with the observation, "They didn't have a platform; they bought airtime. They had no broadcaster paying them money. They had an investment group that gave them money to acquire fighters, but they didn't make progress with the money. We have a platform behind us. We have rights fees. We don't have an amount of money to build a brand to sign fighters. We have rights fees to deliver shows."

There was—and still is—a widespread belief that only the first two years of the Matchroom-DAZN contract are guaranteed and that the announced numbers are an exaggeration. Still, Hearn was far from shy in saying, "We're here to change the game and elevate boxing to a new level for fight fans in America. We can televise the fights on the days we want at the time we want. We don't have to come on at ten o'clock after a movie. We have the dates, the money, and the platform. We were dangerous without this. But with this money and this platform, omigod!"

Two months later, on July 17, Hearn met again with the media. This time, there were questions regarding what appeared to be a thin roster of American fighters. Addressing this issue, Hearn declared, "We live in a world where people say, 'Ah, he didn't get Charlo or Spence.' Calm down. We've just had seven or eight weeks. We're getting so much resistance from advisers and networks, which is really good news because it means they're concerned. We're out there actively talking to Mikey Garcia, talking to the Charlos. We can pay them more money than other promoters. There are contracts out with another dozen fighters. We've signed three world champions [Maurice Hooker, Daniel Roman, and former champion Jesse Vargas]. We've signed a number one middleweight in Demetrius Andrade. We've signed a load of really good amateurs. I'm really pleased with the start. We're going to cause nightmares. We are resilient. We are absolutely ruthless. We won't stop. And we've got a team of people behind us who have a bottomless pit of money who will back us to the heavens. We've got eight years to make it work."

In many respects, the DAZN–Matchroom venture is personality driven. That personality is Eddie Hearn. He recruits fighters, engages the media, and sells to the public. His team in the United States includes, inter alia, director of boxing Frank Smith (widely regarded as one of the most capable young guns in boxing today), head of media Anthony Leaver (efficient and popular with the media), and the head of operations for Matchroom USA, Josh Roy, who handles logistics well.

In July, the incomparable Michael Buffer signed a two-year exclusive agreement to serve as ring announcer for Matchroom's fights worldwide and forego announcing for other promoters. Buffer is slated to work all of Matchroom's shows that originate in the United States and most of its shows that originate in Europe.

Meanwhile, DAZN is positioning itself as a combat sports destination in the United States and has already moved beyond Matchroom in acquiring boxing content. On July 2, 2018, it announced that it would televise all seven fights in each of the three weight divisions in season two of the World Boxing Super Series. It will also showcase mixed martial arts bouts promoted by Bellator and Combate Americas.

The list of European-based boxers with promotional ties to Matchroom includes Anthony Joshua, Oleksandr Usyk, Dillian Whyte, Dereck Chisora, Kell Brook, Amir Khan, Katie Taylor, and popular local fighters like Tony Bellew, Conor Benn, Ricky Burns, Ryan Burnett, Anthony Crolla, Callum Johnson, Gavin McDonnell, Scott Quigg, and Callum Smith. But Matchroom USA's roster is thin, and it's having difficulty signing world-class American fighters for its DAZN venture.

One problem Hearn has had in signing American fighters is that all world-class boxers like to think of themselves as potential pay-per-view attractions. Hearn has said that DAZN will eschew pay-per-view fights. Also, to date, Matchroom USA has reportedly been reluctant to enter into contracts with American fighters that last for more than two years.

DAZN costs $9.99 a month for up to three devices. It launched in the United States on September 10, 2018, and distributed its first fight card on September 22 when Anthony Joshua defended his WBA, IBF, and WBO belts against Alexander Povetkin.

Joshua is a huge star in the United Kingdom and a power center unto himself, which in part is a tribute to Hearn's promotional skill. In four fights over the past seventeen months, Joshua has put 320,000 fans in seats and engendered more than three million pay-per-view buys in the UK. Anyone who asks why Perform Group chose to invest as heavily as it has with Matchroom should consider this: If you go to an Anthony Joshua fight and are engulfed by eighty thousand screaming fans, you'll be impressed.

Hearn says that he's trying to duplicate in the United States what he has done successfully in England. But what works in England won't necessarily work in America. The social media strategy that sparks ticket sales for boxing in the UK hasn't been as effective to date on this side of the Atlantic.

One area where Matchroom says it's determined to change the paradigm for boxing in the United States is in improving the experience for fans who are on site. This also matters to DAZN because onsite enthusiasm translates into a more entertaining experience for viewers at home. The experience of watching Joshua knock out Wladimir Klitschko on television was enhanced by the fact that it happened in front of 90,000 screaming partisans.

However, the two Matchroom USA fight cards currently slated for DAZN are unlikely to engender on-site pandemonium. The first will take place in Chicago on October 6 and features four fights: Artur Beterebiev vs. Callum Johnson, Jessie Vargas vs. Thomas Dulorme, Daniel Roman vs. Gavin McDowell, and Jarrell Miller vs. Tomasz Adamek. Beterbiev, Vargas, Roman, and Miller are expected to win. Miller-Adamek is widely regarded as a travesty.

Adamek is just shy of 42 years old. He has life-style issues, is eighty pounds lighter than Miller, and was knocked out two years ago by Eric Molina. He also has a loss to Artur Szpilka on his record. If Matchroom needs Tomasz to sell tickets to Chicago's Polish-American community, he should be on the card against someone other than Miller. Expectations for the fight are so low that, if it turns out to be competitive, Jarrell will be devalued.

Two weeks later—on October 20—Matchroom's second American-based fight night on DAZN is scheduled to showcase IBF 160-pound beltholder Billy Joe Saunders against Demetrius Andrade. Saunders is promoted by Frank Warren, but the fight went to a purse bid which Hearn won. Katie Taylor vs. Cindy Serrano, Scott Quigg vs. TBA, and Tevin Farmer vs. James Tennyson will also be on the card.

Earlier this month, the *Daily Mail* posted a video that showed Saunders promising a woman 150 pounds (currency, not weight) worth of crack if she performed a sex act on one of his friends and punched an innocent passerby. The punch was captured on video. The sex act was not.

Then, on September 27, it was revealed that a recent test for performance enhancing drugs administered to Saunders by VADA came back positive for oxilofrine (a banned stimulant). It's unknown at the present time whether Saunders-Andrade will proceed as planned.

Meanwhile, Matchroom's signing of Farmer has raised eyebrows. Tevin began his career on a tenuous note with four losses and a draw in his first twelve fights. He has been unbeaten since then and, on August 3, 2018, won the vacant IBF 130-pound title by decisioning the very beatable Billy Dib. But there are many fighters who are more exciting to watch than Tevin and would be favored to beat him. One can argue that collecting belts will enable Matchroom to attract quality fighters who want to fight for these belts. But at some point, this pursuit has to translate into entertaining fights.

Farmer-Tennyson might be an area where the interests of Matchroom and DAZN don't fully coincide. Hearn has signed Farmer to a four-fight deal potentially worth $2,000,000 plus what Matchroom pays to Farmer's promoter, Lou DiBella. That's well above market value.

Tennyson is from Northern Ireland and has fashioned a 22–2 (18 KOs) record against suspect competition. One of his losses was a second-round knockout defeat at the hands of a fighter with 2 wins in 71 fights. Signing Farmer might eventually get Matchroom another belt for one of its UK fighters and boost its ratings on Sky-TV. But how much would that benefit DAZN?

There are still big names that Matchroom might lure to DAZN. Canelo Alvarez, Gennady Golovkin, Mikey Garcia, and Manny Pacquiao come to mind, although Pacquiao now speaks more to boxing's past than its future.

The larger question facing Matchroom and DAZN today is the nature of the platform.

The key to Top Rank's deal with ESPN is the platform. ESPN+ has the entire ESPN empire to advance its boxing franchise. It can push fights and fighters into the consciousness of sports fans across America.

Fox and Showtime (whose relationship with PBC will be explored in Part Three of this series) have built-in sports marketing machines. FOX is a major broadcast network. Showtime has permeated the boxing market.

DAZN can't equal this level of marketing and promotion. It's an over-the-top streaming video service that relatively few people in America are aware of. And because DAZN is largely unknown at present, fighters who appear on DAZN risk becoming close to invisible insofar as most sports fans in the United States are concerned. How can Matchroom USA build fighters as commercial attractions if virtually no one sees them?

Or phrased differently; if the same content that Top Rank is putting on ESPN now was on DAZN, that content would cause less of a stir than it does on ESPN. ESPN is reaching out to the broadest audience possible and hoping to convert casual sports fans to boxing. DAZN is reaching out to hardcore combat sports fans.

That said; it's important to remember that the Matchroom-DAZN alliance is only four months old. They're just starting. They need time to build a brand. A crash program won't do it. As Wernher von Braun (an early architect of America's space program) observed, "Crash programs fail because they are based on the theory that, with nine women pregnant, you can get a baby in a month."

The key questions are: How many subscribers will DAZN attract? And what programming will attract them? At some point, DAZN could add more supplemental boxing programming (as it has already done with the World Boxing Super Series). It could invest heavily in non-combat sports, particularly as current license-fee agreements between television networks and various leagues expire. For now, the destinies of DAZN and Matchroom are linked. But they're two separate entities. Each is capable of surviving without the other.

Can DAZN build a successful platform in the United States? Who knows? Twenty years ago, virtually no one had heard of Netflix.

Part Three

Top Rank and Matchroom each have one basic platform in the United States. Premier Boxing Champions started with seven (Showtime, CBS, NBC, ESPN, Fox, Bounce, Spike) and will have at least two for the foreseeable future.

On August 30, 2018, Showtime announced a three-year agreement with PBC that calls for monthly events to be televised live on Showtime with additional fights to be presented by Showtime Sports on other platforms.

On September 5, Fox Sports announced a four-year agreement with PBC. This deal includes ten prime-time "marquee fight nights" annually on Fox and twelve fight nights each year on FS1 and Fox Deportes. These fights will also be streamed live on the Fox Sports app, and there will be ancillary programming to spur interest in PBC fights and boxing. Pay-per-view telecasts are likely.

PBC's original investors weren't investing to build an over-the-top streaming video platform. They were investing to build a promotional company. And make no mistake about it; PBC is a promoter. The Fox deal, which calls for the payment of significant license fees rather than a time buy, marks the turn of a corner for PBC. Showtime, of course, has paid license fees to PBC from the start.

PBC's investors appear to have lost hundreds of millions of dollars. It's unlikely that they'll get the bulk of this money back, let alone see a profit on their investment, anytime soon—if ever. Also, PBC's plan to dominate professional boxing no longer seems viable. The question now is, where does PBC go from here?

Al Haymon lured many of PBC's original investors into the fold with a narrative that included developing PBC fighters to Floyd Mayweather's level as pay-per-view attractions. So far, that hasn't happened.

Errol Spence, the fighter who many think could be Mayweather's successor, is largely unknown. Deontay Wilder will take a step forward if he beats Tyson Fury on December 1. But Fury (who's promoted by Frank Warren) has more to gain by beating Wilder than Wilder has by beating Fury. And as long as Anthony Joshua remains undefeated, he's likely to be a more valuable commercial property than either of them.

It should also be noted that conflicts of interest have been built into PBC's business model from the start. Al Haymon has moved back and forth between trying to get as much money as possible for his fighters (his manager-advisor hat) and trying to maximize profits for the promotional side of his many companies (his promoter hat). Now we'll see a different kind of conflict as Showtime and Fox vie for PBC's best content.

The supervening question for boxing fans is whether boxing's new order and all of the recent activity at ESPN, Top Rank, DAZN, Matchroom, Showtime, Fox, and PBC will be good or bad for boxing.

HBO's departure from the live boxing scene won't have the impact it would have had a dozen years ago. Many of today's best fighters were introduced to a national audience by HBO. But the network was no longer the force in the sweet science that it once was.

ESPN, DAZN, and Fox are bringing new money into the system and creating new financial opportunities for fighters. ESPN+ announced on September 20 that, after five months of operation, it has more than one million paying subscribers.

But there's cause for concern. Historically, when promoters have had an output deal with a network, the quality of fights they deliver has diminished over time. That's because the network has given away its biggest bargaining chip: the date.

The bifurcation of boxing into separate "leagues" also poses chal-
lenges to giving boxing fans the fights that they want to see. At present, no
one promoter has a monopoly on boxing's most prominent fighters. Vasyl
Lomachenko and Terence Crawford are with Top Rank. Errol Spence,
Deontay Wilder, Keith Thurman, Shawn Porter, and the Charlos are with
PBC. Matchroom has Anthony Joshua, Danny Jacobs, and Oleksandr
Usyk. That leaves Canelo Alvarez, Gennady Golovkin, Mikey Garcia,
Manny Pacquiao, Tyson Fury, and Dmitry Bivol unattached for the time
being or with other promoters.

There's more boxing available in the United States on television and
streaming video now than ever before. Ideally, this would lead to competition among fighters and promoters to put on the best fights possible.
But early signs are that this won't happen. Instead, promoters are likely
to build their own empires and fighters will go in as soft as possible in a
quest for belts that increase marketability. We'll see developmental fights,
stay-busy fights, sanctioning-body mandatory fights, and match-ups dictated by which belts are available rather than what looks to be a good
fight. To a great degree, promoters with output deals are likely to keep
their most valuable assets out of harm's way. Each promoter will have its
own niche in a niche sport.

Boxing owes its place in sports lore to fights between great fighters.
Match-ups like Dempsey-Tunney, Louis-Schmeling, Marciano-Walcott,
Ali-Frazier, Robinson-LaMotta, Leonard-Duran, and Hagler-Hearns
have linked their participants forever in history's eye.

In the near future, we can expect fewer historic fights. When it comes
to making big fights that truly matter, not only isn't everyone in boxing
on the same page today, they're not even reading the same book.

Sports are satisfying because of the belief that each team or individual who deserves to compete for the ultimate prize in a given sport has
the opportunity to do so. If boxing is to get to where Top Rank, PBC,
Matchroom, ESPN, Showtime, DAZN, and the other major players say
they want it to be, the best will have to fight the best. But the expectation is that there will be fewer mega-fights in the near future than "when
HBO was HBO."

Meanwhile, there's so much boxing available now on television and
streaming video that one might analogize the situation to an all-you-can

eat buffet. Which buffet tables have the best food? Is it worth eating? And how much will boxing fans want to eat?

No one watches every college football game on television. In the near future, boxing fans will become more selective in what they watch. It won't just be the investment of $4.99 or $9.99 or $15.99 a month. It will be the investment of time at a time when there's an overflow of product.

Get ready for the ride. This might be fun.

The use of illegal performance enhancing drugs is an ongoing problem in boxing.

Wilder–Ortiz and the PED Shadow

Last year (2017), in an article titled "Congratulations to the WBC and VADA", I praised the World Boxing Council and Voluntary Anti-Doping Association for their stand against the use of performance enhancing drugs in boxing. The article was written after the WBC withdrew its sanction of a scheduled November 4, 2017, title fight between Deontay Wilder and Luis Ortiz in the wake of Ortiz testing positive for chlorothiazide and hydrochlorothiazide—banned diuretics that are sometimes used to treat high blood pressure but are also used to mask performance-enhancing drugs.

The test was administered by VADA as part of the WBC Clean Boxing Program. VADA is still in the forefront of the fight against the use of illegal performance enhancing drugs in boxing. But the WBC has sent ambiguous signals recently regarding the scope of its commitment to VADA.

Meanwhile, Wilder–Ortiz has been rescheduled for March 3, 2018, at Barclays Center in Brooklyn. And the New York State Athletic Commission, which has jurisdiction over the bout, has taken steps to date that bring the enforcement of New York's rules and regulations regarding illegal PED use into question.

The WBC Clean Boxing Program was inaugurated last year under the leadership of WBC president Mauricio Sulaiman. It requires all WBC champions and fighters ranked by the WBC in the top fifteen of any weight division to be available for random PED testing by VADA at any time.

Over the years, VADA has tested hundreds of boxers pursuant to contracts with various individuals and organizations. Roughly four percent of these fighters have tested positive for the presence of a banned substance. Among those who tested positive are Ortiz, Alexander Povetkin, Andre Berto, Lamont Peterson, Lucas Browne, and Brandon Rios.

The WBC Clean Boxing Program isn't keyed to specific fights. Fighters in the program are tested at random. However, as a practical matter, VADA is more likely to test fighters who have a significant fight coming up than it is to test other fighters.

VADA is also retained by promoters and other third parties to over-see drug testing for specific fights such as the upcoming March 31 bout between Anthony Joshua and Joseph Parker.

VADA testing isn't perfect. Given the sporadic nature of the testing and the sophistication of PED cheaters today, the likelihood is that VADA fails to catch some fighters who are dirty. But there's a better chance that boxers tested by VADA are clean than there is for other boxers.

That brings us to Luis Ortiz.

Ortiz first tested positive for illegal drug use in conjunction with a first-round knockout of Lateef Kayode in 2014. In that instance, a urine sample taken from Ortiz by the Nevada State Athletic Commission prior to the bout tested positive afterward for the banned anabolic steroid nandrolone. Ortiz was fined by the NSAC and suspended for eight months.

Ortiz also raised eyebrows on April 14, 2017, when he pulled out of a fight against Derric Rossy scheduled for April 22 at Barclay's Center, claiming that he had suffered a thumb injury while sparring on April 12. This injury was asserted shortly after the New York State Athletic Commission instructed Ortiz to be available for a random drug test because, as stated in the NYSAC directive, "Mr. Ortiz has previously tested positive for PEDs."

With regard to the more recent finding of chlorothiazide and hydro-chlorothiazide in his system, the Ortiz camp claims that Luis took the banned diuretics to combat high blood pressure. However, there are multiple problems with this explanation: (1) Ortiz failed to previously state on required forms that he had high blood pressure; (2) Ortiz nei-ther applied for nor received a therapeutic use exemption for the banned diuretics; and (3) there was an issue as to whether a fighter with blood pressure so high that it that requires the use of chlorothiazide and hydro-chlorothiazide should be allowed to fight.

Moreover, the doctor who the Ortiz camp claimed wrote the pre-scription for the banned diuretics has a checkered past. Richard Allen Hill is a Fort Lauderdale, Florida, physician. A June 27, 2005, press release issued by the United States Attorney for the Southern District of Florida reveals that Dr. Hill was sentenced to 21 months in prison for financial misconduct related to the wholesale distribution of prescription drugs. Just as troubling, the *Palm Beach Post* reported in 2016 that at least six women had complained to the authorities that Hill sexually molested them during medical examinations. As part of a plea deal, Hill pled "no contest" to five misdemeanor battery charges.

On October 4, 2017, the WBC Board of Governors issued an "emergency ruling" with regard to Luis Ortiz as follows:

(1) Ortiz's use of and failure to disclose his use of the prohibited substances on various VADA forms constituted violations of the WBC's Clean Boxing Program protocol.

(2) The WBC withdrew its sanction for the previously-scheduled November 4, 2017, championship fight between Ortiz and Deontay Wilder.

(3) Ortiz was ordered to undertake a complete physical examination pursuant to a protocol designed by the WBC Medical Advisory Committee and performed by one or more licensed physicians approved by the WBC.

(4) Ortiz was to submit to a specific random testing protocol designed by VADA as soon as feasible, such testing to continue for six months or up to the date of Ortiz's next fight, whichever time is longer.

(5) Ortiz was fined $25,000.

Then, on November 30, 2017, the WBC issued a "final ruling" that declared:

(1) Ortiz had undergone the medical examinations as ordered and arranged by WBC Medical Advisory Committee chairman Dr. Paul Wallace.

(2) Dr. Wallace had reviewed the results of all the medical examinations, each one of which was "completely normal and revealed no ongoing adverse health condition whatsoever."

(3) Dr. Wallace had also examined Ortiz's medical history and "confirmed the medical justification for Mr. Ortiz to ingest a blood pressure medication which eventually resulted in Mr. Ortiz's adverse finding."

(4) The WBC Board of Governors ratified the previous ruling that Ortiz's failure to disclose his ingestion of chlorothiazide and

hydrochlorothiazide constituted a violation of WBC Clean Boxing protocol and confirmed the $25,000 fine imposed on Ortiz.

(5) Ortiz would be allowed to compete in WBC-sanctioned events subject to PED testing based on a specifically designed testing protocol.

Now we come to the heart of the matter: Money.

Since the inception of the Clean Boxing Program, VADA has received $10,000 a month from the WBC to underwrite the direct cost of PED testing. This represents a good-faith commitment to clean sport on the part of the WBC. But in the grand scheme of things, it's not a lot of money.

There are seventeen weight divisions in professional boxing. Multiply that by fifteen fighters and one champion in each weight division, and there are 272 fighters who are subject to mandatory PED testing at any given time. There are also "interim" champions and fighters who aren't ranked by the WBC but have voluntarily enrolled in the Clean Boxing Program. All told, almost 400 fighters are subject to testing. That averages out to twenty-five dollars per month per fighter.

In recent months, the WBC has slowed its payments to VADA. A reliable source says that, as of January 23, 2018, VADA had received none of the $25,000 fine paid by Ortiz. Concurrently, and perhaps more significantly, a $250,000 fine paid to the WBC by Alexander Povetkin after Povetkin tested positive for banned substances on multiple occasions seems to have disappeared into a black hole.

Povetkin was scheduled fight Wilder in Moscow on May 21, 2016, but failed a pre-fight drug test when he tested positive for meldonium. The fight was postponed. The WBC then ruled that Povetkin should fight Bermane Stiverne for an interim belt. But twenty hours before that bout, the WBC withdrew its sanction and placed Povetkin on indefinite suspension because he tested positive for Ostarine.

Thereafter, the WBC lifted Povetkin's indefinite suspension but ordered that he pay a $250,000 fine.

On December 24, 2017, the WBC confirmed that the $250,000 fine had been paid. At that time, Mauricio Sulaiman pledged that the money would be "used for the development of the Clean Boxing Program."

Do the math. In the past, the WBC has given VADA $10,000 a month for PED testing. A VADA test led to the WBC receiving $250,000 from Alexander Povetkin. The fine paid to the WBC by Povetkin is double the annual budget for VADA testing. Without VADA testing, the WBC wouldn't have received the $250,000. But as of January 23, 2018, VADA had not received any of the $250,000 fine paid by Povetkin.

Sulaiman has declined to respond to repeated requests for information regarding what portion, if any, of the $250,000 fine paid to the WBC by Povetkin has been given to VADA and also whether any of the $25,000 fine paid to the WBC by Ortiz has been given to VADA. He has also declined to state whether the specifically designed testing protocol for Ortiz has been implemented.

"Mauricio believes in the Clean Boxing Program," one WBC insider says. "He took a lot of flak from outside the WBC, and also internally, when he instituted the program. But he wants Wilder-Ortiz to happen. And the WBC always seems to need money."

It would be a shame if the WBC turned its Clean Boxing Program into just another revenue stream for the sanctioning body.

Meanwhile, the New York State Athletic Commission seems to be stumbling when it comes to its own PED testing program.

On January 10, 2018, NYSAC director of boxing Matthew Delaglio sent a letter to Lou DiBella and Ron Rizzo at DiBella Entertainment advising them that, as a condition of licensure, Ortiz would be required by the commission to undergo testing for anabolic steroids, diuretics, masking agents, and a ten-panel drug urine test no later than January 19, 2018, and, again, fifteen days before the March 3, 2018, fight against Wilder. In addition, Ortiz was told that the commission would require a clearance letter from a cardiologist.

The tests that were ordered are appropriate. The collection process is not.

What were the administrators at the NYSAC thinking? Did they want to give Ortiz notice so he could clean up any possible drug violation and thus proceed with a big fight in New York? Ortiz might now be a clean fighter. But with nine notice, these tests won't prove it.

Moreover, the New York Department of State, which oversees the NYSAC, has refused to respond to inquiries regarding when tests were conducted, where were they conducted, and by whom were they conducted.

The WBC took a huge step forward when it inaugurated its Clean Boxing Program. It would be if a shame if the WBC were to backtrack on that program now.

As for the New York State Athletic Commission; its handling of the situation to date is the equivalent of law enforcement authorities giving a suspect in a drug investigation nine days' notice before executing a search warrant to raid his apartment for drugs.

Coming as it did from Donald Trump, Jack Johnson's pardon seemed like an empty gesture.

Jack Johnson's Pardon

Boxing has a long history of rich white men exploiting black fighters for their own personal gain. Donald Trump did it as a casino magnate before his holdings in Atlantic City devolved into bankruptcy. He did it again on May 24, 2018, when he pardoned Jack Johnson.

Johnson's story is well known. He was the greatest heavyweight of his era and a symbol of towering importance.

Thirty years ago, Arthur Ashe told me, "I think that, within the United States, Jack Johnson had a larger impact than Muhammad Ali because he was first. Nothing that Frederick Douglass did, nothing that Booker T. Washington did, nothing that any African-American had done up until that time had the same impact as Jack Johnson's fight against Jim Jeffries on July 4, 1910. It was the most awaited event in the history of African-Americans to that date. Lincoln's Emancipation Proclamation was not done with widespread prior knowledge. Half of black America didn't know it was going to be issued. And even after it was, many African-Americans didn't know about it for weeks. But virtually every black American knew that Johnson versus Jeffries was going to take place. They knew it; they knew what was at stake; and they also knew they could get the results almost immediately because of the advent of the telegraph. And when Johnson won, it completely destroyed one of the crucial pillars of white supremacy—the idea that the white man was superior in body and mind to all the darker peoples of the earth. That was just not true as far as anybody was concerned anymore because now a black man held the title symbolic of the world's most physically powerful human being. It had an emotional immediacy that went beyond what Ali, Joe Louis, or even Jackie Robinson did because it was the first time anything like that had ever happened. It provided a tremendous spiritual and emotional uplift."

In 1913, Johnson was convicted of violating the federal Mann Act (a statute aimed at combatting prostitution). He was alleged to have transported several women across state lines "for immoral purposes." One of the women was a prostitute named Belle Schreiber. Another was a 19-year-old runaway named Lucille Cameron who Johnson later married.

There's little doubt that Johnson was singled out for prosecution because of his status as heavyweight champion, his flamboyant lifestyle, and, most of all, his color. He was sentenced to a year in prison, fled the country, and returned in 1920 to serve ten months in prison.

As noted by Jeffrey Sammons (author of *Beyond The Ring: The Role of Boxing in American Society*), "Johnson never saw himself as a racial symbol. He felt he was as good as anybody else and that he shouldn't be denied anything that anybody else had, but he didn't think in racial terms. He never became part of a movement or aligned himself in a crusade with others the way Muhammad Ali chose to do."

That theme is echoed by historian Randy Roberts (author of *Papa Jack: Jack Johnson and the Era of White Hopes*), who recounts, "Johnson was treated as a black menace, but he didn't have a highly developed racial consciousness. Most of his friends were white and he made a number of derogatory comments about blacks, particularly black women, throughout his life. By contrast, Ali's message was racial pride, the glorification of being black, a refusal to accept that black was anything less than best, a demand for dignity and full entitlements for all black people."

This brings us to Donald Trump's pardon of Jack Johnson. It was signed one day after the National Football League announced a policy requiring that "all team and league personnel on the field shall stand and show respect for the flag and the Anthem" when the National Anthem is played before a game. Teams whose players kneel or otherwise fail to "show respect for the flag" will be fined. Teams may also choose to fine their own players directly for such conduct.

The National Anthem controversy began in August 2016 as a protest against the inappropriate use of force by a small number of police officers against people of color and the inadequate response of the criminal justice system to these incidents. Thereafter, Donald Trump got into the act, demanding that players who kneel be precluded from playing.

Trump's position on the anthem issue is very much in keeping with his support of laws that have the effect of keeping people of color from voting, his reference to the white supremacists who marched in Charlottesville last year as "good people," and his stand on immigration.

Now Trump has pardoned a person of color who has been dead for 72 years. But the living people he pardons are men like sheriff Joe Arpaio (convicted of violating court orders with regard to racial profiling and other discriminatory conduct) and Lewis "Scooter" Libby (a corporate lawyer and former adviser to Dick Cheney, who was convicted of obstruction of justice and perjury in conjunction with the leak of classified government information).

The Jack Johnson pardon ceremony in the Oval Office at the White House was marked by hypocrisy.

Sylvester Stallone, who for 42 years has said that Muhammad Ali was the inspiration for Apollo Creed, rewrote history by saying, "The inspiration for Apollo Creed was Jack Johnson."

World Boxing Council president Mauricio Sulaiman, a self-described "proud Mexican" who lives on the south side of the wall that Donald Trump wants to erect between the United States and Mexico, declared, "Mr. President, I would like to praise, congratulate, and thank you for taking this gigantic step for human equality and inclusion."

One of the most disheartening things about the ceremony was Donald Trump suggesting that he's more sensitive to minority issues than Barack Obama because Obama failed to pardon Jack Johnson.

"They thought it [the pardon] was going to be signed in the last administration, and that didn't happen," Trump proclaimed. "So that was very disappointing for a lot of people. The Congressional Black Caucus supported it very, very powerfully, very strongly, But they couldn't get the president to sign it."

Here it should be noted that one reason Barack Obama chose to not pardon Jack Johnson was Johnson's history of physically abusing women. But we already know that Donald Trump has limited respect for women.

The issue here isn't whether Jack Johnson should have been pardoned. The issue is that, coming from Donald Trump, it's a cynical, politically-calculated gesture that will be used as cover to justify his ongoing assault against human dignity and human rights; an assault that has particularly harsh consequences for people of color.

Legacies are important.

Irregularities Mar New York State Boxing Hall of Fame Election

On January 10, 2018, the New York State Boxing Hall of Fame announced the names of 22 individuals who will be inducted into the hall in April. This year's class runs the gamut from former heavyweight champion James J. Corbett (who dethroned John L. Sullivan in 1892) to Jake Rodriguez (28–8-2 with 8 KOs and 7 KOs by). As in years past, some of the inductees were well-chosen. Other selections have the feel of cronyism rather than merit.

This year's inductees include, among others, Melvina Lathan.

Ms. Lathan is best known to boxing fans for her role as chairperson of the New York State Athletic Commission. During her time in office, the dangerous job of fighting was often more dangerous than need be. An investigation by the New York State Inspector General's Office detailed the travesty of such instances as Yuri Foreman fighting Miguel Cotto on a knee that was so badly damaged that Foreman kept falling down during the fight and the horrific injuries suffered by Magomed Abdusalamov in a bout against Mike Perez, both of which unfolded against a backdrop of substandard NYSAC medical protocols. The Inspector General also uncovered a pattern of inappropriate gratuities that were received by some NYSAC personnel, including Ms. Lathan, on her watch.

Interviews conducted this month with several members of the New York State Boxing Hall of Fame Selection Committee and a review of related documents reveal that Ms. Lathan's selection was the result of a seriously flawed process.

The New York State Boxing Hall of Fame operates under the auspices of Ring 8, a tax-exempt charitable organization designed primarily to help retired boxers in financial need. The hall has been in existence since 2011 and inducted its first honorees in 2012.

The selection process is haphazard at best. Numerous deserving candidates have been passed over in favor of less-qualified but better-connected

individuals. Among the oversights, A. J. Liebling, Jimmy Cannon, Budd
Schulberg, Bill Cayton, Barney Nagler, and Seth Abraham come quickly
to mind.

A press release heralding the 2018 enshrinements advised, "The 2018
inductees were selected by the NYSBHOF nominating committee members: Jack Hirsch, Bobby Cassidy Jr, Randy Gordon, Henry Hascup, Don
Majeski, Ron McNair, and Neil Terens."

There's one notable omission from this list. And a troubling back-story.

The NYSBHOF inducts members in four categories: living boxers,
deceased boxers, living non-participants, and deceased non-participants.
The 2018 selection committee had eight members, not seven, and held
two meetings.

The first meeting took place in October 2017. Jack Hirsch (committee chairman at the time) recounts, "People came to the first meeting
with names to put into nomination in each category. All of the names
were discussed, and the list in each category was cut to a more manageable
number with somewhere around twelve to fifteen names in each category.
Then, in November, we met again to finalize the inductees."

Several committee members were troubled by the presence of Bob
Duffy in the room at each meeting. Duffy is a former president of Ring
8 and current chairman of the New York State Boxing Hall of Fame.
These members were of the view that Duffy, however well-intentioned
he might be, has interfered with the committee's autonomy in the past
and inappropriately tried to influence the selection process.

This concern was underscored by the fact that Duffy has been known
to influence how many people will be inducted into the hall in each
category in a given year while a meeting is in progress.

Also, Duffy insisted on bringing Charley Norkus Jr. to the November
meeting. Norkus is the son of Charley Norkus (33–19, 19 KOs, 6 KOs
by), a heavyweight who plied his trade in the 1950s and died in 1996.
Norkus, like Lathan, was chosen for induction in the class of 2018.

Duffy advocated strongly for Lathan at the November meeting but
was overruled. Instead, the selection committee voted to admit five other
living non-participants: Dave Anderson, Pete Brodsky, Herb Goldman,
Bobby Goodman, and Ron Scott Stevens.

"So we were ready to go home," Randy Gordon, a committee member, recalls. "People had their coats on. We're walking out the door. And Bob stepped in again to advocate for Melvina."

Among other things, to accommodate Lathan's selection, Duffy ruled that the number of living non-participants to be inducted in 2018 could be expanded from five to six.

"So we voted again," Gordon says. "And again Melvina didn't make it. Some committee members had serious issues with her performance when she was chairperson of the New York State Athletic Commission. And it didn't help that, a few months earlier [September 8], it was announced that the State of New York had agreed to pay $22,000,000 to Magomed Adbusalamov and his family. We left the meeting thinking that Melvina had not been chosen for induction. And then strange things started happening."

On the afternoon of November 17, 2017, (one day after the meeting), Jack Hirsch (who is also the current president of Ring 8) sent an email to the selection committee members. Hirsch had supported Lathan in the committee's deliberations. But even with his support and Duffy's lobbying, Lathan had failed to secure the majority of votes necessary for induction. The electors' final tally in the last-minute re-vote had been 4-to-4.

Hirsch's email advised selection committee members that he had just telephoned 87-year-old Angelo Prospero, a former committee member who now lives in South Carolina. In Hirsch's words, "Angelo is of sane mind but is a little hard of hearing. He had his wife Terry on the other line so he would fully understand what I was saying." The email concluded with the news that Prospero had voted in favor of admitting Lathan, thus theoretically breaking the tie in her favor.

Hirsch later acknowledged to this writer that "Bob Duffy wanted me to call Angelo."

Reaction was swift. Two hours after receiving Hirsch's email, Steve Farhood (who was on the selection committee and had participated in the voting on all of the nominees in each category) sent a return email with a copy to each committee member. In his email, Farhood advised Hirsch that he was resigning from the committee, adding, "I don't care for the manner in which we were manipulated and dictated to. I wish the committee all the best in the future."

The following day, Farhood elaborated on those thoughts in an email to a fellow committee member, writing, "My decision had nothing to do with Melvina, at least personally. From the start of the NYSBHF, Duffy has repeatedly spoken of not interfering and allowing our autonomy. That has never been the case, usually because of his ties to Ring 8. The only thing I wonder: Why did he push so hard? It was as if he was desperate to get her through."

More recently, on February 7, 2018, Farhood, while declining to discuss the matter further, did tell this writer, "I would like one thing made clear. My objection, and the reason for my resignation from the nominating committee, was not regarding the merits of any particular candidate, but rather the process in which candidates were being introduced and voted on."

Also on February 7, Jack Hirsch resigned from the selection committee.

"I wanted some things changed and they weren't," Hirsch told this writer. "One of the things that bothered me in particular was Charley Norkus Jr. being in the meeting when we were discussing his father, but I was overruled on that by Bob Duffy. And the situation with Melvina was a factor in my resigning. What can I say? I was committee chairman and I take responsibility for my part in what happened."

There's a school of thought that Hirsch was pushed into the line of fire by Duffy last November. But Jack says, "Please make it clear that I think Bob Duffy is a great guy and I consider him a friend."

"I love Bob Duffy," Randy Gordon concurs. "But he had a personal agenda last November and he got it through."

There are some very deserving inductees in the New York State Boxing Hall of Fame, and this controversy shouldn't take away from their accomplishments. That said, to be fully credible, the NYSBHOF needs an independent selection committee.

"It's a no-brainer," promoter Lou DiBella says. "Of course, Errol Spence and Terence Crawford should fight each other. But even in boxing, making a no-brainer requires some brains."

A Plea for Spence–Crawford Now

For the past eight years, this writer has administered polls in various weight divisions.

The concept behind the polls is to take the leading contenders in a given weight class and ask what would happen if they fought each other in a round-robin tournament. A panel of knowledgeable boxing experts then predicts the results of each hypothetical fight with one point being awarded for each predicted win and a half-point for each match-up that's deemed "too close to call."

The process is about what would happen if the fights were held now, not what the fighters accomplished two years ago or what they might do two years down the road.

Overall, the electors have been on the mark. By way of example, not a single elector picked Manny Pacquiao, Miguel Cotto, or Canelo Alvarez to beat Floyd Mayweather at a time when many knowledgeable observers were split on the outcome of those fights.

In the past, there has always been clear separation in the poll results between the #1 and #2 finishers.

In this month's "boxing industry poll," 27 electors were asked to predict the results of each fight in a round-robin tournament featuring (listed alphabetically) Terence Crawford, Danny Garcia, Shawn Porter, Errol Spence, and Keith Thurman. Thus, each elector predicted the outcome of ten fights. All told, 270 fight predictions were entered into the data base. A perfect score (every elector predicting that the same fighter would win all four of his fights) would have been 108 points.

How close were the results? TERENCE CRAWFORD AND ERROL SPENCE TIED FOR FIRST PLACE WITH EACH MAN RECEIVING 91 POINTS. Crawford won the head-to-head battle with

Spence by a 13-to-10 margin with four electors calling the fight "too close to call." But Spence did slightly better than Crawford against the other three fighters in the tournament.

I don't care whether the fight is styled Spence-Crawford or Crawford-Spence. The two designations are used interchangeably in this article. Each man is deserving of lead billing. What I care about is that Crawford and Spence fight each other.

The 27 electors brought varying perspectives to their task.

Some are former fighters (Tim Bradley, Kelly Pavlik, Gerry Cooney, and Frank Lotierzo). Others are trainers (Teddy Atlas, Pat Burns, and Barry Hunter). Bradley has a special association with the welterweight division, having beaten Manny Pacquiao, Ruslan Provodnikov, and Juan Manuel Marquez in 147-pound title fights. So does Hunter, who has trained Lamont Peterson throughout his ring career including fights against Spence and Garcia.

The media was represented in the poll by Al Bernstein, Harold Lederman, Brian Kenny, Ron Borges, Gareth Davies, Norm Frauenheim, Michael Rosenthal, Tom Gerbasi, Bart Barry, and Randy Gordon. Michael Buffer and David Diamante also participated and are included in the media group.

Finally, seven matchmakers took part in the voting: Bruce Trampler, Russell Peltz, Ron Katz, Mike Marchionte, Eric Bottjer, Brad Goodman, and Don Elbaum. They were joined by Craig Hamilton, an insightful observer and knowledgeable boxing historian.

The final point totals are:

Terence Crawford	91
Errol Spence	91
Keith Thurman	42
Shawn Porter	26–½
Danny Garcia	19–½

Twelve of the 27 electors thought that Crawford would win all four of his fights, and ten thought that Spence would win all of his fights. Four electors said that Crawford-Spence was too close to call but that each of them would beat everyone else in the tournament. The final elector thought that the tournament would unfold as a three-way tie for first place with Crawford beating Spence, Spence beating Thurman, and Thurman beating Crawford. Rock-paper-scissors. Styles make fights.

Breaking the vote down by each category of electors, fighters and trainers favored Spence over Crawford by a one-half point margin (which came about when one elector called Crawford-Porter too close to call. The media favored Spence over Crawford by a three-point margin. But matchmakers gave the edge to Crawford over Spence by 3–½ points.

Charts #1 AND #2 contain a detailed statistical breakdown of the voting.

CHART #1	Terence Crawford	Errol Spence	Keith Thurman	Shawn Porter	Danny Garcia
Crawford 91	–	15	25	24–½	26–½
Spence 91	12	–	26	26	27
Thurman 42	2	1	–	18–½	20–½
Porter 26–½	2/½	1	8–½	–	14–½
Garcia 19–½	½	0	6–½	12–½	–

CHART #2	Fighters–Trainers	Media	Matchmakers
Spence	1	1	2
Crawford	2	2	1
Thurman	4	3	3
Porter	3	4	5
Garcia	5	5	4

Many of the electors offered thoughts about the fighters in elaborating on their predictions. A common refrain was, "None of these guys is easy to fight."

Thurman has actual victories over Porter and Garcia on his resume. But because of injuries and recent inactivity (one fight in the past two years), there's an issue as to what kind of condition Keith will be in, physically and mentally, when he returns to the ring. Among the electors' comments in this regard were:

* "I don't know if Thurman wants to fight anymore. And if he does want to fight, I don't know if he wants to go in tough."
* "If Thurman can get back to where he was in terms of his physical condition and desire, it's one thing. If he can't, it's another."
* "At his best, Thurman would be tough for Crawford and Spence. I might even favor him over Crawford. But we're talking about now, and I think we've seen the best we're going to see of Keith Thurman. He's not the fighter he was, and I don't think he'll ever be that fighter again."

Shawn Porter was praised for his toughness and non-stop-action assault. Comments included, "Porter is tough. He keeps coming and coming" . . . "With each guy who fights Porter, you have to ask whether he can survive the pressure" . . . "Stylistically, Porter could give Crawford and Spence trouble. His aggressiveness might be his biggest strength. But I think that aggressiveness would get him in trouble against Spence. He'd run right into Errol's power."

A common refrain with regard to Garcia was, "Danny is much trickier than people give him credit for."

The open issue for some electors regarding Spence is his toughness. "If it goes into the late rounds and Spence is tested" one voter said, "I'm not sure how he holds up."

"I'm enjoying the ride with Errol," another elector noted. "But I haven't completely bought into it."

As for Crawford, one elector observed, "He has an impressive body of work, but he has yet to beat an elite fighter."

Spence and Crawford did more than finish in a tie for first place. In the six years that the poll has been conducted, there has never been an instance when two fighters separated themselves from rest of the field as dramatically as they did here.

The electors' offered varying thoughts with regard to Crawford and Spence fighting each other:

* "Spence is dangerous all the time, every second of every fight."
* "Crawford is easier to hit. But I think he's tougher than Spence and has the better chin."
* "Spence is bigger than Crawford and probably hits harder. That, to me, is the difference."
* "Crawford seems to really want the fight. Spence seems a bit ambiguous about it. That tells me something."
* "These guys don't just outpoint opponents. They beat them up."
* "Crawford has a will of iron. I'm confident that he can fight through adversity. I'm not sure about Spence."
* "Crawford-Spence is a pick 'em fight. And right now, I can't make a pick. This is really one where I'd want to see how each guy carries himself during fight week. And I'd also look at things like, did either guy miss a week of training because of an injury. Did either guy have trouble making weight?"
* "I can see this fight unfolding like Leonard-Hearns I, with Spence counterintuitively outboxing Crawford through the middle rounds and Crawford, at some point, throwing caution to the winds and trying desperately to knock Spence out. But today's championship fights are twelve rounds, not fifteen like Leonard-Hearns was."
* "It's a great fight. I hope they do it. And I hope they do it more than once."

Boxing is entering an era when premium cable, basic cable, streaming video, and other options are making more fights available to the viewing public than ever before. But very few of the fights that are currently available matter in a significant way.

Spence-Crawford would matter.

In "the old days," Crawford and Spence would appear in co-featured bouts on an HBO telecast with a binding commitment, assuming that each of them won, to fight each other in their next bout. But as writer Jimmy Tobin recently noted, we're living in an era when "greatness is bestowed at the outset and opponents approved to preserve it. A fighter can have developmental fights even after winning multiple titles, and every stern challenge provides license for at least one unwatchable one."

Thus, Crawford-Spence is unlikely to happen in the near future. Top Rank president Todd DuBoef (who, with Bob Arum, oversees Crawford's promotion) recently told this writer, "I don't look at it as a negative. To me, the question isn't why isn't the fight being made now. The question is when will the fight be ready to be made. The fuel that makes big fights is money. When these guys are household names, the pot will be big enough and the fight can happen. There's no timetable. Big fights happen organically. When the public demand is there, when a switch flips, when both fighters are at a certain point, it organically happens. I can't speak for Errol Spence because we don't promote him. But I think the path we've put Terence on will get him to that point."

One of boxing's many problems today is that it delays—and sometimes never gets to—what would otherwise be its biggest fights.

Other sports find a way to make the match-ups that fans want to see. The Golden State Warriors proved their mettle this year by facing the Houston Rockets in the Western Conference Finals. No one said, "Let's wait until the two best teams are in separate conferences so they can meet for the NBA Championship; it will be bigger that way."

If Crawford and Spence were to fight now, it would be a big fight. Pay-per-view buys would be good, not astronomical. But the fight would imprint both men in the public consciousness in a way that they haven't been so far. The winner—and possibly, the loser—would become a more valuable commercial attraction. And the winner wouldn't just move to the top of boxing's pound-for-pound rankings. He'd be widely touted as "Floyd Mayweather's successor" with the inside track on becoming Mayweather's heir as a pay-per-view draw. He would also have done something that Mayweather never did: beat another great fighter in his prime.

Famed matchmaker Teddy Brenner was fond of saying, "Fights make fights." In other words, the result of a given fight leads naturally to the next match-up. After Spence-Crawford, boxing would have a new star, and a new list of big fights would be on the horizon. There could be a rematch. The winner could fight an unbeaten Keith Thurman, not as a stop along the way to Spence-Crawford but as a destination in itself.

And the loser could rebuild. Ray Leonard lost to Roberto Duran and came back to defeat Duran, Hearns, and Marvin Hagler. Manny Pacquiao lost to Erik Morales before reaching the summit by devastating Oscar De La Hoya, Ricky Hatton, and Miguel Cotto.

Losing to a great fighter is sometimes simply a stop along the road to greatness.

Some observers have likened non-action on Spence-Crawford to the failure to make a fight between Anthony Joshua and Deontay Wilder. But there are significant differences between the two situations. Joshua-Wilder hasn't happened to date because, despite their public posturing, both sides took positions and did things (or failed to do things) that impeded the making of the fight. Also, Joshua doesn't need to fight Wilder to be a hugely marketable commodity. He can make eight figures by fighting fringe contenders. Neither Spence nor Crawford has that luxury.

At first glance, Spence might appear to have more big-money options at 147 pounds than Crawford does. After all, Keith Thurman, Danny Garcia, and Shawn Porter are all under the Premier Boxing Champions umbrella, as is Spence. But while it appears as though Porter will go in tough at the drop of a hat, Thurman and Garcia seem disinclined to share a ring with Errol.

And despite his remarkable ring skills, Spence is languishing as a commercial attraction. Look at his last four fights. Spence vs. Leonard Bundu was televised on NBC on August 21, 2016, immediately after the United States men's basketball team's gold medal victory over Serbia on the last day of the 2016 Olympics. That fight averaged 4.8 million viewers and peaked at 6.3 million. It could have been the launching pad in terms of building Errol as a crossover star. But instead, Spence retreated into a cocoon. He has fought three times since then—against Kell Brook (in a bout that was televised from England live in the United States during the late afternoon), Lamont Peterson, and Carlos Ocampo. These three fights, all on Showtime, averaged 291,000, 637,000, and 683,000 viewers respectively.

Meanwhile, time is ticking away. Spence and Crawford are in their prime years as fighters. Spence is 28. Crawford will turn 31 in September. But Terence is only 5-feet-8-inches tall, won his first belt at 135 pounds, and has never fought above 146–½ (when he moved up to welterweight to challenge Jeff Horn on June 9). Spence is a shade over 5-feet-9-inches tall, turned pro at 149 pounds, and has fought at weights as high as 156–½. At some point in the near future, Errol is likely to outgrow the welter-weight division. Thus, unless Spence-Crawford is made soon, contract weight is likely to be an issue.

Crawford-Spence is makeable now if the powers that be want to make it. Unlike many fighters who talk big but shrink from a chal-lenge, the two men seem to genuinely want to fight each other. For sure, Crawford does. And my read on the situation is that Spence does too.

In the ring immediately after he beat Jeff Horn, Crawford told Bob Arum, "I want the other champions, I want the big fights. Bob, make it happen."

At a late-June media sit-down in New York, Spence declared, "I want to be known as a guy who fought the best, who was willing to fight the best, always came in the ring one hundred percent and always gave it my all, had a big heart, and never shied away from a challenge. I want to be considered as an all-time great."

So let's take a vote. To achieve these goals, should Crawford and Spence enter the ring next to fight a pair of 10-to-1 underdogs or should they fight each other?

I thought so.

Crawford and Top Rank are aligned with ESPN. Spence is with PBC and Al Haymon. Showtime may, or may not, have Spence locked in contractually.

There's no reason that ESPN and Showtime can't work together to promote Spence-Crawford as a pay-per-view attraction the way that HBO and Showtime worked together on Lennox Lewis vs. Mike Tyson and Floyd Mayweather vs. Manny Pacquiao. Can anyone imagine execu-tives at either network saying, "We think this is a bad fight, and we don't want to be part of it."

But the unfortunate likelihood is that boxing fans will be fed a string of unsatisfying Crawford and Spence mismatches for the foreseeable future. None of these fights will tell us anything we don't already know about Crawford and Spence or advance either man's quest for greatness.

It's not brain surgery or rocket science. It's arranging a fist-fight.

And a parable in closing . . .

A man had a longing for filet mignon, so he went to a steakhouse with a reputation for having the best filet mignon in town. There was filet mignon in the kitchen. But the restaurant owners—two brothers named Bob and Al—wouldn't serve it to him.

"We're marinating the beef for a while," Bob told the man. "That way, we can charge you more when the marinating is done. But we'll sell you a rib-eye or some chopped sirloin now."

"I don't want a rib-eye or chopped sirloin," the man said. "I want filet mignon."

"Sorry."

So the next time the man went out for dinner, he went to a different restaurant where they served him what he wanted. And on top of that, when the beef at the first restaurant had finished marinating, it wasn't so prime anymore.

Should the rounds boxed by men and women be of equal duration?

Two Minutes or Three for Women?

Ronda Rousey demonstrated that a female mixed martial arts combatant can be a bigger draw than her male counterparts. But no woman boxer has come close to achieving the level of acceptance and fame that the top men have.

One of many reasons for this disparity is that the overwhelming majority of women's boxing matches are waged in two-minute rounds rather than three.

Most state athletic commissions default to two-minute stanzas for women, although New York, California, and Nevada have permitted three-minute rounds in instances where both boxers agreed.

World Boxing Council president Mauricio Sulaiman has proclaimed that the WBC will "never" sanction three-minute rounds for women or allow women's bouts that are more than ten rounds in duration.

The case for two-minute rounds for women boxers rests partly on tradition and partly on an interpretation of medical data.

Dramatic knockouts are largely absent from women's boxing, primarily because the women don't hit nearly as hard as men. That said, relying on medical research conducted at UCLA, Sulaiman has declared, "The bone structure of women is different than men, specifically in the neck region. Women have almost eighty percent more concussion probability than men and they have a slower recovery time. The more time you fight, the higher the dehydration and fatigue. The risk factor increases. It is also a fact that women have stronger symptoms after concussion and suffer more pain."

Jill Diamond, co-chair of the WBC Women's Championship Committee, adds, "It's not about the ability of women to fight three-minute rounds. It's a safety issue. Women are capable of doing it, but at what cost?"

Diamond also maintains, "A majority of the women I've spoken with don't want three-minute rounds. And if they do want three-minute rounds, they expect to be paid more for it."

These thoughts are echoed by two-time Olympic gold-medalist Claressa Shields, who says, "If fighting three minutes will get us paid equally to the men, I'm all for it. Otherwise, I'll take two. I've been fighting for two minutes since the amateurs. With two-minutes, you don't have time to feel someone out. You start fast, you go fast, and you finish fast. I can go three minutes. I spar three-minute rounds with men all the time. But I think two is better."

By contrast, Olympic gold-medalist Katie Taylor supports the idea of women fighting three-minute rounds. And promoter Barry McGuigan says of the two-minute limit, "It's disrespectful. Women are either boxers or they are not and therefore should be allowed to contest championship bouts over twelve three-minute rounds like the men. Anything less is sexist and fails to recognize the quality, commitment, and hard work that women put into the sport."

Here, one might also note that, in UFC bouts, both women and men fight five-minute rounds with no difference in the number of rounds per fight based on gender.

That brings us back to the medical research.

Dr. Margaret Goodman has served as chief ringside physician and chair of the medical advisory board for the Nevada State Athletic Commission and is one of the most knowledgeable advocates for fighter safety in the world today.

"My impression," Dr. Goodman says, "Is that the WBC is relying on old data and incomplete data.

This thought is backed by Dr. Charles Bernick (director of the Lou Ruvo Center for Brain Health at the Cleveland Clinic) who is overseeing the most comprehensive study to date of brain damage suffered by fighters.

Last year, Bernick told writer Tom Gerbasi, "If you take a woman fighter and matched her up to a male who has the same number of fights, the same age, the same education, we don't really find much difference looking at the brain itself or even how they test out on certain reaction time and processing speed and so on. You can always find some differences, but they're not huge. Nothing has come out that women are more prone to long-term changes. The biggest risk factor is the number of blows you're on the receiving end of. Anytime you reduce that, you're going to, in some sense, improve the safety of that sport. But I don't know if it's really been established yet that for women that's going to make a big difference. It's making a policy change based on indirect evidence. It certainly can't hurt from a safety standpoint. But how much it's going to help, I don't know."

All of the above leads to a host of collateral issues.

Would a state athletic commission countenance a men's fight with four-minute rounds if both boxers agreed to it? A twenty-round championship fight?

"Look," Dr. Goodman says, "exposure to head blows isn't good for anyone. We know that. The less the better. One-minute rounds would do less damage than two-minute rounds. With three-minute rounds for women, there would be more damage. That's a given. There would be less damage in men's boxing if rounds were cut from three minutes to two."

"But there are other ways to make boxing safer," Dr. Goodman continues "You make boxing safer with proper pre-fight medical screening. You make boxing safer with good referees and doctors and cornermen who know when to stop a fight. I favor three-minute rounds for women."

And suppose it turns out that, in fact, women are more easily concussed, suffer worse symptoms, and take longer to heal than men?

"If that's true," Dr. Goodman answers, "then maybe women shouldn't be fighting at all."

There are times when Oscar De La Hoya seems to be struggling as hard outside the boxing ring as he did in it.

An Hour in the Life of Oscar De La Hoya

It's 11:00 a.m. on the morning of Thursday, September 13, 2018. In two days, Gennady Golovkin and Saul "Canelo" Alvarez will meet in the ring at T-Mobile Arena in Las Vegas to do battle for the middleweight championship of the world.

Oscar De La Hoya is sitting on a bronze-colored, metal-framed, cushioned chair in the holding lobby of the KA Theatre at the MGM Grand Hotel and Casino. The hotel is hosting most of the fight week media activities. Golden Boy (De La Hoya's promotional company) is co-promoting the bout.

Oscar is seated opposite a single TV camera. A Canelo-Golovkin backdrop has been erected behind him. A sign taped to the outside of a door leading to the holding area says, "Do Not Enter." Inside the room, a plaque affixed to the wall declares "Authorized Personnel Only."

During the next hour, De La Hoya will be interviewed by eight television networks in an exercise known as "the satellite tour." Alvarez and Golovkin will be similarly engaged later in the day. The interviews are designed to remind viewers that a can't-miss fight is scheduled for Saturday night and encourage pay-per-view buys.

Oscar earned a reservoir of respect during his Hall of Fame ring career. He was an icon in the Hispanic-American community and a genuine crossover star. One can check off the boxes . . . Olympic gold medal . . . Movie-star handsome . . . Bilingual . . .

And he could fight. De La Hoya won his first world championship at 130 pounds at age 21. Ten years later, he surrendered his final belt in a middleweight title-unification bout. His only losses were to Felix Trinidad, Shane Mosley (twice), Bernard Hopkins, Floyd Mayweather, and Manny Pacquiao. All five of these men were in their prime when De la Hoya fought them. The loss to Trinidad and second loss to Mosley are widely regarded as bad decisions. Along the way, Oscar defeated Julio Cesar Chavez (twice), Pernell Whitaker, Ike Quartey, and Fernando Vargas. He was always willing to go in tough.

It has been said that no fighter gets out of boxing unscathed. No fighter goes into boxing unscathed either. For much of his time as an active fighter, De La Hoya battled demons outside the ring as well as in it. His subsequent problems with substance abuse and other issues have been well-chronicled. There were worries when he missed the final pre-fight press conference for Canelo-Golovkin on Wednesday because of what was said to be a sore throat.

But Oscar is still boxing royalty. He still stops a room when he enters.

De La Hoya is wearing faded blue jeans, black loafers without socks, and a light-blue short-sleeved shirt that's hanging out below his waist. He looks heavy. His face is puffy and his eyes are hooded, evoking the image of a fighter in the closing rounds of a hard fight. His voice is less expressive this morning than it usually is. Normally, his smile lights up a room and flows out over the airwaves. Today it seems forced. His delivery is less smooth than usual. There are a lot of "umm"s and "ah"s.

Publicist Ed Keenan is overseeing the satellite tour. A handful of technicians monitor the proceedings. It's not easy to coordinate one interview after another. There are times when a station's turn comes up and it's on a commercial break.

Oscar waits patiently between interviews. He transitions seamlessly from English to Spanish and back again. Three days earlier, he'd told TMZ that he was "seriously considering" a run for president of the United States. Most of the questions today are about the fight. But more often than not, at some point in each interview, he's asked about the possibility of a presidential campaign.

"America was built on dreams," De La Hoya answers. "If Ronald Reagan and Donald Trump can do it, why can't I? . . . I want to be a voice for the people. The way I fought in the ring, I want to fight for the people. . . . I'm seriously discussing it with my team. I don't have a definitive answer yet. . . . This is America. I can be anything I want to be. . . . I won a gold medal at the Olympics for the United States. This would be another way to serve my country."

The lobby holding area is stuffy and uncomfortably hot with no air conditioning and no windows. The temperature outside has risen past ninety degrees. During the short breaks between interviews, a door is opened for fresh air.

"Can someone get a Red Bull for Oscar?" an aide asks.

A production assistant leaves and returns with three bottles of water.

Oscar stays on message with regard to the upcoming fight, although his comments are sometimes hyperbolic.

"Fans will be on the edge of their seats, begging for more. It will be a thrilling night for boxing . . . I've never seen Canelo act this way. He really dislikes Triple-G. He says he wants to knock out GGG. And to me, that's music to my ears . . . It can be a trilogy. Or maybe even four, five, six fights between them like Sugar Ray Robinson and Jake LaMotta."

When asked about Canelo having tested positive for clenbuterol earlier in the year, De La Hoya answers, "People trust Canelo. People love Canelo. People believe in Canelo."

Five minutes after noon, Canelo Alvarez enters the room. His satellite tour is scheduled next. The old champion rises from his chair, embraces his successor, and departs from the holding lobby, leaving the stage to the new king.

For those who were so inclined, the build-up to Deontay Wilder vs. Tyson Fury was a time for reflection.

Reflections from the Flight Deck of the USS Intrepid

The last time that I was on the USS Intrepid prior to the October 2, 2018, press conference for the upcoming fight between Deontay Wilder and Tyson Fury, I saw a man beaten to death. His name was Beethaeven Scottland. He died because of the nature of the sport he was involved with and because a referee let a fight go on too long and the ring doctor assigned to his corner was less than vigilant.

That night—June 26, 2001—began as a festive occasion. Duva Boxing was promoting the first professional fight card ever held on the flight deck of the Intrepid, a decommissioned 900-foot aircraft carrier. Arriving fans were greeted by roundcard girls styled as World War II pin-ups. There were panoramic views wherever one turned. The towering skyscrapers of midtown Manhattan to the east; the George Washington Bridge to the north; the Hudson River and New Jersey Palisades to the west. And to the south, the World Trade Center.

Red, white, and blue ring ropes cordoned off the red, white, and blue ring canvas. Everything sparkled. The sky was a perfect, almost surreal, backdrop for the fighters. Aquamarine at first, then dark with just enough haze to resemble a black velvet curtain.

George Khalid Jones faced off against Scottland in the next-to-last fight of the evening. In the tenth and final round, tragedy struck.

Seventeen years later, most athletic commissions in the United States still have substandard medical protocols. And even these are poorly enforced. It's all too easy to connect the dots from Beethaevan Scottland to Magomed Abdusalamov to the sham testing for performance enhancing drugs that plague boxing today.

As I made my way toward the Wilder-Fury press conference on October 2, there were reminders of that long-ago night on the Intrepid.

Several flights of long winding stairs led from street level to the flight deck. The stairs and a tiny elevator were the only routes available for the medical team that brought Scottland from the ring to the hospital in a futile struggle to save his life. One end of the gurney that he was strapped to had to be lifted up and held at a sharp incline to fit it into the elevator.

Now, instead of a boxing ring, there was stage on the flight deck. Deontay Wilder and Tyson Fury were the center of attention, not Scottland and Jones.

At a press conference in London one day earlier, Steven Espinoza (president of Showtime Sports, which will distribute the fight on pay-per-view) said of Wilder and Fury, "We have two mythical figures. They are almost superheroes." After Espinoza's remarks, the two mythical figures got into a shoving match when Fury questioned Wilder's punching power and suggested that they "have a little spar."

On the flight deck of the Intrepid, Fury called Wilder "a skinny runt" and declared, "I'm gonna beat this bum because he can't box." Wilder proclaimed, "He knows his face is gonna get smashed in," and simulated masturbation for the viewing audience. On several occasions, the two men stood nose to nose. They also shouted at each other and said "fuck" a lot. Fury seemed a bit mad at times while Wilder looked genuinely angry.

Neither fighter is strong on impulse control. CRAZY will be a major selling point for the fight.

In truth, it's an intriguing match-up. Fury has skills. But in recent years, he has abused his body with heavy drinking, drug abuse, and rampant obesity. Regardless of what happens in the early rounds, Tyson can be expected to tire late. And when that happens, he's likely to get hit flush.

Fifteen years have passed since the Staples Center in Los Angeles hosted Lennox Lewis vs. Vitali Klitschko, the last big heavyweight championship fight in the City of Angels. Wilder and Fury will meet in the same arena. As they ranted on October 2, it was hard to not contrast their demeanor with the more dignified conduct of Lewis and Klitschko.

As Jerry Izenberg (the dean of American sportswriters) recently said of the Wilder-Fury promotion, "This isn't how sportsmen are supposed to act. It isn't boxing; it's burlesque."

Maybe. But it reflects what's happening now in our society. People were appalled when Mike Tyson bit Lennox Lewis on the leg at a 2002 press conference. If that happened today, it would be treated as a marketing tool.

The USS Intrepid symbolizes the defense of traditional American values. It set out to sea for the first time in 1943 and saw extensive action during World War II. Later, it was at the heart of other military missions and served as a NASA recovery vehicle for the Mercury and Gemini space capsules.

So much has changed since then and since the last time I was on the flight deck of the Intrepid . . . 9/11 . . . The election of Barack Obama . . . The rise of Donald Trump.

The Manhattan skyline looks different when viewed now from the Intrepid than it did seventeen years ago. Massive building projects have reshaped its contours to the north and east. To the south, the Twin Towers are gone.

Bart Barry recently wrote, "It's not like anyone with access to YouTube could mistake this era for a great one."

Comparing Today's Fighters
with the Past

Modern boxers, more than athletes in other sports, suffer from comparisons with the past. No one looks at Los Angeles Angels superstar Mike Trout and complains, "He isn't as good as Mickey Mantle was." People accept and appreciate Mike Trout for what he is. And that's true of other sports. But in boxing, elite fighters are constantly judged against their long-ago predecessors and hear, "So and so would have beaten him."

At times, boxing fans over-romanticize the past. Previous "golden ages" of boxing weren't always so golden. There was a five-year period from 1932 to 1937 when the heavyweight championship resided with Jack Sharkey, Primo Carnera, Max Baer, and James Braddock. The light-heavyweight champions immediately preceding Billy Conn were Bob Olin, John Henry Lewis, and Melio Bettina. I could go on. And on.

Was Benny Leonard a great fighter for his time? Absolutely. But put Benny Leonard in his prime (his prime being the 1920's) in the ring against Vasyl Lomachenko, and I'm betting on Lomachenko. That's not to say that Lomachenko is as great in his era as Leonard was in his. It's to say that times change.

Terence Crawford, Vasyl Lomachenko, Canelo Alvarez, Gennady Golovkin, Errol Spence, and their brethren would have been competitive in any era. They might not have beaten the best, but they would have been competitive against them. The same hold true for Andre Ward, Floyd Mayweather, and Bernard Hopkins.

Was Ray Leonard (who peaked in the 1980s) better than any welterweight fighting today? Absolutely. But Ray Leonard was also arguably better than any welterweight ever except Sugar Ray Robinson.

By and large, athletes today are better than their counterparts were decades ago. Babe Ruth is widely regarded as the greatest baseball player ever. Put Ruth in the game now against pitchers who are attacking him with forkballs, sliders, fastballs, split-finger fastballs, two-seam fastballs, cut fastballs, curveballs, knuckleballs, and change-ups, and I doubt that he'd have a .342 career batting average. The men who won gold medals in swimming at the 1932 Olympics wouldn't have qualified for the *women's* finals at the past three Olympic games.

Where do boxers fit into the equation?

Today's fighters are better conditioned than their predecessors as a consequence of advances in nutrition and conditioning technique.

Boxing technique is a different matter.

"You can look back over time and see how technique evolved," trainer-commentator Teddy Atlas offers. "It didn't happen all at once. You see it advance in stages. Fighters learning to use their legs. Fighters learning to punch effectively to the body. Fighters learning to move their head. Jack Johnson was a great pioneer for black people. But he was also a great pioneer in blending defense with offense and controlling the distance between himself and his opponent. Benny Leonard made history as a great Jewish fighter, but he also advanced boxing technique."

Hall-of-Fame matchmaker Bruce Trampler is in accord and says, "Fighters like Joe Gans, Jack Johnson, and Benny Leonard had skill sets that were advanced for their era but wouldn't be today. I think the post-war 1940s and 1950s were the era when, overall, fighters had the best technique. I don't think there have been any significant breakthroughs in technique since then."

As for today, Trampler declares, "The knowledge is still available. But I don't think fighters today are as well-rounded as a group as they once were. The coaching is inferior to what it used to be, so most fighters aren't being taught what they should be about technique."

And there's another factor in play today that has led to a decline in the number of great fighters.

Athletes in all sports get better when they compete against the best. In tennis, for example, Roger Federer, Rafael Nadal, and Novak Djokovic have learned from their battles and pushed each other to new heights

Boxers, like other athletes, learn and improve their skills by competing against the best. When boxing was boxing (as the saying goes), fighters had to go in tough and beat other, equally talented fighters to be considered great.

But boxing's current business model deprives fighters of the opportunity to prove and improve upon their skills by fighting other great fighters. Now slick PR and marketing create the illusion of greatness.

Part of the beauty of sports is that a team or individual athlete has to compete successfully at the highest level to be acknowledged as great.

Baseball's historically great teams won the World Series. Football's historically great teams won the Super Bowl. In basketball, the Holy Grail is the NBA Championship. Great athletes excel in their sports' flagship events whether in team competition or individual endeavors like track and field, tennis, and golf.

There's sad irony in the fact that boxing—the world's purest sport—has been manipulated by parochial economic interests to the point where it no longer has that level of competition. Except on rare occasions, the best no longer fight the best. We no longer know which fighters are great. Instead, we're left to speculate as to which fighters might someday be great or might have been great if only they'd fought the best.

In that regard, Teddy Atlas observes, "No matter how good a trainer a fighter has, no matter how hard he works in the gym, a fighter learns what's most important about the craft of boxing in fights. There's no teacher like the fight itself. And the problem we have today is that the priorities aren't centered around fighters learning the craft of boxing. They're about navigating a fighter to a belt and getting him a name while traveling down the easiest path possible. And that hurts because tough hard great fights make great fighters, and tough hard great fights make great fighters greater."

"Ray Leonard became a greater fighter because of what he learned fighting Roberto Duran," Atlas continues. "Then he took what he learned fighting Duran and used it to beat Thomas Hearns. After that, he took what he learned fighting Duran and Hearns and it helped him beat Marvin Hagler. And he fought Wilfred Benitez before he fought any of those guys. It was the hard fights, not the easy ones, that led Leonard to understand that there was always one more move he could make and taught him how to make that move to turn things around and win. Great fighters aren't born great or trained to greatness, although, obviously, natural physical gifts and a good teacher are important. Great fighters are forged in the fire."

As a contrast to "Fistic Nuggets," these "Notes" were on the serious side.

Fistic Notes

On November 2, 2013, Russian heavyweight Magomed Abdudsalamov suffered life-altering brain damage in a fight against Mike Perez at Madison Square Garden.

People with injuries like Magomed's tend to be hidden from view. They fade into the shadows. We conjure up positive images of their condition with phrases like "he's in rehab" and "he's doing well." They come from all walks of life. None of us is promised a life that's immune to horrible suffering.

Magomed was fighting to provide for his family. That much he has done. Last year, the State of New York, which was responsible for overseeing the fight, agreed to pay $22 million to Adbusalamov and his family after almost four years of litigation that focused on substandard New York State Athletic Commission medical protocols and haphazard implementation. The case against three individual defendants is still pending.

Some of the $22,000,000 has gone to lawyers. Magomed's wife, Bakanay, received a lump sum payout. The bulk of the settlement is structured in annuities that will provide income to Magomed over the next thirty years. If he dies before this period has run, $2,000,000 will revert to New York State and the remainder of the annuity will be paid to Magomed's estate. All of his medical expenses and related costs are paid for out of the annuity which is overseen by Charles Thomas, a former Queens County Surrogate's Court judge.

Magomed and Bakanay live in Greenwich with their three daughters, now 11, 8, and 4 years old. Greenwich is part of Connecticut's "gold coast," home to hedge fund managers and other members of the financial elite. The town has a few less desirable pockets. The Abdusalamovs live in a modest house surrounded by asphalt and gravel on a small plot of land with no lawn or garden.

Each morning, Bakanay bathes and shaves Magomed and dresses him in clean clothes. Three days a week, she takes him to Stamford Hospital for physical therapy, not to improve his condition—little further physical or cognitive improvement is expected—but to prevent his muscles from atrophying further.

The right side of Magomed's body is fully paralyzed. There's a scar the shape and size of a horseshoe on the right side of his head. He can control his left hand to a degree and part of his left arm. He tires easily and suffers from seizures. He cannot walk or control his bodily functions. He's at a high risk of choking, so everything he puts in his mouth is closely monitored.

His voice is soft. He tries to speak, sometimes in English and sometimes in Russian. Often what he says is unintelligible. At best, only a few words come out at a time. Sometimes they're appropriate to the situation. Other times, they're not.

He can follow simple commands such as "take my hand."

Magomed knows he's injured. The extent to which he understands his condition is uncertain. He responds to kindness. He recognizes familiar faces like his wife and children and knows that they're objects of affection. His strongest personal connection is with Bakanay. Asked if he knows who she is, he answers, "Big love."

His mind wanders. Almost always, there's a vacant look in his eyes.

He will never be independent or self-reliant again.

He's still Mago.

★ ★ ★

The Association of Boxing Commissions took a natural next step at its 2018 convention in Orlando when it voted 34-to-2 to make BoxRec. com the sole official record keeper for boxing in the United States.

The Ali Act, which went into effect in 2001, mandates that the ABC keep certain boxing-related records. Thereafter, the ABC granted Fight Fax the status of what was essentially a government-mandated monopoly. Every state athletic commission in America was required by law to send bout results, suspensions, and federal ID numbers to Fight Fax (as were ABC associate members in Canada). In exchange for its favored position, Fight Fax provided an updated list of suspended boxers to these commissions free of charge. But everyone else had to pay for the list. And more significantly, the ABC required that promoters submit a Fight Fax record for each boxer on a proposed fight card before the card was approved by the governing athletic commission. Fight Fax charged promoters (and everyone else other than commissions) for these records.

Meanwhile, BoxRec.com was growing. The site was founded by John Sheppard in 2000 and has become far-and-away the most heavily-trafficked boxing website in the world.

On a typical day, BoxRec.com has well over 100,000 visitors who view three-quarters of a million pages. These numbers increase significantly in the week before a big fight.

BoxRec's core content consists of more than 2,156,000 bouts that have been entered into its data base. This includes roughly 23,000 active (having fought within the past 365 days) and 602,000 non-active fighters. The site also has data on more than 74,000 referees, judges, managers, promoters, matchmakers, supervisors, and other "non-fighters." All of these numbers keep growing as new fights take place and more old ones are recorded.

Sheppard has steadfastly resisted the temptation to turn BoxRec.com into a pay site. The undertaking is fueled largely by his efforts and the work of two hundred editors from around the world who contribute their services for free. For years, he tried to get fight reports and other data such as suspension lists from governing state athletic commissions. Some commissions provided the information to BoxRec as a matter of course. Some sent it upon request. A few refused to send it even when asked.

That changed in 2016 when the ABC designated both Fight Fax and BoxRec as official registries and entered into separate two-year contracts with each. Thereafter, all athletic commissions subject to Ali Act jurisdiction were required to send fight reports to both record keepers. At the same time, the ABC requested certain system upgrades from Fight Fax. Fight Fax did not implement these upgrades and did not send a representative to the 2018 ABC convention. Therefore, only BoxRec's contract with the ABC was renewed.

The two holdout states in the voting were Pennsylvania and Texas, both of which felt that Fight Fax should be afforded the opportunity to remain as an alternative record keeper in light of its past contributions. But it wasn't to be.

Congratulations to BoxRec.com. Now, more than ever, it's boxing's indispensable website.

★ ★ ★

Hall-of-Fame linebacker Lawrence Taylor was incredibly gifted physically and arguably the most ferocious football player of his time. More than a few admirers looked at him and marveled, "What a fighter Taylor would have been."

LeBron James elicits a similar reaction. I haven't seen anyone on the basketball court or elsewhere pick a fight with LeBron.

But what would have happened if Lawrence Taylor caught a few Larry Holmes jabs on the nose? We don't know, do we? LeBron James is imposing and has lots of heart. But if Deontay Wilder cranked up a big right hand and landed, who knows how good LeBron's chin would be?

Fighters are a breed apart. They have toughness—physical and mental—that often goes unappreciated.

Appreciate it.

★ ★ ★

Does getting knocked out change a fighter? Don Turner has trained myriad world-class boxers including Larry Holmes, Evander Holyfield, and Michael Grant. When asked that question, Turner responded, "It depends on the fighter. When Evander Holyfield got knocked out by Riddick Bowe, it didn't change him at all. I don't think he even thought about it when he went back in the ring. But with a guy like Michael Grant, it changed his whole mindset toward being in boxing. After Lennox Lewis knocked Michael out, he was never the same."

★ ★ ★

Earlier this month (January 2018), World Boxing Council president Mauricio Sulaiman acknowledged that the WBC is considering adding a Floyd Mayweather medallion to its championship belts. That would place Mayweather in the company of Muhammad Ali, Joe Louis, Sugar Ray Robinson, and Jose Sulaiman.

We're living in an age when basic human dignity is under attack. At the same time, a large segment of the population is finally becoming aware of, and concerned about, the indignities that are regularly visited upon women.

Floyd Mayweather has been criminally convicted on multiple occasions of being physically abusive to women. On one of these occasions, he spent time in prison. Yet he has shown no remorse and continues to act in a way that objectifies and demeans women.

In defending Donald Trump's "grab them by the pussy" comment to *Hollywood Unlocked* last year, Mayweather declared, "People don't like the truth. Real men speak like, 'Man, she had a fat ass. You see her ass? I had to squeeze her ass. I had to grab that fat ass.' Right? So he's talking locker room talk. 'I'm the man. You know who I am. Yeah, I grabbed her by the pussy.' I feel people shy away from realness."

In an interview with *Men's Health* this month, Mayweather voiced ignorance of the "Me Too" movement which is in the vanguard of combatting sexual harassment and assault against women. He also owns and operates what is sometimes referred to as an "adult club" in Las Vegas.

I hope Mauricio Sulaiman understands the message that adding Mayweather's image to the WBC championship belt would sent to young men and women. Is this what he wants the WBC to stand for? Is this what he wants his father's legacy and his legacy to be?

★ ★ ★

Muhammad Ali vs. George Foreman was scheduled to take place in Zaire on September 25, 1974. On September 17, Foreman was sparring with Bill McMurray, a thirty-three-year-old journeyman fighter. Raising his arms to defend against a barrage of blows, McMurray accidentally jammed an elbow into George's face, slicing open the skin above Foreman's right eye. The bout was postponed and rescheduled for October 30.

Fast-forward to Caesars Palace on June 7, 1996. Oscar De La Hoya was challenging Julio Cesar Chavez for Chavez's WBC 140-pound title. Early in round one, a deep cut opened above Chavez's left eye. In round four, the cut necessitated stopping the fight. Afterward, Chavez acknowledged that he'd suffered the cut five days earlier while sparring and had covered it up with make-up during fight week activities. Nevada State Athletic Commission executive director Marc Ratner maintained that the cut had gone undetected during the pre-fight physical examination that the NSAC administered to Chavez.

If a fighter and his camp choose to move forward with a bout despite a cut that hasn't fully healed, the governing state athletic commission is charged with determining whether or not the fight should proceed.

In theory, it's a medical decision. How deep is the cut? Where is the cut? How likely is it that the cut will reopen? Fights aren't stopped because blood is lost. They're stopped because the flow of blood is impairing a fighter's vision or the nature of the cut threatens permanent damage. The magnitude of the fight shouldn't be a determining factor.

But we live in the real world. On one side of the equation is the safety of the fighter, the integrity of the fight, and protecting the buying public. On the other side, there are practical considerations. Economics matter.

And while we're at it; is a cut different from a bruised hand? A broken nose? The flu? Manny Pacquiao went into his bout against Floyd Mayweather with a tear in his right rotator cuff.

State athletic commissions respond to economic interests. The Nevada State Athletic Commission is mindful of what the big casinos want. Its primary function is to facilitate bringing big fights to Las Vegas and to regulate them in a manner that's acceptable to the powers that be.

A big fight hasn't been taken down in New York since 1998 when a card headlined by Henry Akinwande vs. Evander Holyfield was cancelled after Akinwande tested positive for hepatitis B. But here, one should note, Holyfield-Akinwande was shaping up as an economic disaster, and the New York Daily News reported that Madison Square Garden stood to lose more than a million dollars on the evening because of an overly optimistic financial guarantee.

Greg Sirb is executive director of the Pennsylvania State Athletic Commission and a staunch advocate for fighter safety.

"It's a tough call," Sirb says. "It happens more often than you'd think, particularly with big fights where there's definite pressure to get the fight on. The fighter says, 'I've won before with cuts.' And let's be realistic. It's rare that a fighter goes into a fight at one hundred percent. Fighting hurt is part of boxing. They're like football players in that regard."

And there are other considerations that go beyond the governing commission's deliberative process. Is it the A-side fighter or the B-side fighter who's cut? The A-side fighter can usually afford to pull out. Often, the B-side fighter can't.

If the fight goes forward, should bettors know about the cut? What about the opponent?

Meanwhile, as boxing maven Ron Katz notes, "The fighter should bring a good cutman. That's for sure."

* * *

Lewis Dial, a sportswriter for the *Amsterdam News* in the 1930s, once opined, "You can fight better with a broken hand than with a broken heart."

Here are more words of wisdom from boxing writers:

* Randy Roberts: "Far more boxers' careers have been ruined by free time than by punches."
* Brin-Jonathan-Butler: "Boxers don't just walk out onto a tightrope with no net. Everyone's cheering to help jiggle the rope."
* Charles Farrell: "No one can disabuse you of the notion of being a tough guy faster than a professional fighter."

* * *

Twenty-five years ago, Craig Hamilton founded Jo Sports, one of the leading boxing memorabilia companies in the world today. When Hamilton started Jo Sports, roughly eighty-five percent of his business came from the United States. That number is now down to forty percent because of burgeoning sales in Europe.

Recently, Hamilton offered some thoughts for those interested in the boxing memorabilia market.

(1) The value of an item is determined by its historical significance, scarcity, and condition. A photograph signed by Cus D'Amato is worth more than a photo signed by Mike Tyson because of scarcity. A nicely-signed photo of Tex Rickard will sell for between $800 and $1,000, while a nicely signed photo of Don King can be bought for $30. Again, scarcity is the key.

(2) "Vintage" signatures signed while a fighter is active are worth more than a signature from the fighter's later years.

(3) Most mass-produced items created for the memorabilia market fade in value. Limited-edition LeRoy Neiman lithographs of Muhammad Ali signed by Neiman and Ali are an exception to this rule.

That brings us to Ali.

When Muhammad died in 2016, the market was saturated with Ali memorabilia. Many potential sellers had been waiting for him to die in the belief that his passing would increase the value of their holdings. But so much content went on sale in mid-2016 that the price of Ali memorabilia actually dropped a bit.

Still, in Hamilton's opinion, Ali will always be a big seller. Babe Ruth has been dead for seventy years, and Ruth memorabilia has retained its value.

Hamilton says that, to his knowledge, the most valuable piece of boxing memorabilia that exists today are the gloves Cassius Clay wore when he defeated Sonny Liston in 1964. They were sold at auction in 2014 for $836,500. But that's a small number compared to what Hamilton estimates the "Holy Grail" of Ali collectors—Clay's *Ring Magazine* championship belt—would bring if it were found.

Ali cornerman Bundini Brown, who died in 1987, is believed to have had the belt at one time. It's unlikely that the belt was broken down for its content because it was made of base metal and contained no precious stones. Possibly, Bundini sold it. But it has never surfaced.

"You could start the bidding on that one at five million dollars," Hamilton posits.

Many collectors build their collection around a particular fighter, class of individuals (such as famous trainers), or fights at a particular venue (e.g. Madison Square Garden). Others look for a particular type of collectible such as vintage posters, uncut fight tickets, or onsite programs. Autographs are very much in demand.

The fly in the ointment for collectors of Ali signatures is that, in Hamilton's words, "it's probably the most forged signature of all time." In part, that's due to heavy demand. And more significantly, Ali's signature is difficult to authenticate because, as he aged and his health deteriorated, his signature varied dramatically from day to day.

Hamilton has this advice for collectors: "Don't buy something because you think it will appreciate in value. Buy what you like. Then you can enjoy it while you have it. And make sure it's real. Check the provenance. Buy from reputable sellers. Make sure you get what you're paying for."

★ ★ ★

A bit of boxing trivia . . .

One man fought both Jack Dempsey and Joe Louis. And the loser was . . . Jack Sharkey.

On July 21, 1927, in the next-to-last fight of Dempsey's storied ring career, the Manassa Mauler knocked out Sharkey at Yankee Stadium in the seventh round. Five years later, Sharkey won a split decision over Max Schmeling to claim the heavyweight throne. But a year after that, he lost the crown by knockout to Primo Carnera.

Fast-forward to August 18, 1936, when Sharkey had the misfortune to enter the ring against Louis. It was the Brown Bomber's first fight after suffering a devastating knockout defeat at the hands of Schmeling. The feeling was that Louis still might not be right.

The feeling was wrong. He KO'd Sharkey in the third round.

And talking about going in tough; one man fought Muhammad Ali, Joe Frazier, and George Foreman. That was George Chuvalo, who was knocked out by Foreman and Frazier respectively in the third and fourth rounds and lost by decision twice to Ali.

★ ★ ★

There were times when David Haye conducted himself like a jerk. But his June 12, 2017, retirement statement was eloquent and poignant.

Referencing his May 5 knockout defeat at the hands of Tony Bellew in the final fight of his 15-year ring career, Haye acknowledged, "I saw punches coming but wasn't quick enough to avoid them. I created openings but lacked the speed and agility to capitalize on them. Quick counterattacks, the sort I've effortlessly thrown since my teenage years, are no longer in my armory. And when I take shots, they now shake me to my boots. The things I used to be able to do in the ring instinctively now exist only in my mind and in video clips of my old fights. My ego would have loved to have retired on a win. But deep down, I know my effort was the very best I had left to give. That underwhelming effort revealed the truth about my current abilities in a world-class boxing arena. The boxing gods have spoken."

Haye also had this bit of wisdom to offer: "If I could go back in time and give advice to my 21-year-old self, or anyone setting off on their own adventure, I would say this. Live in the moment. Don't only appreciate the good times once they become a memory."

★ ★ ★

An observation from Ann Wolfe, perhaps the most dangerous female fighter of her era: "This is a savage murderous sport. We're punching each other in the damn head. If you ain't trying to kill somebody, why the hell are you punching people in the head until you make them unconscious?"

★ ★ ★

Bigtime boxing is doing reasonably well in New York City with Barclays Center and Madison Square Garden at the center of the action. But club fights are struggling. That's due in part to the high cost of promoting in the Big Apple. It's also because suitable venues keep disappearing, particularly in Manhattan.

Four years ago, Roseland Ballroom (which hosted 27 fight cards) was demolished to make way for a high-rise office building. The latest casualty of the Manhattan real estate wars is B.B. King Blues Club and Grill, located nine blocks north of Madison Square Garden in Times Square.

B.B. King opened in 2000. It was primarily a music venue. Artists who performed there, in addition to B.B. King, included Little Richard, James Brown, Chuck Berry, Bo Diddley, Boyz II Men, Ice Cube, Public Enemy, Dionne Warwick, Roberta Flack, Al Green, Judy Collins, Don McLean, Gregg Allman, Billy Ray Cyrus, Eric Burden, Peter Frampton, and Jerry Lee Lewis.

The first fight card at B.B. King took place on August 6, 2008. Randall Bailey knocked out Dairo Esaias in the main event. All told, 29 cards were promoted at the venue by Lou DiBella as part of his "Broadway Boxing" series.

The room had the feel of a fire trap. Its tiny dressing rooms and backstage corridors were suffocatingly hot during the summer months. The ring was set up just below the front of the stage, which gave credentialed media, who were seated on the stage, an incredible view of the action. Most of the sightlines for patrons were good, although there was an inconvenient pillar or two. Many fans stood all night by a large bar in the back of the room.

DiBella used the shows to develop fighters that his promotional company had signed. If he was lucky, he broke even on a given night. Over the years, "Broadway Boxing" at B.B. King showcased Guillermo Rigondeaux, Yuri Foreman, Badou Jack, Sadam Ali, Andy Lee, Charles Martin, Joe Smith, Seanie Monaghan, Sergey Lipinets, Tevin Farmer, and Sergey Derevyanchenko. The last fight card at the club was contested on February 2, 2018. Rising rent forced it to close at the end of April.

"I adored B.B. King, "DiBella says, looking back on it all. "Doing a show there always made me feel better. The atmosphere was great. We had some future champions on the cards. But what made me feel particularly good was when a club fighter came in, upset a heavy favorite, and had the best night of his career right there. Losing B.B. King as a venue is a loss for me and a loss for boxing."

★ ★ ★

I recently watched *Paterno*, the HBO film about former Penn State football coach Joe Paterno.

Paterno was one of college football's greatest coaches. But his image was forever tarnished by an inadequate response to allegations, later proven true, that longtime assistant coach Jerry Sandusky was sexually abusing underage boys. Paterno's failure was particularly disappointing given the fact that he was an intelligent man who wasn't afraid to venture outside the parameters that often restrict the thinking of bigtime college football coaches.

When I was researching *Muhammad Ali: His Life and Times*, I interviewed a number of iconic sports figures. Paterno was one of them.

We began by talking about football.

"Ali would have made a great linebacker and an outstanding tight end," Paterno told me. "I don't know if he had the foot speed for any of the other skill positions, but his strength, quickness of hands, and balance were awfully good. Now maybe football wouldn't have been the right game for him. Certainly, at age eighteen or nineteen, he'd have needed guidance as to what he could and couldn't do as far as alienating his teammates was concerned. I'm liberal politically, but I'm conservative in terms of lifestyle and how I coach the team. Here at Penn State, we have a rule about players getting along with each other. You can only say you're sorry so many times. But I don't want to underestimate Ali's ability to accommodate any situation. If he'd made a commitment to it, I'm sure he would have been a team player. I know, I'd have loved the chance to coach him."

Then the conversation turned to weightier matters.

"Ali was important," Paterno noted. "I think every black person who's able to overcome the problems that surround them as he did and serve as a role model is important. Kids today are in desperate need of role models who not only succeed in the sports world, but once they've done that, have the ability of a Jackie Robinson or a Muhammad Ali to change the social attitudes of black and white Americans, and make blacks understand that they don't necessarily have to do what whites want them to do to be respected. Ali achieved that. I always admired him as an athlete. But I think the stand he took on the draft was what spoke most about him. That he had the courage to jeopardize his career and accept all the implications of his position showed a man of great principle."

"The world was different then," Paterno continued. "It's hard for some people now to remember the—'despair' might be too strong a word, but the fear in young people over what was going on. I had a friend, a bright young man I admired greatly who'd covered our team for the student newspaper here at Penn State. Then he'd become editor of the paper and gone into the service after college. One day, he came back to visit and had a long talk with me about deserting. He wanted to know how I'd react. I said, 'Well, as far as our personal relationship is concerned, it would have no effect on me.' And he did desert. He went up to Canada and wrote me every once in a while. And when he did that, and when Ali took his stand, it made me wonder, 'What the devil is going on?' I started thinking about what was happening in Vietnam. Now, if I'd been drafted, I probably would have gone because of my traditions. But that doesn't mean I'd have been right to go. And the truth is, I started to become very sympathetic to people like Ali and that young man. I began to understand that they had very good reasons for what they were doing. I began to see Vietnam as a white man's war in the sense that it was being fought by blacks, but in support of a white colonial mentality. I began to think that the war was very wrong."

Not your typical bigtime college football coach.

★ ★ ★

Greg Sirb (executive director of the Pennsylvania State Athletic Commission) is a staunch advocate for fighter safety. Sirb regularly reviews fight schedules and fight results from around the country with an eye toward determining which commissions need to upgrade their standards. Recently, he turned an eye toward the National Football League.

The causal link between football and chronic brain damage is no longer in doubt. After years of waffling and covering up, the NFL is now addressing the issue in a more substantive way. A massive financial settlement with former players and a new "concussion protocol" are part of the mix. But Sirb still believes that the NFL is behind boxing in some respects.

"Look at [New England Patriots all-pro tight end] Rob Gronkowski," Sirb said in a recent telephone conversation. "On January 21st, Gronkowski suffered a concussion after a helmet-to-helmet hit in the AFC conference championship game. But he was cleared to participate in a full practice on February 1st and to play in the Super Bowl on February 4th."

"In other words," Sirb continued, "two weeks after Gronkowski suffered a concussion, he was back on the field where he risked getting hit in the head again. Now let's take the same scenario for boxing. Say, Gronkowski was a boxer and got hit with a big right hand, went down, maybe got to his feet, and the referee stopped the fight. And just like he did on the football field, Gronkowski the boxer suffered a concussion. In boxing, he would have been suspended for at least thirty days."

"The NFL can say all it wants about its so-called concussion protocol," Sirb concluded. "But football is behind boxing when it comes to caring about participant safety. Look, football is a great game. I love football. My son plays college football. And I regulate a sport where one guy is paid to punch another guy in the face. But those guys at the NFL have to get off their high horse and stop all this sanctimonious talk about concussion protocol. You tell me which sport is more dangerous."

★ ★ ★

A thought from boxing historian Peter Benson: "The original purpose of the boxing ring wasn't to keep the boxers in but the crowd out; not to protect the crowd from the fury inside the ring, but the boxers from the fury outside it."

★ ★ ★

We've seen it countless times. Two fighters are in the ring. One of them is the aggressor and hits harder. But he can't get within punching range because the opponent keeps running. Invariably, one of the commentators says, "So-and-so doesn't know how to cut the ring off."

But it's not that simple.

Standard operating procedure for cutting off the ring is as follows.

The ring is a square. Imagine your opponent moving around the perimeter. The first thing you have to say to yourself is, "I own the center of the ring. I own the middle."

Next, whichever side of the ring your opponent is on, draw an imaginary line from one corner of the ring to the opposite corner and stand on that line with one shoulder pointed toward each corner. That cuts the ring in half.

Let's assume both boxers fight out of an orthodox stance. If the opponent moves to his left, step forward with your left foot and slide to the right with your right foot. If the opponent moves to his right, you still step forward with your left foot, take another short step with your right, and then slide to the left with your left foot. What you're doing now is making the ring smaller and cutting down on your opponent's avenues of escape. If you do give him an avenue of escape, make him go to his right because it's hard for an orthodox fighter to punch effectively when he's moving to his right. And you repeat the process again and again until you're on top of your opponent.

"It's really not that complicated," says Pat Burns (who trained Jermain Taylor during the glory years). "It's all about footwork. If you and I got in the ring together, I could teach you how to do it in fifteen minutes, yell at you for six weeks, and you'd be a master at cutting off the ring. It's a basic skill, but it has to be taught and then practiced again and again until each step becomes instinct."

Still, there's more to cutting off the ring than knowing how. It takes footwork, speed, and athleticism. And it's not just about closing the gap between a fighter and his opponent. The pursuing fighter has to get within range and, at the same time, accurately throw one or more punches.

Also, it's more difficult to cut the ring off against some fighters than others.

When Muhammad Ali was young, he was able to escape because he was incredibly fast on his feet. And if someone got inside, Ali knew how to tie him up. Hector Camacho could escape all night because he was fast on his feet and a southpaw to boot. And if a fighter is being pursued, he can evade being pinned in by getting off first with a jab and forcing his pursuer to reset while he starts moving again.

Further in that regard, veteran trainer Don Turner notes, "If Larry Holmes stuffed a jab in your face, all of a sudden you didn't want to cut the ring off on him so much."

★ ★ ★

Oscar De La Hoya and Bernard Hopkins did battle at the MGM Grand in Las Vegas for the unified middleweight championship of the world on September 9, 2004. Miraculously—or so it seems—the two men have coexisted as equity participants in Golden Boy since November of that year.

I was going through some old files recently and came across a handful of thoughts from Oscar and Bernard that I haven't used in articles before. Now seems like a good time to share them:

* Hopkins: "If you don't know how to control your emotions, that's a signed death warrant in boxing."
* De La Hoya: "Greed is good when you're a fighter."
* Hopkins: "I don't like buffets. You pay to try to kill yourself."
* De La Hoya: "Nothing can save you in that ring except yourself."

★ Hopkins:"James Toney makes out like he's this big gangsta. He makes out like he's from Detroit. The man came up in Ann Arbor. The only Big House they got there is the Michigan football stadium."

★ De La Hoya: "When you start losing to fighters you know you should beat, it's time retire."

★ Hopkins: "It's not enough to fight like you're broke. That's easy. You have to train like you're broke."

★ De La Hoya: "I went through the fire and I'm still here."

★ ★ ★

The Boxing Writers Association of America is honoring Lou DiBella this year with the Sam Taub Award for excellence in broadcast journalism. The award is long overdue. It harkens back to a Golden Era when HBO redefined the sport and business of boxing, and the sweet science enjoyed a renaissance built around fighters and fights that truly mattered.

The television executive widely regarded as most responsible for that era was Seth Abraham, who built HBO's boxing program from the ground up. But if Abraham was HBO's Batman, then Lou DiBella played the role of Robin.

DiBella joined HBO in 1989 after a four-year stint as an attorney on Wall Street. He rose quickly through the ranks and was the driving force behind HBO's *Boxing After Dark* as well as an integral member of the team that elevated *World Championship Boxing* to an industry-wide standard.

Speaking of DiBella, Abraham said simply, "I became a much better boss when I came to understand and accept the fact that Lou knew more about boxing than I did."

While at HBO, DiBella also developed a reputation as a white knight within the boxing community.

"I felt a fiduciary duty to the sport when I was a TV executive," Lou acknowledged. "With the checkbook I had at HBO, in addition to my corporate responsibilities, I felt an obligation to be a force for reform. I put a lot of pressure on myself in a way that most TV executives don't."

DiBella left HBO Sports in 2000 to form a promotional company of his own. Eighteen years have passed since then. An entire generation of writers and others in the boxing community know him only as a promoter.

But some things never change. DiBella is still passionate about the sport. And having a conversation with Lou about boxing on a bad day exposes a person to more profanity than gansta rap. As Jeff Wald, one of the creators of *The Contender*, observed, "Lou could start a fistfight in an empty room."

And Lou is still a good guy.

"A lot of people told me that, when I left my lofty perch at HBO, I'd see how nasty and dirty this business really is," DiBella has acknowledged. "They were right. The truth is, boxing is a miserable business, and there's a part of me that wonders if I wouldn't be happier if I redirected away from it. But there's also part of me that loves the sport and loves the fighters and thinks I can make money and have a positive impact on boxing at the same time."

Meanwhile, there's a poem surrounded by DiBella's other favorite sports memorabilia in the den of his Long Island home. It's two lines long and reads as follows:

Lou DiBella
Is a wonderful fella

The poet's signature is inscribed beneath the poem: Muhammad Ali.

★ ★ ★

The BWAA honors one of its own each year for the craft of boxing journalism. This year's recipient of the Nat Fleischer Award for career excellence is Michael Rosenthal.

Rosenthal was born in Chicago and grew up in Los Angeles. After he graduated from Fresno State with a BA in journalism, his journey led him to a year in Italy and another year in Israel, where he lived on a kibbutz. He worked as a reporter for two small newspapers in California—the *New Hall Signal* and *Simi Valley Enterprise*—and then spent fourteen years as a reporter and assistant sports editor for the *Los Angeles Daily News*. That was followed by five years as Assistant Sports Editor for the *San Diego Union-Tribune* and eight years as a writer for, and editor of, *The Ring*.

Rosenthal became a fixture on the boxing scene during the ten years that he covered big fights and wrote a weekly boxing column for the *Daily News*. "I love the sport in its purest form," he says. "The actual fighting is incredible. I don't like the business of boxing, but I suppose I could say the same thing about a lot of businesses."

"The best story I ever wrote," Rosenthal continues, "was about the problems that Bobby Chacon had after his career as a fighter ended. The most memorable fight I covered was Holyfield-Tyson II. The image of the ear bite is as clear in my mind now as if it happened yesterday. We saw Holyfield jumping up and down, and then someone shouted, 'He bit his ear.' Being around Tyson after he got out of prison wasn't much fun, but it was important and it was big. Foreman-Moorer was memorable because of the drama of it all. The roar of the crowd when George knocked Moorer out was the loudest sound I've ever heard. Chavez-Haugen in Mexico City was unforgettable. And I became very close to Rafael and Gabriel Ruelas because I'd covered them from the time they started their careers in the valley. Both of them won world titles. That was special for me."

Rosenthal has earned the respect of the public and his peers as both a writer and editor. Reflecting on these dual roles, he says, "Editing is primarily about taking someone else's work, making it better, and ensuring that it conforms to basic journalistic standards. There are times when it's gratifying. But I prefer writing because writing allows you to be more creative and also to express yourself and connect with your subject more fully."

"But the best thing for me about being a boxing writer, Rosenthal notes, "is that I get to see things from up close as they unfold. And then I have the privilege of conveying my impression of what I've just seen to the world."

★ ★ ★

Elvis Presley was intrigued by the sweet science. He tried out for the boxing team at Humes High School in Memphis but quit after one day when he suffered a bloody nose. Years later, he played the lead in a 1962 remake of the classic film, *Kid Galahad*.

The original version of Kid Galahad was good for its time.

Ward Guisenberry (played by Wayne Morris) is a naïve, gullible, handsome farmboy who's working as a bellhop at a Florida hotel so he can get enough money to buy a farm. Defending a woman's honor at a party thrown by fight manager Nick Donati (Edward G. Robinson), Ward punches out a big lug who, it turns out, is heavyweight champion Chuck McGraw. This piques Donati's interest. He gets Ward a trainer, puts him in the ring, and watches as the newly-christened "Kid Galahad" moves quickly up the ladder to challenge for the heavyweight crown.

There's also a love triangle involving Wade, Louise "Fluff" Phillips (Nick's assistant played by Bette Davis), and Jean Donati (Nick's sister played by Jayne Bryan).

Bette Davis has some of the better lines in the film. "They'll all be talking about you someday," she tells Wade. "And then they'll forget about you." Speaking with Wade about McGraw's manager, mobster Turkey Morgan (Humphrey Bogart) Fluff confides, "He'd just a soon kill me or you as take a drink." And in a moment of anger, she tells Nick, "I've never liked you, and I'm not going to start now."

That sentiment is understandable, since Nick has told Fluff, "There isn't any room for feelings in this game. A fighter is a machine, not a violin player." Or as Mama Donati (Soledad Jimenez) tells her daughter, "Nicky is a manager of fighters, not of people's hearts."

The original *Kid Galahad* plays nicely on the emotions. The black-and-white cinematography is wonderful. The heroes are heroes, and the villains are villains. There's the usual skullduggery of double-crosses and fixed fights (which are choreographed like cartoons). It's unrealistic, hokey, and lots of fun.

As for the remake . . . Once Elvis Presley was discharged from the Army in 1960, his manager, Andreas Cornelis Van Kuijk (who preferred to be called "Colonel Tom Parker"), locked him into a series of Hollywood movie contracts that lasted for the better part of a decade. During this time, Elvis starred in twenty-seven films in which the character he played was always a thinly-veiled version of himself. *Kid Galahad* was one of these films.

Elvis plays Walter Gulick, a young man recently discharged from the Army who's seeking employment as an automobile mechanic. He winds up in the Catskills, where he takes a job as a sparring partner for five dollars a round to make ends meet. Lo and behold, it turns out that Walter has one-punch knockout power. Things go from there.

Gig Young plays Willy Grogan, a smalltime manager in trouble with the mob. The ever-forgiving, Walter says of Grogan, "He's not a bad guy. Maybe he's got a reason for being a liar." Meanwhile, transfixed by Walter's power and ability to take a punch, Grogan declares, "He's got an ax in his right hand and a bowling ball for a head."

Lola Albright plays Dolly Fletcher, Grogan's love interest. Joan Blackman is cast as Rose (Grogan's sister and the object of Elvis's affections). Charles Bronson plays Lew Nyack, Walter's camp buddy and trainer, who at one point counsels his charge, "Hey Walter. In case you want to duck once in a while, it ain't against the rules."

The fight scenes with Elvis are as realistic as a theatrical production would be if Adrien Broner played *Hamlet*. It's a mediocre movie with Elvis singing some of his lesser songs.

"I'd like to make better films than the films I made before," Presley said ruefully when his Hollywood sojourn was over. "I didn't have final approval of the script, which means I couldn't say, 'This is not good for me.' I don't think anyone was consciously trying to harm me. It was just, Hollywood's image of me was wrong, and I knew it and I couldn't do anything about it. The pictures got very similar. I'd read the first four or five pages, and I'd know it was just a different name with twelve new songs in it. It worried me sick. I didn't know what to do. I was obligated a lot of times very heavily to things I didn't believe in and it was very difficult. I had thought they would get a property for me and give me a chance to show some acting ability, but it did not change. I became very discouraged. I would have liked to have something more challenging instead of Hollywood's image of what they thought I was."

Presley was a one-of-a-kind superstar, known and idolized the world over. There was, of course, another global superstar of equal if not greater magnitude who shared the spotlight with Elvis—Muhammad Ali.

The King of Rock and Roll and the King of Boxing met on two occasions. The first was in Las Vegas, when Ali saw Elvis perform. "All my life, I admired Elvis Presley," Muhammad said afterward. "It was a thrill to meet him."

The two men met again in a Las Vegas hotel suite just prior to Ali's February 14, 1973, fight against Joe Bugner. Elvis presented Muhammad with a faux-jewel-studded robe emblazoned with the words "The People's Choice." Ali wore it in his next fight, which was against Ken Norton. But as The Greatest later recalled, "I got my jaw broke and stopped wearing it."

"I felt sorry for Elvis," Ali said a decade after Presley's death. "He didn't enjoy life the way he should. He stayed indoors all the time. I told him he should go out and see people. He said he couldn't because, everywhere he went, they mobbed him. He didn't understand. No one wanted to hurt him. All they wanted was to be friendly and tell him how much they loved him."

★ ★ ★

Boxing has a PED problem. And Barclays Center has its own drug problem. At times—and Saturday, January 14, 2018, was one of them—the smell of weed is so strong that non-smokers are in danger of getting a contact high. Sitting in the media section during Errol Spence vs. Lamont Peterson was like hanging out in a legalized-marijuana dispensary. The odor was so intense that several New York State Athletic Commission inspectors assigned to the fighters' corners noticed it.

Someday, someone driving home from Barclays Center after a fight will be in an accident. Tetrahydrocannabinol will be found in his or her blood. There will be a lawsuit. And a jury will find that second-hand smoke from Barclays Center was a contributing causal factor. Or a fighter will say that his or her performance was adversely affected by the "Barclays buzz."

It's a difficult situation to control. But Barclays should do more to control it. That would include announcements over the public address system, security personnel with the proper equipment looking for vapor-izers, and similar measures.

I appreciate the pleasures of marijuana as a recreational drug and also its benefits as a medicinal aid. But it shouldn't be forced on those who don't want it.

★ ★ ★

On July 27, 2018, *The New Yorker* published an article by Ronan Farrow that details multiple allegations of sexual misconduct lodged against Les Moonves (chairman and CEO of CBS Corporation).

On July 30, the CBS board of directors voted to keep Moonves in his present position pending an investigation of the allegations against him as well as the broader culture at CBS. This investigation will be conducted by an outside law firm.

Moonves, for his part, issued a statement that reads, "I recognize that there were times decades ago when I may have made some women uncomfortable by making advances. Those were mistakes, and I regret them immensely. But I always understood and respected—and abided by the principle—that 'no' means 'no,' and I have never misused my position to harm or hinder anyone's career."

A corporate CEO creates a culture in which values—good and bad—trickle down. The *New Yorker* article also references allegations of sexual harassment lodged against several other CBS executives, some of which resulted in quiet financial settlements.

What does this have to do with boxing?

A lot.

The first anniversary of the August 26, 2017, fight between Floyd Mayweather and Conor McGregor is approaching. For those with short memories, it's worth recounting how Showtime (part of the CBS empire) promoted the pay-per-view telecast of that fight.

The Mayweather-McGregor media tour was marked by blatant misogyny, racism, and homophobia. There were stops in Los Angeles, Toronto, Brooklyn, and London. During a promotional event at Barclay's Center, McGregor told 13,165 screaming fans, "A lot of the media seem to be saying I'm against black people. That's absolutely fucking ridiculous. Do they not know I'm half-black? Yeah. I'm half-black, from the belly button down. And just to show that that's squashed, here's a little present for my beautiful, black female fans."

McGregor then began thrusting his pelvis back and forth with his microphone strategically placed between his legs to simulate sexual intercourse.

All four press conferences were posted online in their entirety by Showtime. During these events, Mayweather and McGregor branded each other a "cunt," "bitch," "pussy," or "ho" more than fifty times. This was regarded as effective marketing by the promotion. Showtime offered no criticism of the misogyny, just as it was institutionally silent when Mayweather branded McGregor a "faggot." After all, the network was increasing its visibility and stood to make a lot of money from the promotion.

One might add here that Mayweather has been criminally convicted for being physically abusive to women on multiple occasions and served 63 days in jail for one such offense. But there was no mention of that by Showtime during the Mayweather-McGregor promotion.

If Mayweather had called Les Moonves "a money-grubbing, hook-nosed Jew bastard," that might have gotten Showtime's attention. But in the context of Mayweather-McGregor, the network showed no concern for the women who work at Showtime or any other women.

As I wrote at the time, "Somewhere, as you read this, men who think that Floyd Mayweather and Conor McGregor are really cool role models are abusing women. The abuse will psychologically scar some of the women for life. Maybe one of the abusers will kill his victim."

Now, thanks to Ronan Farrow, we know a little more about the culture at Showtime's parent company.

* * *

A word of remembrance regarding Bill Nack, who died on April 13, 2018, at age 77 after a battle with lung cancer.

Nack is best known for his literary output during a 23-year sojourn at *Sports Illustrated* and a 1975 book that remains the definitive study of Secretariat, horse racing's greatest champion.

The horses were Nack's first love. But he was a talented wordsmith who could write well about anything. He didn't turn his attention to boxing often. But when he did, it was worth reading.

Among the articles Nack wrote about the sweet science (collected in a 2003 book entitled *My Turf*) were a ground-breaking exploration of the dark side of Rocky Marciano; a portrait of "Young Cassius" that celebrated Muhammad Ali's fiftieth birthday; a study of the lasting enmity that Joe Frazier felt for Ali (written on the twenty-fifth anniversary of Ali-Frazier I); an insightful look back at the Dempsey-Tunney "long count" fight; and a piece that humanized Sonny Liston.

Nack's work was always well-researched and beautifully written. He was a good writer and a nice man.

★ ★ ★

I was thinking recently about a conversation I had with Joe Frazier years ago. Joe was reminiscing about his first fight against Muhammad Ali—"The Fight of the Century."

"That night at Madison Square Garden," Joe told me, "fifteenth round when I put Ali down. I stood where no one else ever stood."

Other sports stir passions. But no matter how much glory there is in winning the Super Bowl or World Cup, those are team sports. It's nice to win an individual championship at Wimbledon or Augusta. But no sport has been invested with more social and political symbolism than boxing. And no sporting events have demanded more attention than the biggest fights of all time.

A significant portion of the population doesn't know who won the World Series the day after it's over. Sports fans do. Your eighty-year-old grandmother might not.

But virtually everyone on the planet knew that Joe Frazier beat Muhammad Ali. on March 8, 1971. Joe Louis's first-round knockout of Max Schmeling in 1938 sent similar shockwaves around the globe. And Ali experienced his ultimate moment of glory when he reclaimed the throne against George Foreman in Zaire.

Just winning a championship is enthralling. In his autobiography, Sugar Ray Robinson recalled his first world title, a fifteen round decision at Madison Square Garden over Tommy Bell: "The ring announcer was holding a microphone and blaring 'The new world welterweight champion . . .' And even though he was only a few feet away, I could hardly hear him. My ears were almost bursting with the noise. The most noise seemed to come down out of the balcony; a steady roar, like a waterfall splashing all over me. Unless you've been in that ring when the noise is for you, there's no way you'll ever know what it's like."

Now magnify that feeling exponentially by adding the hopes and fears of millions of people around the globe to the drama. To be Joe Louis, knowing that this is the first time many people have heard a black man referred to simply as "the American." To be Jack Johnson or Joe Frazier or Muhammad Ali.

To be standing in the center of the ring—for one night, the center of the world—and know you've done it. Think about that feeling for a moment.

That's boxing at its greatest.

There's boxing. And then there's heavyweight boxing.

The Heavyweight Triangle: Anthony Joshua is Still The Man

When 2018 began, Anthony Joshua was the dominant force in heavyweight boxing as a fighter and as a commercial attraction. Joshua was basking in the afterglow of a dramatic comeback win against Wladimir Klitschko in front of 90,000 adoring fans at Wembley Stadium. Deontay Wilder was largely unknown with a resume as thin as rice paper. And Tyson Fury was mired in a cycle of self-destruction.

Times change. Joshua looked ordinary this year in defeating Joseph Parker and Alexander Povetkin. Wilder scored a dramatic knockout victory over Luis Ortiz. And Fury came back from the abyss. Then Wilder and Fury engaged in a dramatic struggle that left fight fans buzzing. All of a sudden, people were asking, "What would happen if Joshua, Wilder, and Fury fought each other in 2019?"

Boxing needs one heavyweight champion, not three. It needs a round-robin tournament with Anthony Joshua, Deontay Wilder, and Tyson Fury as the participants. But it won't happen anytime soon. So *Sporting News* has done what we can to create the tournament for you.

We put together a panel of forty experts. Then we asked them to predict the results of a rematch between Tyson Fury and Deontay Wilder and also Anthony Joshua vs. Fury and Joshua vs. Wilder. The panel includes nine fighters, three trainers, seven matchmakers, and twenty-one media representatives.

Four legendary heavyweight champions—George Foreman, Lennox Lewis, Larry Holmes, and Evander Holyfield—are among the electors. Other fighters on the panel include Gerry Cooney (one of boxing's hardest punching heavyweights ever), Paulie Malignaggi and Matthew Macklin (both of whom have retired as active fighters and are now among the best TV analysts in the business), Dominic Breazeale (who fought Joshua and is now the mandatory challenger for Wilder's WBC belt), and Bernard Hopkins.

Teddy Atlas, Pat Burns, and Russ Anber bring a trainer's perspective to the proceedings.

Bruce Trampler, Russell Peltz, Ron Katz, Eric Bottjer, Mike Marchionte and Don Elbaum are among the savviest matchmakers in boxing. It's their job to know who will win fights. Craig Hamilton is one of boxing's most knowledgeable historians.

The media is also well-represented. Joshua and Fury are from England, so we enlisted the services of Matt Christie, Gareth Davies, John Dennen, Tris Dixon, Don McRae, and Jeff Powell (six of the best boxing writers in the UK). They're joined on the panel by Al Bernstein, Harold Lederman, Larry Merchant, Brian Kenny, Ron Borges, Jerry Izenberg, Mark Kriegel, Keith Idec, Norm Frauenheim, Michael Rosenthal, Randy Gordon, Tom Gerbasi, and Bart Barry.

Michael Buffer and David Diamante (fixtures at ringside for countless fights) round out the panel.

Each of these forty electors predicted the outcome of all three fights. A fighter was given one point for each predicted win. In the event an elector thought a fight was "too close to call," each fighter received a half point. A perfect score—all forty electors thinking that the same fighter would win both of his fights—would have been 80 points.

The final point totals are:
Anthony Joshua   51–½ points
Tyson Fury   36–½
Deontay Wilder   32

Breaking the point totals down, Joshua's predicted record in the tournaments is 50 wins, 27 losses, and 3 draws with 26 knockouts and 14 KOs by

Fury's record in the tournament is 33 wins, 40 losses, and 7 draws with 2 knockouts and 23 KOs by

Wilder's record in the tournament is 29 wins, 45 losses, and 6 draws with 26 knockouts (the same number as Joshua) and 17 KOs by.

The electors predicted that 54 of the fights would end in a knockout and 66 would go the distance. Of the 66 fights going the distance, eight were considered too close to call.

Eighteen of the electors thought that Joshua would win both of his fights.

Nine of the electors thought that Fury would win both of his fights.

Seven of the electors thought that Wilder would win both of his fights.

Analyzing the electors by category, fighters and trainers (grouped as one), matchmakers, and media all ranked Joshua first. The fighter-trainer grouping and matchmakers ranked Fury second and Wilder third. The media electors ranked Wilder second and Fury third.

"One of the things I love about these match-ups," one elector said, "is that they're all hard to predict. No outcome could be called an upset in any of these fights."

Other comments included, "You have three radically different personalities with vastly different skill sets. Wilder can punch but he can't box. Fury can box but he can't punch. Joshua punches better than Fury and boxes better than Wilder. But Fury boxes better than Joshua and Wilder can outpunch Joshua . . . Fury is a paradox. He has less power than you'd expect from someone his size and is more skilled as a boxer than you'd expect from someone his size . . . My perception of Fury changed after his showing against Wilder. Now Wladimir Klitschko's performance against Fury doesn't seem so inept. And that elevates Joshua's performance against Klitschko . . . Wilder's strengths and flaws are written large. But he can punch."

Wilder, at 33, is the old man in the group. Fury is 30. Joshua is 29.

Let's look further at the predictions and some of the electors' comments for each fight.

Tyson Fury vs. Deontay Wilder (Rematch)

Fury by knockout	1
Fury by decision	19
Wilder by knockout	13
Wilder by decision	2
Too close to call	5

The Case For Fury Over Wilder

"Fury abused his body with massive overeating, alcohol, and drugs. Then, after thirty months away from boxing and two glorified sparring sessions, he fought Wilder on even terms. He'll be in better shape and more fight-ready for the rematch . . . Give Fury credit. He was a lot better against Wilder than most of us thought he'd be, and he showed that his boxing skills are for real . . . Deontay depends on one thing—his power. Find a way to neutralize that, and he's lost . . . Both guys will know what they're getting into this time. But Fury will make adjustments off of their first fight better than Wilder . . . Wilder has had 41 fights and been fighting professionally for ten years. It's a little late for him to get better . . . Fury will put his punches together better the next time around . . . Wilder-Fury II will be the same as Wilder-Fury I, but Fury won't get as careless . . . The Gypsy King reigns."

The Case For Wilder Over Fury

"Fury is tricky and hard to figure out the first time you fight him. But Wilder learned from their first fight. He got a good look at Fury and will make the necessary adjustments . . . Wilder now knows what he's up against with Fury. He'll have a greater understanding of the need to be busier and use his jab more . . . All Wilder needed against Fury was more left hooks to follow the missed right hands. If Wilder works the left hook more in the rematch, he'll knock Fury out . . . Fury surprised me against Wilder with his conditioning, his boxing skills, and his heart. He surprised Wilder too, and Deontay still almost knocked him out. This time, Wilder will be ready for all that . . . Wilder is the biggest puncher in boxing. The next time he fights Fury, he'll catch Tyson earlier and more often than he did in their first fight and finish the job . . . Wilder started to figure Fury out as their first fight went on. Don't forget; he knocked Fury down in two of the last four rounds . . . Fury wants to win. Wilder has to win. Deontay will want it more . . . Wilder will win because, before the rematch happens, Fury will go on another binge and come in out of shape and out of his mind."

Anthony Joshua vs. Tyson Fury

Joshua by knockout	10
Joshua by decision	15
Fury by knockout	1
Fury by decision	12
Too close to call	2

The Case For Joshua Over Fury

"Joshua learned from what Wilder did wrong against Fury. And Joshua is a good enough boxer that he'll take that knowledge and use it to break Fury down . . . Joshua will do a much a better job of figuring out how to get to Fury than Wilder did . . . Joshua's workrate and the mix of his arsenal will be a problem for Fury. Against Wilder, Tyson had to be on guard for one punch: the big right hand. Joshua has more weapons than that and he can fire them at any time . . . Joshua has the tools to grind Fury down by cutting off the ring and applying pressure. He knows how to turn up the pressure when he has to . . . Joshua will put his punches together better than Wilder did and be able to land on Fury in ways that Wilder couldn't . . . Fury doesn't have the power to keep Joshua from doing what he has to do . . . Joshua has the edge in power over Fury. With a good game plan, he'll beat him . . . Joshua beats Fury. He's more athletic. He has a better variety of punches, and more power. It won't be easy, but he'll solve the puzzle . . . So much depends on Fury's state of mind. If he's clear of the old demons, he could beat Joshua. But my gut tells me that the coming months won't be trouble-free for Fury . . . Joshua is too well-rounded a fighter for Fury. He does everything a little bit better than Tyson . . . Joshua can fight. And he rises to the occasion."

The Case For Fury Over Joshua

"When it's time to perform, Fury performs . . . Fury is massive. His size is a problem for anyone. And that includes Joshua. You have to understand how hard it is to box a man with Fury's size, skill, and mobility . . . Joshua will face the same complications against Fury that Wilder did. Tyson is a very clever, elusive boxer who drives his opponents crazy. He knows how to blunt an opponent's attack with his jab and long arms . . . Fury has an uncanny ability to frustrate opponents with his size and style. Joshua won't be able to figure him out any better than Tyson's other opponents have . . . Fury befuddled Klitschko for twelve rounds. And Klitschko wasn't some green kid. He was a seasoned pro. Tyson will do the same thing to Joshua that he did to Klitschko and Wilder, and A.J. won't know how to deal with it . . . Joshua is too readable to beat Fury. Fury will keep Joshua turning and not let him get set . . . Fury is a boxing man. He has been boxing his whole life. Joshua is an athlete who took up the sport late . . . Fury had the strength, courage, and heart to get off the canvas in round twelve against Wilder. The only way to beat him is to knock him out. And I don't think Joshua will do that . . . Just because Joshua put ninety thousand people in Wembley doesn't mean he's Superman. He was life and death against a 40-year-old Wladimir Klitschko and looked ordinary against Alexander Povetkin, Joseph Parker, and Carlos Takam . . . Joshua is used to fighting at home and having the crowd solidly behind him. But he might not have that support if he fights Fury. How will that affect him?"

Anthony Joshua vs. Deontay Wilder

Joshua by knockout	16
Joshua by decision	9
Wilder by knockout	13
Wilder by decision	1
Too close to call	1

The Case for Joshua Over Wilder

"Joshua has seen enough of Wilder to know what he has to do and can't do, and he has the skills to implement the right fight plan . . . Wilder can punch but he doesn't know how to box. Joshua is a much better boxer than Wilder, and he'll hit Wilder harder than Fury hit him . . . Joshua is a much better inside fighter that Wilder. He'll find a way to get inside and stop Wilder with an uppercut . . . Joshua is a good finisher once he gets his man hurt. And he'll exploit Deontay's lack of ring skills to hurt Wilder . . . Joshua has far more dimensions to his game than Wilder. If Plan A isn't working, he can go to a Plan B and Plan C . . . Joshua has beaten a big puncher, Wladimir Klitschko, who knows how to box, which Wilder doesn't. And Joshua got up against Klitschko, which showed tremendous resilience and heart . . . If Joshua can't put Wilder away, Wilder will put Joshua away. But Joshua will get there first . . . If Joshua can't knock Wilder out, then everything we think we know about the craft of boxing is wrong."

The Case for Wilder Over Joshua

"Joshua's defense leaves a lot to be desired. And that's a poor quality to have against Wilder . . . Klitschko knocked Joshua down with a right hand and almost put him out. If Wilder lands that way, Joshua won't get up . . . Joshua is much easier to hit than Fury. He likes to punch. And when Anthony goes for it, he'll get hit. Wilder knocks Joshua out . . . Joshua doesn't punch as hard as Wilder. He's more of a wear-the-opponent down type of puncher. And that won't be good enough against Wilder. Wilder has tremendous resilience. Eventually, he'll get to Joshua . . . Being careful is one thing. Being intimidated is another. I think Joshua will be intimidated by Wilder's power and lay back, which will give Deontay the time and space he needs to knock Joshua out . . . Joshua-Wilder is a question of who gets to who first. Either Wilder lands the big one first or he doesn't. I think he will . . . The remarkable thing about Wilder isn't just his power. It's that he keeps his power late . . . Wilder and Joshua both make too many mistakes for this to go the distance. Somebody goes to sleep. It could be either one. But I think Wilder is the more devastating puncher, and he takes a good shot too. I'm betting his chin holds up better than Joshua's . . . If ever a fighter had an appropriate last name, Deontay Wilder is the guy. He can punch and he pulls the trigger in a hurry."

So . . . Where does that leave us?

"These guys aren't Ali, Frazier, and Foreman," one elector notes. "But at least we have heavyweights we can talk about. I'd love it if they fought these three fights for real so we could see which of them comes out on top."

And a word of caution. This is boxing. One punch can end the narrative with the referee performing a simple act arithmetic that begins with "one" and ends with "ten." The composite scoring of the four legendary champions—George Foreman, Lennox Lewis, Larry Holmes, and Evander Holyfield—who took part in this poll placed Deontay Wilder first, Anthony Joshua second, and Tyson Fury third.

More on boxing's literary tradition.

Literary Notes

A word of explanation regarding the process by which I review books.

Each year, I'm sent dozens of books about boxing. I don't have time to read all of them in their entirety, but I read at least part of each book. Some of them are informative, beautifully written, and demand attention. I read these books from cover to cover. Others don't rise to that level but are solid research efforts. And some are mediocre.

I write for a living, so I'm sensitive to the time and effort that go into writing a book. I know that a good review can move the needle a bit, particularly for authors who receive little marketing support from their publisher or self-publish. But I also have an obligation to readers who rely on my reviews when they decide which books to buy and read.

In recent years, Pitch Publishing has published more than its share of books about the sweet science. *Born to Box* by Alex Daley—a sad story of what might have been versus what was—is its latest offering.

Pat Daley removed the "e" from the spelling of his last name and fought as "Nipper Pat Daly." The story of his life has been written by his grandson. That raises a red flag with regard to objectivity, but it's a credible book.

Daly was born in Wales on February 17, 1913. He entered the ring for his first pro fight seven weeks before his tenth birthday. By his mid-teens, he was hailed by the British press as a boy wonder, the future of British boxing, and a worthy successor to flyweight great Jimmy Wilde. At age 16, he was ranked among the top-ten bantamweights in the world by *The Ring*. He was, his grandson writes, "handing out boxing lessons to grown men in 15-round fights, trouncing pros with whom, by any logic, he had no business sharing a ring."

Want more?

In 1927, at age 14, Daly fought four 15-round fights against grown men in the course of 38 days, winning three and battling to a draw in the fourth.

In 1928, he fought 25 fights totaling 280 rounds.

In 1929, when Daly was 16, these numbers increased to 33 fights and 319 rounds. That same year, the British publication, *Boxing*, proclaimed, "We may hope with increasing confidence to see the day when he is acknowledged as absolutely the best and greatest there has ever been."

"It was becoming increasingly hard to believe," Alex Daley writes. "Hard to believe that a boxer could be so good at such a young age, and harder still to believe that he could keep on going fifteen rounds week after week against grown men yet each time emerge unscathed. So far, Pat's toughness, fitness, speed, and skill had made a mockery of age and strength disadvantages."

But the seeds of Daly's destruction were being sown. His handsome young face had been marred a cauliflower ear from age 14. Scars and other visible reminders of his trade began to accumulate.

The worst damage was unseen.

"Pat was aware of the dangers of fighting so often and at the level he was," Daley notes. "But his immense self-belief, the illusion of invincibility that comes with youth, and a reluctance to let down others would have helped him to purge such thoughts from his mind. What he needed was a wise and compassionate guiding figure who valued his health above short-term financial gain. Sadly, there was no one close to him who fitted this mold."

Manager-trainer Andrew Newton (who fancied being called "Professor Newton") cashed in on his prodigy as early and often as possible. He exploited Daly financially and did his best to cut off any avenue that might lead to the fighter's education or independence.

On June 13, 1929, Daly was knocked unconscious in the first round of a fight in Sunderland, England. Five days later, he fought 15 rounds in Liverpool. He was in the ring again eight days after that. This led the *Daily Mirror* to warn, "It looks as though Nipper Pat Daly is running the risk of having his career ruined before he has reached his best by being rushed along at too great a pace. His advisers ought to bear in mind the fact that he is not strong enough to oppose boxers who are fully matured and exceptionally strong for the weight."

On October 9, 1929, Daly suffered another knockout defeat, and Trevor Wignall of the *Daily Express* wrote, "The whole thing was a tragedy for this child of boxing. He has been worked too hard, his jaw has been made glassy and vulnerable to one accurate smack, and a very promising career has been blighted. He should now be given a long rest and be allowed to grow in a normal way. If this is not done, his life as a fighter will end long before he is twenty."

Faced with this criticism, Newton responded, "Burned out? Wait for another few years and then see whether any intelligent boy can get burned out so long as I train and manage him. Some boys may get burned out. But if they were, it was only because their trainers did not know their business."

However, contrary to Newton's self-justification, Daly was all used up as a fighter at an age when most young men are just starting their ring career.

"He'd seemed destined to rule the boxing world," Alex Daley writes. "But now, at age 17, he felt like he was on boxing's scrapheap. Surely, that was absurd. The scrapheap was for washed-up old pugs who had gone on too long, and the old fighter was the only one who didn't know it. You couldn't be washed up at 17, could you?"

Daly's 118th and final fight was contested on January 27, 1931, three weeks before his eighteenth birthday. BoxRec lists his professional ring record as 99 wins, 11 losses, and 8 draws with 26 knockouts and 7 KOs by.

Daly rarely complained about his lot in life. But in 1949, at age 36, he told Ron Oliver of *The People* newspaper, "I loved to fight. I used to say to myself, 'If I can do this at sixteen, what shall I be able to do when I'm 26?' But they never allowed me to grow up naturally."

Thereafter, the story grew sadder. In his later years, Daley was given to mood swings and erratic behavior and suffered from dementia. His final years were spent in an assisted living facility. He died on September 25, 1988.

In an introduction to *Born to Box*, Alex Daley writes, "To my regret, I never really knew my grandfather. He died just before my eighth birthday. I have only hazy memories of him."

But drawing on a manuscript written by his grandfather in the late-1970s and his own independent research, Daley has fashioned a moving cautionary tale. And a 1985 observation from boxing writer O.F. Snelling is used to sum up well:

"The boy was so potentially great, so keen and gifted, that with judicious handling it is no exaggeration to say that he might have boxed his way to a world championship had he been allowed to reach his full growth and potential. But he went up like a rocket, burst into sparks well before he had reached his peak, and sank into darkness. A great memory now, but that is all."

★ ★ ★

Given the popularity of boxing in England, we can expect a stream of books about Anthony Joshua from across the pond. *Joshua* by John Dennen (Yellow Jersey Press) is one of the early arrivals.

Dennen had access to Joshua from Anthony's early days as an amateur. The book is a thorough recounting of AJ's life in the ring from his first visit to a boxing gym in 2004 through his April 29, 2017, conquest of Wladimir Klitschko.

Joshua was widely hailed after winning a gold medal in the super-heavyweight division at the 2012 London Olympics. Most people forget how close he came to defeat. In the first round, he squeaked by Cuba's Erislandy Savon by a 17–16 margin. In the gold-medal bout, he was dead even with Roberto Cammarelle of Italy at 18 points apiece and prevailed on the basis of supplemental points. His other two Olympic bouts (against Ivan Dychko of Kazakhstan and Zhang Zhilei of China) were decided by two and four points respectively.

An Olympic gold medal gives a fighter the economic advantage of being fixed in the public consciousness before he turns pro. Cassius Clay (soon to be Muhammad Ali), Joe Frazier, George Foreman, Lennox Lewis, and Wladimir Klitschko all capitalized on their Olympic fame. Super-heavyweight gold-medalists Audley Harrison and Tyrell Biggs met with far less success in the aftermath of their amateur years.

Combining his natural ability and work ethic with the guidance of promoter Eddie Hearn, Joshua has climbed steadily through the professional ranks as a fighter and as a commercial attraction. Dennen takes us on this journey.

There are some evocatively written passages. One that comes to mind is the description of Dominic Breazeale after his seventh-round knockout loss to Joshua.

"Breazeale," Dennen writes, "was no longer the enemy. He was just a man cutting a forlorn figure as he picked himself off the canvas. A man who had come up against the limits of his ambition. At a time like that, you remembered that his wife and child were in the crowd. You hoped Breazeale had been well paid for what he suffered. You hoped he'd be the same afterwards."

Dennen has a nice feel for boxing. Among the thoughts he shares are:

* "The boxing ring is a lonely place. In few other areas are limitations of skill and character so painfully and so publicly exposed. In no other sporting endeavor is a small lapse so brutally punished. Miss your attack, drop your guard, and prepare to eat a fist thrown by a man whose business is knowing how to hurt."
* "In many ways, boxing is a simple morality tale. Nothing comes for free. If you want something, by all means take it. But you can't take it without the work."
* "In professional boxing, pain is constant. Boxers suffer. No other sport compares."
* "You can't live a normal life and box."

Dennen's insights into the essence of boxing are so on the mark that it's frustrating when he lapses into what seems like hero-worship of his subject. The cover of *Joshua* proclaims that it's "the unauthorized biography." This suggests a warts-and-all exploration. But at times, the book has the feel of a look through rose-colored glasses.

Also, the portrait of Joshua as a person apart from his identity as a fighter is superficial. His relationships with his parents and the other important non-boxing people in his life are given short shrift. So are the years that Anthony spent in Nigeria during early childhood.

Similarly, Joshua's experiences with the criminal justice system in 2009 and 2011 for what AJ later called "fighting and other crazy stuff" are treated in a single paragraph. The "other crazy stuff" (not fully discussed by Dennen) includes an arrest after Anthony was stopped for speeding in North London and the police found eight ounces of cannabis in a sports bag in the car he was driving. Joshua was charged with possession of a controlled drug with intent to distribute, an offense that carried a maximum 14-year sentence. A guilty plea to a lesser charge followed.

Joshua today gives every indication of being a model citizen. But it's important to acknowledge the valleys he passed through on the way to his current place in society, not just the mountains he has climbed.

At one point, talking generically about boxing, Dennen quotes Charlotte Leslie, a former member of Parliament who once chaired the All Party Parliamentary Group for Boxing.

"What do human beings need to be happy?" Ms. Leslie asked. "They need a sense of identity. Who am I? A sense of purpose. What am I here for? And a sense of community. Who am I with? If kids are not given that through mainstream society, they'll find that somewhere else. If a gang says, 'You are for this and you are with us,' they go there. But that's exactly what boxing clubs provide. So for the kids who haven't got any of those things in their lives, the boxing club is there. Boxing clubs provide them with identity, community, and purpose."

Dennen then writes, "If you have standing within your peer group, you don't have to do other things to get standing. You don't have to do criminal stuff, you don't have to vandalize things, because you have that standing." But he never applies these thoughts directly to Joshua's personal journey.

The best writing in the book is a chapter that recounts Dennen's own abbreviated experience as an amateur boxer.

"I tried boxing myself," Dennen reminisces. "It was a joyful as well as a hurtful experience. In training, I could haul myself round the Oxford University track where Roger Bannister broke the four-minute mile. I got to try to punch people in the head. I took plenty of blows myself. I bled. I felt the pain. I felt fear. I felt free. I heard the sound, briefly, of a crowd shouting my name. Boxing, for the short time I did it at the low level I did it, let me feel like someone bigger, someone better. Made me feel like I was getting something done. It was a strange kind of magic."

"The sport may be called amateur boxing," Dennen continues, "but the name is deceptive. The standard gets very high very quickly. After ten bouts, if you're not good enough, you can start getting hurt. It's a dangerous sea if you swim too far out of your depth. I had five bouts in total. Then the coaches advised me to pack it in, to give it up before I came up against someone who knew how to handle themselves and I contrived to get myself hurt. My attempt to box had not been successful, but nevertheless it was a great gift to me."

"Boxing matters," Dennen concludes. "Its dangers can't be ignored. There is an ugliness to it, in wrong decisions, in the damage, in the bad deals. But there is a beauty to the sport." And reflecting on the end of his own in-ring experience, he writes, "I could only imagine what it took to make it in boxing, to keep driving yourself into that place. I could imagine it. I couldn't do it. And it left me in awe of those who could."

★ ★ ★

Never Stop by Simba Sana (Bolden Books) isn't a boxing book. It's a coming-of-age memoir written by a man who grew up in inner-city poverty, escaped, and then had to navigate the world outside it. But boxing keeps popping up in his life.

There's a warning flag in an "author's note" at the beginning of *Never Stop* that states, "This is a work of creative nonfiction. The events are portrayed to the best of Simba Sana's memory. While all the stories in this book are true, some names and identifying details have been changed to protect the privacy of the people involved."

Changing names to protect privacy is understandable. And memory is what it is. The phrase "creative nonfiction" should leave readers a bit wary.

But Sana writes well and his work demands attention from the start. The opening paragraph reads, "My mother never told me anything about her past—not one thing. This may be hard to believe, but she talked to herself more than she ever actually spoke to me. I grew accustomed to this at home. But as I got older, I became keenly aware that her habit of engaging in intense conversations with herself was not ordinary behavior."

As Sana (then named Bernard Sutton) moved through adolescence, he trained at several boxing gyms and developed an affinity for the sweet science. Later, he earned master's degrees from Howard University and St. John's College and moved into the corporate world.

The most intriguing portion of *Never Stop* insofar as boxing is concerned deals with the period of time that Sana managed Beethavean Scottland.

During his sojourn through various gyms, Sana established a rapport with Scottland. By 1997, "Bee" had fallen out with his manager and walked away from boxing with an 11–4–2 record. In 1998, Simba began managing him on a handshake agreement. Scottland won his first fight back and, by late-2000, had a 20–6–2 record. Meanwhile, Sana was roughly $5,000 in the hole, not having cut Bee's purses for most fights and having advanced money for various expenses.

In November 2000, Scottland dumped him. It hurt.

"All the work I'd put in with Bee," Sana recalls, "and then bam! Just like that. I was no longer Bee's manager. It was like all my work meant nothing. Bee avoided me, and I didn't go out of my way to find him either."

On June 26, 2001, Scottland fought his first fight under new management against unbeaten George Khalid Jones and was knocked out in the tenth round. Sana watched it unfold on ESPN2 and acknowledges, "As Bee lay on the canvas, I felt vindicated. I had been wronged and part of me wanted him to pay for what he did to me."

That's impressive honesty given what soon turned Sana's "sense of satisfaction" to concern. Scottland was carried from the ring on a stretcher and died six days later.

★ ★ ★

It's not often that a member of Parliament writes a book about boxing. But Christopher Evans, who represents Islwyn in South Wales, has done just that.

Fearless Freddie (Pitch Publishing) is a biography of Freddie Mills, the Englishman who compiled a 77–18–6 (55 KOs, 7 KOs by) record and reigned briefly as light-heavyweight champion in the aftermath of World War II.

Mills was an aggressive action fighter. He won the crown in London by decision over Gus Lesnevich on July 26, 1948, and was knocked out by Joey Maxim in his first title defense. He was the epitome of a fighter who fought too long, suffering from memory loss, headaches, and blackouts throughout the later stages of his ring career.

After retiring from boxing, Mills parlayed his fame into a brief show business career. He also opened a Chinese restaurant and then a nightclub in which some of the hostesses doubled as prostitutes. He died on July 25, 1965, at age 46. The cause of death was a bullet that entered his head just above the right eye. Evans concurs with the authorities that Mills committed suicide.

At the time of Mills's death, he was in debt to an organized crime syndicate. There were also rumors, which Evans fails to explore, that Mills had a sexual relationship with a nightclub singer named Michael Holliday and that Mills was a serial killer known as "Jack the Stripper" who murdered eight women in London in 1964 and 1965.

Evans sees Mills as a hero to working-class England. But like its subject, the book is flawed. I'm wary of biographies that recreate long-ago conversations and ascribe thoughts to subjects that can't possibly be verified. The most obvious example of this in *Fearless Freddie* is the description of Mills's suicide: "Closing his eyes, Freddie slowly counted backwards from ten before gently and deliberately pushing his thumb down on the trigger."

Let's get real. How could Evans possibly know that?

★ ★ ★

The image has been fixed in the consciousness of fight fans for more than a half-century: a 12-year-old boy wearing boxing trunks, fight shoes, and socks, standing on a crude wood platform. It's the first known photograph of Cassius Clay in a boxing pose and was taken for the *Louisville Courier Journal* by a photographer named Charley Pence.

That photo and many more from the *Courier-Journal* archives are in a new book entitled *Picture: Muhammad Ali*. Warren Winter, who oversaw the undertaking on behalf of publisher PSG, notes that the newspaper chronicled Ali's life for more than six decades and estimates that he reviewed well over ten thousand Ali images in the course of the project.

Louisville was always close to Ali's heart. In the ring, moments after defeating Joe Frazier in their climactic third fight in Manila, an exhausted Ali proclaimed, "I want everybody to know that I'm the greatest fighter of all times and the greatest city of all times is Louisville, Kentucky."

Add in the fact that the *Courier-Journal* was nationally known for excellence in photo-journalism in the second half of the twentieth century (its staff was awarded the Pulitzer Prize for Photography in 1976) and one has a good marriage.

Picture: Muhammad Ali has superb production values. It's a 296-page hardcover book printed on hard glossy stock, 9.25-by-12.4 inches in size. The photographs are divided into eight sections entitled "Young Ali", "Miami", "Home", "Deer Lake", "vs. Spinks", "Retirement", "Bahamas", and "The Later Years".

One might ask why Ali vs. George Foreman in Zaire is missing while Ali-Berbick in the Bahamas gets a whole section. The answer is that staff photographers were given specific assignments (e.g., to photograph Ali while he was training for a particular fight at Deer Lake, to photograph Ali at home with his family, etc.). These are the photos that the *Courier Journal* has.

The text consists of tagline photo captions, a few short essays, and quotes from Ali. The essays are thin and sometimes factually inaccurate (e.g., Ali fought Joe Frazier three times, not twice). But this book is about the photos. And the photos are wonderful. Each one creates a nice sense of the moment.

As for 12-year-old Cassius Clay . . . Pence's photo was published for the first time in the November 11, 1954, edition of the *Courier Journal* with a caption that read, "Flyweight Cassius M. Clay will be making his first fight tomorrow night when he appears on the weekly WAVE-TV amateur boxing program but he is being billed in the feature match. He meets Ronnie O'Keefe, little brother of light-heavyweight James W. O'Keefe."

Bill Luster (a retired staff photographer) says of Pence, "Charley was a gruff old man. At least, he seemed old to me at the time. And he was a good man. He did a lot of sports photography for the paper, college and high school sports. I liked him."

Tom Hardin (who retired from the *Courier Journal* after serving as a staff photographer and director of photography, recalls, "I worked with Charley when I was new at the paper. He was senior at the time. He had a dry sense of humor. He was dedicated to his job. He didn't suffer fools gladly. He was a good guy who knew what he was doing. You could always count on him to get the job done."

Pence had no way of knowing in 1954 that the 12-year-old boy he was photographing would become the most famous person on the face of the earth. Nor could he have imagined that the photograph he was taking would be reproduced millions of times, giving him his own slice of immortality. But he lived long enough to see both of these improbabilities come to pass.

What did that mean to him?

"I don't recall Charley talking about that photograph," Tom Hardin says. "He might have said, 'I knew him when he was a kid.' But that was all."

And what about Ronnie O'Keefe, Clay's opponent on November 11, 1954?

It was the first and last bout of O'Keefe's ring sojourn. Decades later, he would recall, "I weighed 89 pounds, and he weighed about the same. The fight was three rounds, a minute a round. And he hit me a whole lot more than I hit him. I had a heck of a headache that night. He won by a split decision. And right after he was announced the winner by the referee, he started shouting that he was going to be the greatest fighter ever. He was heavyweight champion of the world already, at twelve years old and 89 pounds."

★ ★ ★

Mark Twain was a fight fan. He attended several boxing matches and characterized them as "absorbingly interesting."

On January 25, 1894, heavyweight champion James J. Corbett knocked out Charlie Mitchell in three rounds at the Duval Athletic Club in Jacksonville. Corbett then took a train directly to New York and, two days later, boxed a three-round exhibition at Madison Square Garden against Dan Creedon (a sparring partner who had helped him prepare for the Mitchell fight).

Twain was at that exhibition accompanied by Henry H. Rogers (an industrialist and financier who was one of the richest men in America).

The following day, Twain wrote to his wife, Livy, telling her, "We bought a fifteen-dollar box in the Madison Square Garden. Rogers bought it, not I. There was a vast multitude of people in the brilliant place. [World-renowned architect] Stanford White came along presently and invited me to go to the World Champion's dressing room, which I was very glad to do. Corbett has a fine face and is modest and diffident besides being the most perfectly and beautifully constructed human animal in the world."

What did Twain and Corbett talk about?

According to Twain's letter to his wife, he told the champion, "You have whipped Mitchell, and maybe you will whip {Peter] Jackson. But you are not done then. You will have to tackle me."

And how did Corbett respond to his slightly-built challenger, a man with no apparent physical gifts?

"He answered so gravely," Twain recounted, "that one might easily have thought him in earnest. 'No! I am not going to meet you in the ring. It is not fair or right to require it. You might chance to knock me out by no merit of your own but by a purely accidental blow; and then my reputation would be gone and you would have a double one. You have got fame enough and you ought not to want to take mine away from me.'"

As for the action that unfolded at Madison Square Garden that night, Twain wrote, "There were lots of little boxing matches to entertain the crowd. Then, at last, Corbett appeared in the ring and the 8,000 people present went mad with enthusiasm. My two artists [illustrators who had joined Twain, Rogers, and White in the box] went mad about his form. They said they had never seen anything that came reasonably near equaling its perfection except Greek statues, and they didn't surpass it."

"Corbett boxed three rounds," Twain concluded. "Oh, beautiful to see."

Statistics are subject to interpretation. But the underlying numbers should be accurate.

CompuBox and Muhammad Ali

There's always room for more Muhammad Ali scholarship. *Muhammad Ali: By the Numbers* by Bob Canobbio and Lee Groves (published by New Book Authors) is the latest addition to the fold. The book offers a statistical analysis of Ali as a fighter and is one more resource to be used in studying Ali. But to measure the book's strengths and weaknesses, it's first necessary to understand CompuBox.

CompuBox was created in 1985 by Bob Cannobio and Logan Hobson. One year earlier, they'd been working at a sports data company when they saw a computer program that was capable of tracking every shot in a tennis match. That gave them the idea to apply a similar technology to boxing. They designed a computer program and, on November 28, 1984, brought it to Atlantic City to test it out.

"Trevor Berbick won a ten-round decision over Walter Santemore," Hobson later recalled. "When it was over, we looked at our results. We didn't know the full significance of the numbers, but we knew we had come up with something good."

Since then, CompuBox has changed the way fans and the media view fights.

In calculating statistics for live fights, the CompuBox system utilizes two computers, two keypads, and two operators. Each operator records the efforts of one fighter. Punches are divided into "jabs" and "power punches" (any punch other than a jab). CompuBox totals jabs landed, jabs missed, power punches landed, and power punch missed. The results are codified as "punch stats," a "punch profile," or with some other label depending on which television network has commissioned the statistics.

CompuBox now compiles statistics for approximately one hundred boxing telecasts a year. Its clients include HBO, Showtime, ESPN, FOX, and several other networks. When Matchroom USA begins televising fights on DAZN this autumn, CompuBox is expected to be onboard. There are roughly eight thousand fights in the company's data base.

The invention of CompuBox added an important new tool to the analysis of fights. But there has always been a disconnect with regard to CompuBox technology in that the punch counts don't register the effectiveness of punches. There's a difference between being hit and being hit cleanly by a solid punch. And the distinction between "jabs" and "power punches" is often irrelevant because not all so-called "power punches" are damaging blows.

In that regard, Canobbio has said repeatedly that CompuBox doesn't score fights. Rather, it's a tool to analyze the flow of a fight and contribute to a detailed historical record of the action.

There's a tendency on the part of the media and fans to take CompuBox numbers at face value. Many writers—including this one—cite them in post-fight reports. The numbers are also often relied upon by the media and fans in criticizing judges' decisions.

But there's an issue as to how accurate CompuBox really is and whether the absence of a competitor has led to a decline in the accuracy of CompuBox punch counts. Canobbio has said that there's a two percent margin of error, which would certainly be acceptable. But is that number correct?

There's no magic CompuBox bullet. The system might have the aura of computer science. But in reality, it consists of two operators entering punches into a data base. The data is only as accurate as the split-second judgments of these operators as they enter what they see (or think they see) into their computers. And just as ring judges sometimes get a fight horribly wrong, so does CompuBox.

This writer first examined CompuBox in the aftermath of the March 13, 1999, draw between Lennox Lewis and Evander Holyfield. The widespread impression was that Lewis dominated the fight, and CompuBox credited him with outlanding Holyfield by a 348-to-130 margin. The almost three-to-one advantage in punches landed in favor of Lewis seemed high to me. So I decided to compile my own "punch stats."

I watched a video of the fight twice. The first time, I counted the punches that Lewis landed. Then I repeated the process for Holyfield. When I was done, I was impressed with CompuBox. There were small variations in my calculations vis-à-vis theirs. But some errors are unavoidable in the flash of the moment. And it's possible, if not likely, that the CompuBox totals were more accurate than mine. After all, the CompuBox operators were sitting at ringside, and I conducted my punch count off a VHS tape.

Thirteen years later, I had a very different experience. On June 9, 2012, Tim Bradley won a controversial split-decision over Manny Pacquiao. In the days that followed, much of the criticism of the judges focused on round seven, which was labeled "the smoking gun." The CompuBox "punch-stats" had Pacquiao outlanding Bradley in round seven by a 27-to-11 margin. Yet all three judges scored the round for Bradley.

Thereafter, I studied videos of round seven in Pacquiao-Bradley I from multiple camera angles in their entirety . . . Several times . . . In slow motion . . .

Bradley outlanded Pacquiao 16-to-12 in round seven of their first fight. That's a huge difference between reality and the CompuBox numbers.

You, the reader of this article, can watch round seven of Pacquiao-Bradley I on YouTube and make your own judgment.

Cannobio bristles at the mention of round seven from Pacquiao-Bradley I. "That's history," he told this writer earlier this month. "Pacquiao-Bradley is old news. I've been doing this for thirty-three years. We wouldn't keep getting contracts and new deals if we weren't good."

But if a good historian discovers an error in the historical record that he or she has made, the historian corrects it. When statistics are as far off the mark as the CompuBox "punch stats" were for round seven of Pacquiao-Bradley I (and possibly the rest of the fight), they should be corrected. I'm not talking about a discrepancy of a few punches. I'm talking about significant mistakes.

Also, in the past, CompuBox operators sat at ringside for almost every fight. Now, to cut costs, CompuBox statistics are usually compiled off television by company personnel sitting at home. This practice began in 2014.

I've been in the first few rows at ringside for many fights. Trust me. From that vantage point, an observer sees which punches land and which don't much more clearly than someone watching a fight on television. That's why ring judges sit in elevated chairs by the ring apron rather than watch a fight on a TV monitor.

Calling a fight off a TV screen comes with a loss of visual perspective. It's sometimes difficult to know whether a jab fell just short of the mark and whether what appeared to be a grazing punch slid harmlessly by. Also, compiling punch statistics off a TV monitor leaves the person counting the punches at the mercy of decisions made by a director in a TV truck.

Canobbio defends the practice of compiling statistics off-site. "The more we do remotely," he says, "the less difference I see between working off a monitor and working from ringside."

But there is a difference. And when CompuBox compiles statistics remotely, its keypad operators are seeing the same thing that viewers at home see. This means that, with a little practice, fans can create "punch stats" as reliably as CompuBox.

Once again, a Manny Pacquiao fight is instructive. CompuBox calculated statistics for the July 2, 2017, fight between Pacquiao and Jeff Horn off a TV monitor and reported that Pacquiao outlanded Horn by a 182-to-92 margin with a 10–9 edge in punches landed in round one.

I won't quarrel with the notion that Pacquiao landed ten punches in round one. But I watched round one of Pacquiao-Horn several times the same way that the CompuBox operators watched it. Off a TV screen. And I think that Horn landed 18 punches, not 9. That's a big difference.

One day after Pacquiao-Horn, Tom Gray of Ring Online wrote, "Horn was all over Pacquiao in the opening round. Horn landed to the mid-section and had more success up top. Pacquiao evaded some shots but he was tagged a lot more than Horn was. Not only are the numbers a joke, but this is where CompuBox's legitimacy in this contest ends."

Once again; you, the reader, can go to YouTube and decide for yourself.

This brings us to *Muhammad Ali: By the Numbers*. The book contains punch totals for 47 of Ali's 61 professional fights. Complete film footage of the other fourteen bouts is unavailable. The format for the book is to present a narrative that places each fight in context followed by an account of the action, the judges' scorecards, and complete CompuBox statistics.

The punch totals were compiled by Lee Groves, who tracked 4/4 rounds from Ali's fights. Groves began working for CompuBox in 2004 on a part-time basis and has been with the company on a fulltime basis since 2007.

"I watched each Ali fight twice," Groves recounts. "Once for each fighter. From the start, I had a sense of the historic importance of what I was doing. I knew it would add a new dimension to how Ali is perceived as a fighter."

Groves also put an enormous amount of time into crafting the narrative text.

CompuBox divides Ali's career into four phases:

(1) "The Young Clay"—The six available bouts from Cassius Clay vs. Alonzo Johnson through Clay's first fight against Henry Cooper.
(2) "Prime Ali"—The ten fights from Clay-Liston I through Ali vs. Zora Folley.
(3) "The Comeback Years"—There's some questionable organization here. Ali's "comeback" began with his 1970 fight against Jerry Quarry and culminated in his regaining the heavyweight throne against George Foreman four years later. But in *Muhammad Ali: By the Numbers*, the "comeback years" are extended to include twenty-one Ali bouts from Quarry I through Ali-Frazier III in Manila. There's no material on Ali's decision victory over Rudi Lubbers because footage of the complete fight is unavailable.
(4) Past-Prime Ali—The final ten fights of Ali's ring career.

The conclusion reached by the authors of *Muhammad Ali: By the Numbers* is that, even in his prime (Clay-Liston I through Ali-Folley), Ali wasn't as good as we thought he was. During this period, Canobbio and Groves posit, Ali had a defense that was "surprisingly leaky." As proof, they cite "the high percentage of punches his opponents landed."

"During those rare times they were in range to reach him," the authors write, "they reached him—often. The statistics shatter the myth that the prime Ali was an expert defender. In light of this information, some experts may have to reconsider not only how they perceive the best version of Ali but also how he might fare against the best of the best."

Groves recently elaborated on this theme, saying, "Watching Ali in the past, my eye had always been drawn to his magnetism. Here, I had to watch the opponents. And I was shocked at how often the opponents penetrated Ali's defense. Ali fancied himself an amateur magician. And in the ring, he pulled off his greatest illusion. He was able to erase the memory of his getting hit by not showing it in his facial expression and immediately striking back. Knowing how often Ali got hit, even when he was young, was surprising to me."

Thus, *Muhammad Ali: By the Numbers* states, "As great as he was to watch inside the ring and to listen to beyond the ropes, Ali was hardly the greatest in terms of statistics."

According to CompuBox, over the course of 47 fights, Ali outlanded his opponents by a 7,953-to-7,010 margin, which was attributable to a huge 3,749-to-1,892 advantage in jabs landed. But he was on the short end of power punches landed by a 5,118-to-4,204 tally.

Moreover, *Muhammad Ali: By the Numbers* proclaims, "Ali rated a minus 1.7 on CompuBox's plus-minus scale that compares the fighter's overall connect percentage with that of his opponents. Ali's terrible final nine fights had a lot to do with that. But even if Ali had retired after the Thrilla in Manila, his plus-minus rating would have been a puny plus 0.4 (34.9% for Ali, 34.5% for his opponents) and he still would have been underwater in power-punch accuracy (39.3% for Ali, 41.7% for his opponents)."

Further with regard to this "plus-minus" scale; CompuBox analyzed available video footage for what it calls "twelve notable heavyweight champs" beginning with Joe Louis and ending with Wladimir Klitschko. By CompuBox's calculation, Ali ranks dead last. Joe Louis ranks sixth, while Joe Frazier ranks first.

According to CompuBox, over the course of 47 fights, Ali's opponents landed 34.2% of their total punches and 41.8 percent of their power punches, while Joe Frazier's opponents landed 29.7% of their total punches and 38.5% of their power punches.

In other words, according to CompuBox, Ali was easier to hit than Joe Frazier.

I don't think so.

CompuBox also maintains that Ali was easier to hit than Rocky Marciano. Here, it's worth noting that, on August 29, 1969, two days before being killed in a plane crash, Marciano said of Ali, "From what I've seen, he's as good or better than anybody I fought. I really don't know if I could have beaten him. I would have liked to have fought him. Even if I'd lost, I'd have known that I fought the best."

There are a lot of small errors in *Muhammad Ali: By the Numbers.* For example, the authors say that Cassius Clay's February 21, 1961, fight against Donnie Fleeman (his fifth as a pro) was "his first main event." That's just wrong. Ali was in the main event in his pro debut against Tunney Hunsaker. It's a small point. But mistakes like this, by definition, raise the issue of whether the underlying CompuBox statistics themselves are reliable. More on that later.

Also, statistics in and of themselves can be misleading.

According to *Muhammad Ali: By the Numbers*, the "Prime Ali" was outlanded by Sonny Liston in Clay-Liston I and was even with Liston in punches landed in their second encounter. But as the book acknowledges, Liston's 103-to-95 edge in Clay-Liston I was built largely on a 37–1 disparity in round five, when Clay was blinded and trying simply to survive. And regardless of the punch count, Liston quit on his stool after six rounds. That wasn't an illusion.

Ali-Liston II, of course, ended in a first-round knockout for Ali.

Then there's Ali versus Zora Folley. *Muhammad Ali: By the Numbers* maintains that Folley outlanded Ali by a 66-to-61 margin. But Ali was in total control of the bout that night and knocked Folley out in the seventh round.

After the fight, Folley called Ali "the greatest fighter of all time" and declared, "This guy has a style all his own. It's far ahead of any fighter's today. How could Dempsey, Tunney, or any of them keep up? Louis wouldn't have a chance; he was too slow. Marciano couldn't get to him and would never get away from Ali's jab. There's just no way to train yourself for what he does. The moves, the speed, the punches, and the way he changes style every time you think you got him figured. The right hands Ali hit me with just had no business landing, but they did. They came from nowhere. Many times he was in the wrong position but he hit me anyway. I've never seen anyone who could do that. The knockdown punch was so fast that I never saw it. He has lots of snap, and when the punches land they dizzy your head; they fuzz up your mind. He's smart, the trickiest fighter I've seen. He could write the book on boxing, and anyone that fights him should be made to read it."

That sounds like the description of an all-time great, not a fighter who came out on the short end of CompuBox numbers. And for the record, having viewed a video of Ali-Folley, I think Folley landed far fewer than 66 punches that night.

Similarly, *Muhammad Ali: By the Numbers*, notes that "on the negative side, Ali failed to land a single punch in a given round seven times." But that's like grouping apples with brussels sprouts. There's no rational correlation between round ten of Ali vs. Larry Holmes (when a helpless Ali was being beaten to a pulp) and round one of the first fight between Ali and Floyd Patterson.

In round one of Ali-Patterson I, Ali was playing with Patterson. He feinted a lot but threw no serious punches. Blow-by-blow commentator Don Dunphy observed, "Cassius Clay seems content to just move. Clay is clowning at this point."

Muhammad Ali: By the Numbers acknowledges that Ali "ceded round one to Patterson" and also concedes that all but one of his twelve punches were "half-speed jabs." But even that is an exaggeration. At most, Ali appears to have thrown one punch that was intended to land against Patterson in round one.

Moreover, in terms of Ali's overall ring career, some of his jabs were sharp, cutting, and hurting. Others were of the stay-away-from-me variety designed to dictate distance and the pace of the fight. Whether or not this latter group of jabs landed was secondary to their primary purpose.

The ultimate question, of course, is, "How accurate are CompuBox's Ali statistics?"

Ali's third-round knockout of Cleveland Williams on November 14, 1966, is often cited as Ali's finest performance as a pro. CompuBox says that Williams landed ten punches that night. But is that right?

Decades ago, Bill Cayton (who owned film rights to most of Ali's bouts) and Steve Lott (who worked for Cayton) reviewed films of several Ali fights and determined that Williams landed three punches against Ali. A recent review of Ali-Williams on YouTube seems to indicate that three is the more accurate number.

Ali's first-round knockout of Sonny Liston on May 25, 1965, has long been shrouded in controversy. CompuBox says that Liston landed four punches that night. Cayton and Lott said it was two. A review of the fight on YouTube suggests that Cayton and Lott were right.

CompuBox says that Leon Spinks landed 419 punches in his first fight against Ali. Cayton and Lott said it was 482. That's a significant difference. I don't know who's right because I haven't counted punches for that fight.

"I've been doing this for a number of years," Groves recently told this writer. "I'm confident in my ability to track punches."

To repeat: you, the reader of this article, can go to YouTube and decide for yourself.

CompuBox has made a significant contribution to boxing. But it has the tools to be better.

On November 9, 2015, an independent commission set up by the World Anti-Doping Agency published a 323-page report that accused Russian government officials of overseeing a drug-testing program that covered up positive test results, destroyed drug samples, orchestrated the collection of bogus samples, and received inappropriate monetary payments from athletes. Shouldn't WADA explore the issue of whether or not the United States Anti-Doping Agency has done similar things in boxing?

1,501 Tests, One Reported Positive: What's Going On with USADA and Boxing?

On October 18, 2012, Halestorm Sports (a small website that no longer exists) reported that Erik Morales had tested positive with the United States Anti-Doping Agency (USADA) for clenbuterol, a banned substance. Morales was scheduled to fight Danny Garcia at Barclays Center in Brooklyn on October 20. More significantly, it was later confirmed by the New York State Athletic Commission that USADA hadn't reported the violation to the NYSAC until after the internet disclosure.

USADA has been testing professional boxers for performance enhancing drugs since 2010. Its website states that it has administered 1,501 tests on 128 professional boxers through August 22 of this year. Yet it appears as though, in all these years, USADA has reported only one adverse finding regarding a professional boxer (its belated report of Morales to the NYSAC) to a governing state athletic commission.

Is it possible that USADA has administered 1,501 tests to 128 professional boxers and that only one of these tests has come back positive? Yes. It's also possible that a giant asteroid will obliterate life as we know it on earth tomorrow. But it's statistically implausible and highly unlikely.

USADA, as discussed later in this report, has refused repeated requests by this writer to provide information that would clarify and help explain these numbers.

In the past, I've written extensively about USADA's involvement with professional boxing. Most notably, in a 2015 article entitled "Can Boxing Trust USADA?," I explored how the agency handled the intravenous administration of what it said was a mixture of saline and vitamins to Floyd Mayweather hours after Mayweather weighed in for his May 2, 2015, fight against Manny Pacquiao. As outlined in that article, the evidence strongly supports the conclusion that USADA's actions with regard to Mayweather's IV violated both Nevada State Athletic Commission protocols and the World Anti-Doping Code.

"Can Boxing Trust USADA?" and a follow-up piece entitled "Was Floyd Mayweather Really Dehydrated?" can be found in an earlier book—*A Hard World*—published by the University of Arkansas Press.

Now, in 2018, there's still reason to question USADA's commitment to "clean sport" insofar as professional boxing is concerned. As noted above, USADA reports having conducted 1,501 tests for banned substances on 128 professional boxers from January 1, 2010, through August 22, 2018. Yet it appears as though only one of these tests (that of Erik Morales) resulted in an adverse finding that was communicated to a state athletic commission.

By way of comparison, Dr. Margaret Goodman (president of the Voluntary Anti-Doping Association, which is widely regarded as the most credible testing organization in professional boxing) reports that close to four percent of the tests for illegal performance enhancing drugs conducted by VADA come back positive. Using the four-percent benchmark, one would expect that 60 of the 1,501 tests conducted by USADA from 2010 to date would have yielded a positive result.

Broken down by year, the numbers reported by USADA on its website are as follows:

YEAR	BOXERS	TESTS
2010	2	16
2011	2	29
2012	9	113
2013	11	181
2014	28	310
2015	35	446

YEAR	BOXERS	TESTS
2016	16	171
2017	12	105
2018 thru 8/22	13	130
TOTAL	128	1,501

Virtually all of these tests were administered in conjunction with fights in which companies controlled by Al Haymon had a vested financial interest.

The most common venues for the fights in question were Nevada, California, and New York.

On August 21, 2018, Bob Bennett (executive director of the Nevada State Athletic Commission) told this writer, "I don't recall ever being advised that a boxer who was tested by USADA for one of our fights tested positive for a banned substance. MMA combatants, yes; but no boxers."

One day later, Andy Foster (executive officer for the California State Athletic Commission) acknowledged, "I can't recall an instance when USADA reported a positive test finding for a professional boxer here in California. I know that VADA has, but not USADA."

Multiple sources at the New York State Athletic Commission say that they are unaware of USADA communicating any adverse finding with regard to a professional boxer to the NYSAC other than its belated reporting of Erik Morales for the presence of clenbuterol in his system in 2012.

It should be further noted that three of the professional boxers who tested clean with USADA during the period in question—Andre Berto, Lamont Peterson, and Canelo Alvarez—tested positive with VADA on other occasions. Indeed, it was VADA's finding that Alvarez had clenbuterol in his system that forced the rescheduling of his rematch against Gennady Golovkin from May 5 to September 15 of this year.

Despite its name, USADA is neither a government agency nor part of the United States Olympic Committee. It's an independent "not-for-profit" corporation headquartered in Colorado Springs that offers drug-testing services for a fee. Most notably, the United States Olympic and Paralympic movement utilize its services. Because of this role, USADA receives in excess of ten million dollars annually in Congressional funding.

Travis Tygart, USADA's chief executive officer, spearheaded his organization's expansion into professional boxing. That opportunity arose in late-2009 when drug testing became an issue in the first round of negotiations for a proposed fight between Floyd Mayweather and Manny Pacquiao. Thereafter, Tygart moved aggressively to expand USADA's footprint in professional boxing and forged a working relationship with Richard Schaefer, who until 2014 served as CEO of Golden Boy Promotions. USADA also became the drug-testing agency of choice for fighters advised by Al Haymon.

At present, no state requires as a matter of course that drug testing contracts entered into by USADA or VADA be filed with the state athletic commission. In some states, USADA and VADA aren't even required to report positive test results (although VADA always does).

By and large, state athletic commissions tend to defer to USADA and VADA because of their expertise and because it saves the governing commission money if someone else does the PED testing.

Often, when USADA sends reports to a state athletic commission, it sends only test summaries, not full laboratory test results.

Even when USADA and VADA are uninvolved, some states still don't test for performance enhancing drugs.

It's a haphazard system that's ripe for abuse. And it leads to the question, "How can USADA administer 1,501 tests for banned substances to professional boxers and report only a single violation of anti-doping rules to a governing state athletic commission?"

USADA has shown that it knows how to catch drug cheats. In 2015, it entered into a contract to test mixed martial arts combatants for UFC. UFC wanted USADA to catch the drug cheats. In part, that might have been because a multi-billion-dollar sale of UFC's parent company was in the works and prospective buyers wanted a clean sport. It's also possible that Dana White and the rest of the UFC leadership understand the difference between right and wrong when it comes to illegal PED use in a combat sport.

Since then, some of the biggest names in UFC have been suspended pursuant to tests administered by USADA. This includes Brock Lesnar, Chad Mendes, Junior Dos Santos, Francisco Rivera, Anderson Silva, Jon Jones, Josh Barnett, and Nick Diaz.

Similarly, USADA has issued numerous press releases with regard to positive test results and the resulting suspension of amateur boxers (e.g. Paul Koon, Michael Hunter, Damon Allen Jr, Jesus Gomez, and Jerren Cochran).

So why the absence of reported positive test results with regard to professional boxers?

Let's start with the fact that USADA is often hired by, and contracts with, representatives of the very boxers it's supposed to be testing.

A Major League Baseball team or National Football League player can't choose the drug-testing agency that will conduct tests and then negotiate a fee with that agency. But this is what happens frequently with USADA. Indeed, there are times when it seems as though USADA collects drug-testing payments the way boxing's world sanctioning organizations collect sanctioning fees. It has been known to charge as much as $150,000 to administer tests for a particular fight. By contrast, VADA charges approximately $16,000 for a complete drug-testing program for a given fight.

Also, if one is looking for loopholes, there are many ways to rationalize throwing out an adverse test result: "The collection process was flawed . . . The chain of custody for the sample was improper . . . The sample was somehow contaminated . . . The boxer tested positive for clenbuterol because he ate contaminated beef . . . I know he tested positive, but we're granting him a retroactive therapeutic use exemption."

Judgments regarding mitigating circumstances are properly left to governing state athletic commissions. USADA should test and report the results of these tests to the governing state athletic commission and certain other contractually-designated parties. It should not adjudicate or grant retroactive therapeutic use exemptions. That's what got it in trouble in Nevada in 2015 when it unilaterally granted a retroactive therapeutic use exemption to Floyd Mayweather and later conceded that, without this retroactive TUE, Mayweather would have been in violation of the World Anti-Doping Agency code.

But it appears as though some of USADA's PED-testing contracts for professional boxers don't require it to report violations to the governing state athletic commission. And some of its contracts allow it to adjudicate matters that should be left to other decision-makers.

Here, the contract for PED testing entered into by USADA with Floyd Mayweather and Manny Pacquiao is instructive. Paragraph 30 of this contract states, "If any rule or regulation whatsoever incorporated or referenced herein conflicts in any respect with the terms of this Agreement, this Agreement shall in all such respects control. Such rules and regulations include, but are not limited to: the Code [the World Anti-Doping Code]; the USADA Protocol; the WADA Prohibited List; the ISTUE [WADA International Standard for Therapeutic Use Exemptions]; and the ISTI [WADA International Standard for Testing and Investigations]."

In other words, USADA was not bound by the drug testing protocols that one might have expected it to follow in conjunction with Mayweather-Pacquiao.

Indeed, at one point in the negotiations, USADA presented the Pacquiao camp with a contract that would have allowed USADA to grant a retroactive therapeutic use exemption to either fighter in the event that the fighter tested positive for a prohibited drug. And this TUE could have been granted without notifying the Nevada State Athletic Commission or the opposing fighter's camp. Team Pacquiao thought this was outrageous and refused to sign the contract. Thereafter, Mayweather and USADA agreed to mutual notification and the limitation of retroactive therapeutic use exemptions to certain circumstances.

On August 14, 2015, in the aftermath of the Mayweather IV controversy, Annie Skinner (then a public relations spokesperson for USADA) acknowledged, "At this time, the only professional boxer under USADA's program who has been found to have committed an anti-doping rule violation is Erik Morales."

At that time, USADA, by its own count, had administered 915 tests to professional boxers. Think about that for a minute! VADA's four-percent positive-test-result rate would have yielded 36 positive test results at that point in time. Since then, there appear to have been zero reports by USADA of adverse findings regarding a professional boxer to a governing state athletic commission.

Here it should be noted that, as stated earlier in this article, the USADA website says that USADA conducted 105 tests on professional boxers in 2017. But USADA's 2017 annual report states that USADA conducted 109 tests on professional boxers in 2017.

Drug-testing is a detail-oriented endeavor. Statistics have to be precisely calculated. How does USADA account for the four missing tests?

Victor Conte was the founder and president of BALCO and at the vortex of several well-publicized PED scandals. He spent four months in prison after pleading guilty to illegal steroid distribution and tax fraud in

2005. Since then, Conte has become a forceful advocate for clean sport. What makes him a particularly valuable asset is his knowledge of how the performance enhancing drugs game is played.

Asked about USADA's PED test numbers for professional boxers, Conte declares, "Numbers like this for professional boxing don't make sense. It's just not credible. You have to ask whether there's a genuine interest on the part of USADA in catching these athletes."

"One reason VADA testing is effective," Conte continues, "is that Margaret Goodman uses CIR [carbon isotope ratio] testing on every urine sample that VADA collects from a boxer. CIR testing can increase the number of positive tests in a given situation from one percent to five percent. To my knowledge, USADA doesn't use CIR testing on every sample. But it's common sense. To be successful in any endeavor, you do more of what works and less of what doesn't work."

On multiple occasions in August, this writer requested of USADA that it provide answers to the following questions:

(1) Other than Erik Morales in 2012, has USADA ever reported a positive drug test result with regard to a professional boxer to a state athletic commission? And if so, on how many occasions and to which commission(s).

(2) On how many occasions has the "A" sample of a professional boxer tested by USADA come back positive for a prohibited substance?

(3) On how many occasions has the "B" sample of a professional boxer tested by USADA come back positive for a prohibited substance?

On August 28, Danielle Eurich (a media relations specialist for USADA) responded as follows: "Hi Thomas, Given your previous inaccurate reporting on USADA's role in professional boxing and refusal to correct the record when given the opportunity, our only comment at this time is that we will not be providing you with the requested information as we have no confidence that anything we offer in response to your questions would be used accurately. We believe readers deserve an honest, fact-based account of the state of anti-doping in boxing, but regrettably that need has not been met with your past reporting. We're sure you understand the reasons why we are unable to offer any further comment at this time."

This is known as avoiding the issue.

Meanwhile, where should boxing go from here?

As I wrote three years ago, the presence of performance enhancing drugs in boxing cries out for action. To ensure a level playing field, a national solution with uniform national testing standards is essential. A year-round testing program is necessary. It should be a condition of being granted a boxing license in this country that any fighter is subject to blood and urine testing at any time. While logistics and cost would make mandatory testing on a broad scale impractical, unannounced spot testing could be implemented, particularly on elite fighters.

Without additional federal legislation, the Association of Boxing Commissions can't require PED testing. But the individual states can. Each state should require that:

(1) All contracts for drug testing be filed with the governing state ath-letic commission within seven days of execution.

(2) All test results be forwarded to the governing state athletic commis-sion within three days of receipt by USADA, VADA, or any other testing agency. Such filings should include (a) the name of the boxer who was tested; (b) a summary of the results from each test; and (c) copies of the complete test results. A commission doctor should review all test results as they come in.

The Association of Boxing Commissions could serve as a repository for this information as it's received by the individual states. In today's computer age, that wouldn't be hard to do. This registry would ensure the free flow of information from state to state and also provide a base-line against which future tests for performance enhancing drugs could be evaluated.

Given the amount of money that USADA receives annually from the federal government, it would also be appropriate for Congress to conduct an inquiry into USADA's practices with regard to professional boxing.

Meanwhile, the point can't be made often enough. This isn't about running faster or hitting a baseball further. It's about hitting someone in the head harder in a sport where the aim is to knock an opponent unconscious.

"1,501 Tests, One Reported Positive: What's Going On with USADA and Boxing?" was posted on September 7, 2018. On December 10, I followed up with another investigative report.

USADA, VADA, and the State Athletic Commissions

On September 7, 2018, I posted an investigative report entitled "1,501 Tests, One Reported Positive? What's Going On with USADA and Boxing?"

The article was based on data taken from USADA's own website in addition to interviews with state athletic commission personnel and experts in the field of performance enhancing drugs. It raised troubling questions regarding the role that USADA plays in boxing today.

USADA has been testing professional boxers for performance enhancing drugs since 2010. As of September 6, 2018, its website stated that it had administered 1,501 tests on 128 professional boxers through August 22 of this year. Yet in all these years, USADA had reported only one adverse finding regarding a professional boxer to a governing state athletic commission.

By way of comparison, Dr. Margaret Goodman (president of the Voluntary Anti-Doping Association, which is widely regarded as the most credible testing organization in professional boxing) reported that close to four percent of the tests for illegal performance enhancing drugs conducted by VADA come back positive. Using the four-percent benchmark, one would have expected that 60 of the 1,501 tests conducted by USADA would have yielded a positive result.

Virtually all of USADA's tests were administered in conjunction with fights in which companies controlled by Al Haymon had a vested financial interest. The most common venues for the fights in question were Nevada, California, and New York.

What has happened since then?

First, USADA has now conceded to multiple third parties that there was more than one positive test result but that USADA chose to adjudicate these matters internally without reporting the positive test result to the opposing fighter's camp or state athletic commission that had oversight responsibility with regard to a given fight.

This is consistent with many of USADA's contracts, which purport to allow it to adjudicate positive test results without notice to persons and entities with a legitimate interest in the outcome of these tests. However, it runs contrary to the rule in many states that, in the event of a positive drug test, judgments regarding mitigating circumstances must be left to the governing state athletic commission.

As recently as November 23 of this year, Bob Bennett (executive director of the Nevada State Athletic Commission) stated unequivocally that the NSAC must be notified of any adverse findings related to PED tests in and out of competition and that the NSAC has jurisdiction over all adverse findings for PED's.

It should also be noted that it appears as though every positive test result adjudicated internally by USADA with regard to a professional boxer was adjudicated in favor of the boxer since there have been no reported adverse findings other than the acknowledgement, after the news leaked on the internet, that Erik Morales tested positive for clenbutereol in 2012.

Second, and equally significant, it appears as though USADA—for the time being at least—has stopped testing professional boxers for performance enhancing drugs.

According to postings on the USADA website (updated through December 7, 2018), the most recent tests conducted on professional boxers by USADA were administered to Danny Garcia and Shawn Porter, who fought each other at Barclay's Center on September 8, one day after this writer's investigative report was posted.

In other words, a company that tested more than fifteen hundred professional boxers over the course of eight years appears to have suddenly stopped testing professional boxers.

In recent years, USADA has charged in excess of $30,000 for drug testing for each fight. The amount was $150,000 for Floyd Mayweather vs. Manny Pacquiao. Multiply these numbers by more than 1,500 tests and it's a lot of money to walk away from. Did USADA decide that the spotlight was getting too bright?

The Voluntary Anti-Doping Association (VADA) doesn't catch all of boxing's drug cheats any more than the Internal Revenue Service catches all tax cheats. But it catches some of them.

On September 20, 2018, it was announced that a test for performance enhancing drugs conducted on Manuel Charr by VADA had come back positive for epitrenbolone and drostanolone (banned anabolic steroids).

On September 27, it was revealed that a test administered to Billy Joe Saunders by VADA had come back positive for oxilofrine (a banned stimulant).

In other words, VADA reported more positive tests for banned PEDs to supervising state athletic commissions in eight days than USADA has reported in eight years.

Given the fact that USADA charges roughly twice the amount for PED testing that VADA charges, one might ask why anyone in professional boxing would test with USADA. Unless a "get-out-of-jail-free" card comes with the test results.

Andy Foster is executive officer of the California State Athletic Commission. Multiple sources say that Foster has made it clear to promoters that he is uncomfortable with the pattern of USADA's reported test results for boxing and would prefer that promoters use VADA or another reliable testing agency until the issue is resolved. On December 5, 2018, Foster told this writer, "It's the weirdest thing. USADA has reported lots of positive test results for MMA but none for boxing. When it comes to boxing, I feel much more comfortable with VADA."

The recent PED controversy involving Canelo Alvarez is also instructive.

Alvarez was scheduled to fight a lucrative rematch against Gennady Golovkin in Las Vegas on May 5, 2018. But on March 5, it was revealed that urine samples taken from Canelo by VADA on February 17 and February 20 had tested positive for clenbuterol. Alvarez said that the positive tests were the result of his having inadvertently eaten contaminated meat. But the Golovkin camp refused to let the matter rest and pressed the issue with the Nevada State Athletic Commission.

A March 15 letter sent on behalf of Golovkin to the NSAC and VADA demanded that the commission hold Alvarez to a standard of strict liability insofar as the presence of clenbuterol in his system was concerned. The letter also asked that the NSAC conduct an investigation and hold a full hearing with regard to possible performance enhancing drug use by Canelo.

On March 20, Golovkin raised the ante further when he met with reporters and declared, "I'm a clean athlete. After the first fight, I knew he was not clean. It's not Mexican meat. Canelo is cheating. They're using these drugs and everybody is just trying to pretend it's not happening."

On March 23, 2018, the Nevada State Athletic Commission announced that Alvarez had been temporarily suspended as a consequence of the two positive tests and that the matter would be finally adjudicated at an April 10 commission meeting. On April 3, Canelo announced that he was withdrawing from the fight. Then, on April 18, the NSAC voted unanimously to approve a settlement agreed to by Alvarez that called for Canelo to be suspended for six months retroactive to the date (February 17) of his first positive test for clenbuterol. There was no admission of wrongdoing on Canelo's part. But there was an acknowledgement that clenbuterol had been present in his system.

On May 15, Alvarez signed up for a full year of VADA testing and paid the $50,000 cost out of his own pocket. His rematch against Golovkin was rescheduled for September 15 and Canelo emerged with a majority-decision triumph.

So let's look at what happened. A positive test result was properly reported. There was a sanction. Alvarez then came back, tested clean twenty times in an enhanced VADA program, and beat Golovkin.

Now suppose hypothetically that Alvarez had been tested by USADA, not VADA. Suppose USADA advised the Canelo camp of his positive test for clenbuterol and was told, "Canelo says he never used clenbuterol. It must have come from contaminated beef." And suppose further that USADA said, "That sounds like a reasonable explanation. We'll adjudicate this internally and give the fighter an inadvertent use waiver. There's no need to report it to the Golovkin camp and Nevada State Athletic Commission and bring the fight down."

That would have avoided interfering with a major promotion. But it would also have overlooked the presence of an illegal performance enhancing drug in a fighter's system.

Unfortunately, some jurisdictions still don't understand the implications inherent in the use of illegal performance enhancing drugs. Others would rather pay lip service to the issue than deal forcefully with it. And there are significant loopholes in some testing protocols.

Jermall Charlo and Jermell Charlo are two of the most talented fighters in boxing today. Jermall is the World Boxing Council "interim" middleweight champion. Jermell holds the WBC 154-pound belt. As such, the Charlos are subject to the World Boxing Council Clean Boxing Program which requires them to keep VADA apprised of their where-abouts, be reachable by telephone at all times, and be subject to spot testing for performance enhancing drugs at any time.

On November 1, 2018, VADA collection officers went to pick up blood and urine samples from Jermall and Jermell Charlo at their respec-tive homes and were told that neither brother was at home nor would they be at the gym that day. Neither brother picked up his phone at the contact number given to VADA when he was called. And no one could (or would) tell the collection officers where Jermall and Jermell Charlo were.

This is known in drug-testing as a "missed test" or "unsuccessful collection attempt."

As per the terms of the World Boxing Council Clean Boxing Program, VADA immediately notified the WBC, the Association of Boxing Commissions, and Al Haymon (who represents the Charlos). Because the Charlos are scheduled to fight in separate bouts at Barclays Center in Brooklyn on December 22, VADA also notified Kim Sumbler (executive director of the New York State Athletic Commission) Nitin Sethi (the commission's chief medical officer), and Tom Brown (who is promoting the December 22 fights).

The WBC Clean Boxing Program is an important initiative. The sanctioning body deserves credit for setting up a PED-testing program with protocols pursuant to which missed tests and positive test results are reported to the governing state athletic commission and other appropri-ate parties. But the WBC program allows for two missed tests within a one-year period without the imposition of a significant penalty (such as a fighter being stripped of his title).

On November 28, the WBC issued a statement that read in part, "Every single fighter who is enrolled in the WBC Clean Boxing Program is responsible for his acts. It is important for the WBC to clarify that both Charlos have been tested in the past and that the infraction they are facing is a missed test which has been acknowledged and they will be responsible to pay the corresponding fine. It is very simple. If you are chosen for testing and are not available for the collector to test you, you will be incurring a missed test penalty. It is of extreme importance that every fighter updates their whereabouts forms with VADA at all times."

The WBC declined to reveal the amount of the fine imposed on the Charlos. But in a November 29 email, Alberto Leon (chief legal counsel for the WBC) advised, "In general, for a first whereabouts failure, the fine is limited to the actual costs of collection incurred which so far have fluctuated between $750 and $950 depending on the location of the collection effort."

In today's world of microdosing, many illegal PEDs leave an athlete's system within twenty-four hours. The unfortunate message sent by the WBC regarding the Charlos is, hypothetically speaking, if a fighter takes an illegal performance enhancing drug and, by chance, VADA shows up to test him while the drug is still in his system, the fighter can simply "miss" his test and pay a small fine.

But the matter didn't end there. On November 27, Jermall Charlo tweeted, "Missed the Test not Failed you idiots. It's Random and wbc program or Whoever they are Randomly chose a day we were out of town doing promotional stuff on Fox for the Next fight. Get ya facts straight. I like I said Haters must Hate it's the job."

As previously noted, the Charlos are scheduled to fight at Barclays Center on December 22. The New York State Athletic Commission acknowledges having been advised of the missed tests but initially maintained in a November 30 email to this writer that "The VADA and WADA [World Anti-Doping Agency] programs are separate from the New York State Athletic Commission's Rules & Regulations."

In other words, according to the New York State Athletic Commission, the missed tests were a matter for the WBC, not the NYSAC, to resolve. That was a ludicrous position and, three days later, the commission backtracked, saying, "The NYSAC is indeed investigating this matter fully and takes it very seriously. We are undertaking specific actions as part of this investigation and are in regular contact with the promoter, the combatants involved, and their seconds."

These "specific actions" are said to include additional tests administered to the Charlos at the direction of the NYSAC. That's a case of too little too late given the transitory nature of performance enhancing drugs in a fighter's system.

The NYSAC should have acted on the Charlos' situation in early November. Then, if it felt that a remedy similar to Nevada's handling of Canelo Alvarez was warranted, the December 22 fight card could have been reconfigured. At this late date, no one expects the NYSAC to interfere with the card.

But let's follow up with a few questions in response to Jermall Charlo's tweet. Questions that the New York State Athletic Commission should ask at a hearing with Jermall and Jermell Charlo under oath.

Where were the Charlos doing their out-of-town promotional work for Fox? Presumably, there's a record of their travel. What, specifically, was the promotional work? Who did they meet with? Why didn't they answer their cell phones when the VADA collection officers attempted to reach them? VADA could have sent collection officers to collect blood and urine samples in whatever city the Charlos were in. Jermall and Jermell Charlo might be innocent of any wrongdoing. But suppose it turns out that they weren't out of town that day? That would be a problem, wouldn't it?

Meanwhile, after Jarrett Hurd knocked out Jason Welborn on the undercard of Deontay Wilder vs. Tyson Fury at Staples Center on December 1, Jermell Charlo climbed into the ring to challenge Hurd. The two men jawed back and forth with Hurd saying, "Answer the phone. I got the date."

"My phone is always on," Charlo responded.

Except when a VADA collection officer calls.

As noted earlier, virtually all of the tests that USADA has administered with regard to professional boxing have been in conjunction with fights in which companies controlled by Al Haymon had a vested financial interest. Haymon is known for looking after his fighters' best financial interests. But he has a fiduciary duty to all of the fighters he represents, not just the A-side fighters. This fiduciary duty should include taking all reasonable steps to ensure that none of his fighters are put in the ring to face opponents who have increased their punching power through the use of illegal performance enhancing drugs.

Like the Charlos, Errol Spence is an Al Haymon fighter. He's also deservedly near the top of most pound-for-pound lists.

According to postings on the USADA website, Errol Spence has been tested 35 times by USADA. Did any of these tests come back positive?

Were there any "missed" tests? Did USADA ever give Spence a therapeutic use exemption or inadvertent use waiver?

One person who'd like to know the answer to these questions is Victor Conte.

Conte was first known to sports fans as the mastermind behind the BALCO scandal. In recent years, he has been a positive force for education and reform and now works with athletes as a conditioner and nutritionist at a facility in San Carlos, California, known as SNAC (an acronym for Scientific Nutrition for Advanced Conditioning).

In late-October, Conte agreed to help Mikey Garcia prepare for a scheduled March 16, 2019, fight against Errol Spence. But he made it a precondition to his involvement that both Garcia and Spence enroll in VADA.

"So far," Conte says, "Mikey has been willing to enroll, and Errol has been dragging his feet. Now I'm told that Errol and Al Haymon will agree to ten weeks of testing starting on January 5th. Ten weeks of VADA testing is better than none. But why the wait?"

"It's common knowledge," Conte continues, "that the benefit an athlete retains from using certain performance enhancing drugs carries over for months. In fact, you don't perform at your best when you're actually on the drugs. You get maximum benefit after the use stops. It all depends on what an athlete was taking, how much he was taking, how long he was taking, and when he cycled off. So my question is, 'If Errol Spence and Al Haymon aren't hiding anything, why couldn't VADA testing have started in November?'"

"And there's another point I'd like to make about Errol," Conte continues. "When a person uses testosterone, part of it converts to dihydrotestosterone and the rest converts to estrogen. And when that happens, it can cause the tissue around the nipples to swell. Technically, the condition is called gynecomastia. Some people who use testosterone get gynecomastia. Others don't. It depends on one's genetic disposition. Body-builders treat the condition by using Tamoxifen or Arimidex to shrink the tissue."

And what does that have to do with Spence?

"I was in Las Vegas on September 15 and went to something called the Boxing Fan Expo," Conte answers. "Errol was there. I got within a few feet of him. He was wearing a white shirt, and I saw what I believe were signs of gynecomastia. If you've seen a fighter in the past without gynecomastia and then you see him with it, it causes suspicion. Errol is a hell of a fighter. I have no reason to not like him and I'm not saying that Errol is using anything inappropriate. But I'm suspicious, and Errol knows it."

At present, many state athletic commissions are reluctant to push hard on the issue of performance enhancing drugs because they fear that doing so will lead promoters to take big fights to other jurisdictions. But illegal PED use is analogous to fighting with loaded gloves. In each instance, the aim is to gain a competitive advantage and inflict more physical damage on an opponent by cheating. Everyone in boxing who lets this issue slide is complicit.

It's ridiculous to think that Margaret Goodman and VADA can put a thumb in the dike and stop the flow of illegal performance enhancing drugs in boxing. Accomplishing this end will take a concerted effort by state athletic commission officials, sanctioning body officials, promoters, managers, fighters, members of the media, and law enforcement authorities.

Meanwhile, as an interim step, the New York, California, and Nevada state athletic commissions should ask USADA for the following:

(1) Copies of all contracts entered into by USADA for the testing of any professional boxer in conjunction with any fight that has taken place in their jurisdiction since January 1, 2016.

(2) Copies of all test results (complete test results, not just summaries) and all other documents that embody the results of tests conducted pursuant to these contracts.

(3) Copies of all documents that relate to instances, if any, where USADA, pursuant to these contracts, adjudicated issues that arose in conjunction with a positive test for one or more substances that are prohibited under the WADA code.

(4) Copies of all documents that relate to any instance where, pursuant to these contracts, USADA departed from World Anti-Doping Agency standards in adjusting the permissible level of any drug that might be found, or was found, in a professional boxer.

To help evaluate this data, USADA should also be asked with regard to all fights that have taken place in each respective state since January 1, 2016:

(1) On how many occasions has the "A" sample of a professional boxer tested by USADA come back positive for a substance that is prohibited under the WADA code?

(2) On how many occasions has a professional boxer "missed" a test?

USADA is skating on thin ice when it comes to boxing. An exploration of its conduct here might provide a window onto its testing of other athletes. For example, United States Olympic athletes.

If a government entity with subpoena power decides to seriously investigate, the implications could extend far beyond boxing. Maybe USADA will test clean. Maybe not.